CW00799119

ENTERPRISE INFORMATION TECHNOLOGIES

ENTERPRISE INFORMATION TECHNOLOGIES

Designing the Competitive Company

Bruce Love

VNR VAN NOSTRAND REINHOLD
New York

Copyright © 1993 by Bruce Love

Library of Congress Catalog Card Number 92-40887
ISBN 0-442-00955-0

Printed in the United States of America

Van Nostrand Reinhold
115 Fifth Avenue
New York, New York 10003

Chapman and Hall
2–6 Boundary Row
London, SE1 8HN, England

Thomas Nelson Australia
102 Dodds Street
South Melbourne 3205
Victoria, Australia

Nelson Canada
1120 Birchmount Road
Scarborough, Ontario MIK 5G4, Canada

16 15 14 13 12 11 10 9 8 7 6 5 4 3 2 1

Library of Congress Cataloging-in-Publication Data

Love, Bruce, 1942–
    Enterprise information technologies : designing the competitive
company / Bruce Love.
        p.   cm.
    Includes bibliographical references and index.
    ISBN 0-442-00955-0
    1. Management information systems.   2. Information technology.
3. Information storage and retrieval systems—Business.   I. Title.
HD30.3.L68   1993
658.4'038'011—dc20   92-40887
                                                          CIP

To Betty and Tom

Contents

Preface   ix

Acknowledgments   xv

Part I: Exploiting a Valuable Business Asset   1

Chapter 1   The Hidden Power of Information   3

Chapter 2   Obstacles to Exploiting the Information Asset   16

Chapter 3   A New Vision: Enterprise Information
   Technologies (EIT)   27

Part II: Identifying the Information Opportunities   45

Chapter 4   Information for Critical Business Strategies   47

Chapter 5   Information for Tactical Response   61

Chapter 6   Information for Effective Management   65

Part III: Designing the General Information Solution   75

Chapter 7   Prototypes for an EIT Design   77

Chapter 8   The EIT Information Infrastructure   95

Chapter 9   EIT Information Transformation   105

Part IV: Integrating the Information Technologies   131

Chapter 10   An EIT Integration Model   133

Chapter 11   Enterprise Information Technologies   145

Chapter 12   Vendor Information Visions   170

Part V: Implementing the General Information Solution   197

Chapter 13   Establish the Implementation Environment   199

Chapter 14 Prototype and Justify the Implementation   210

Chapter 15 Implement the Information Solution   224

Appendix Recommended and General Readings   237

Index   249

Preface

THE BACKGROUND OF THE BOOK

My interest in large-scale or enterprise information technologies began in earnest at Teradata Corporation (now part of the NCR unit of AT&T), where, responsible for creating a professional services and consulting organization, I was exposed to some truly massive collections of information. Having worked for over two decades building large, mission-critical mainframe applications for industrial, service, and public enterprises (and several local area network systems as well), I encountered at Teradata a new breed of information system, one that was simply staggering to my previous way of thinking: 10, 50, 100 billion bytes (gigabytes) in one database. Later, I learned of a handful of innovative companies pushing the edge of technology with 300 or more gigabytes of active, on-line information in one database, with hundreds of people plying it constantly with every sort of query imaginable.

Why were these companies doing this? Weren't there already enough thick reports piling up that people didn't have time to read? Couldn't we just be smarter at aggregating information, presenting a few key numbers in a one-page report to senior management?

The answers as it turned out were incredibly complex. It seemed we were crossing the threshold into an era in which organizations would be increasingly required to capture ever larger quantities of information in order to focus on ever more precise and timely responses to problems and opportunities. It appeared that, because of more urgent and demanding marketplace pressures, companies were being forced to wrest critical competitive advantage in any way possible;

that every edge, no matter how small, was critical; and that an increasingly important way was to tap the power of this rising flood-tide of information.

Those business enterprises that knew how to exploit their massive collections of detailed and historically rich data and turn them into timely, useful business knowledge would win the higher competitive ground; the others, using smaller databases of summary and segmented information, would be forced to work with a grosser view of the world, and find themselves responding more slowly and less precisely.

But how to tap into all that data and release its stunning power? And how to do that in such a way that each information success was part of a companywide and continuing process, in which the organization grew ever more effective in utilizing information? *That* was a far-from-certain thing. Beyond a handful of innovative people producing impressive results in isolated settings, it seemed no one really knew how to do it. And it wasn't at all clear that the technologies were available to do the job. But most of all, there seemed to be widespread myopia to the very opportunity itself, of systematically mining a company's ubiquitous data resource for greater business advantage.

With a few impressive exceptions, executives and technologists alike didn't (and still don't) understand the vast promise that lay waiting for those who would harvest the fruits of operational data in a company's "disk farms." Only a very few on the cutting competitive edge seem to grasp this elusive reality. How could this possibility be explored, tested, formulated, and expressed, in order that all business organizations be able to realize the inherent value of their information asset? How could those very unique information success stories, focused as they were on one or two critical business objectives in different enterprises and industries, be understood in a more general way, so that any company awash in oceans of detailed data could achieve similar benefits?

This challenge fired my deepest enthusiasm and led to the idea of *enterprise information technologies,* a promising but still nascent vision for using advanced technologies to transform vast quantities of data into information for ongoing competitive advantage. I left Teradata determined to understand and capture the tantalizing possibility of harnessing information's power. This book is the result of that process.

THE PURPOSE OF THE BOOK

Enterprise Information Technologies helps companies meet the challenge of today's dynamic marketplace by providing a workable vision for transforming data into an asset for lasting competitive advantage. Written primarily for information systems executives, technology professionals, and information users, it provides a basis for understanding the potential of computerized information to enhance radically the management and operation of a business. The book also offers a design, integration, and implementation framework for employing the most promising enterprise information technologies to exploit this potential, helping organizations to build an ongoing information capability that grows in functionality, knowledge, range, and depth.

The demand for results in the face of tough competitive pressures makes ever more urgent the need for radical new solutions. Business cycles grow shorter and more complex. Decisions require ever larger perspectives, greater precision, and faster reaction. Stock responses such as mass media promotions, "repackaged" goods and services that aren't much different from the current ones, or marginally better pricing tactics, are increasingly ineffective for retaining the most profitable customers. Nasty surprises lurk in the bowels of the large complex organization. Assets, whether a company's people or its plants, its money or its materials, must be constantly optimized to get the kinds of returns needed to survive and prosper.

Information mirrors those business demands and contains the power to meet them. The company that learns to exploit fully its information asset reaps a critical advantage that grows in importance as the competitive stakes increase and the sources of advantage from conventional automation diminish. This book presents one way information technologies can be used to strongly differentiate a particular company from others. *Enterprise Information Technologies* not only helps create order from information chaos; it helps executives understand the opportunities and risks of pushing the limits of information technology and the necessity for bolder use of technology to achieve orders-of-magnitude improvements.

Enterprise Information Technologies also provides a basis upon which the application of information technology can be guided and ultimately unified. Using information as the focal point—rather than hardware or software—this approach calls for separate but linked development of Business Automation (systems that support a company's business operations and procedures) and Information Automation (systems concerned with the transformation of information for critical decision-making and strategic purposes). Each is driven by its own set of methods, needs, and requirements, and under broad guidelines these two "automation worlds" separately evolve and gradually merge to where they share a common information resource.

Most important, *Enterprise Information Technologies* shows the information technologist and executive how to use information to improve the company's bottom line and net worth. It illustrates the importance of liberating information users (the non-technical knowledge worker) from the clutches of today's unresponsive systems. It illustrates why the information opportunity is great and why it is too often overlooked in many corporations. The book describes real-world examples (most of them unidentified due to their extremely competitive nature) that demonstrate the levels of success some organizations are having in seizing this opportunity. And it describes how to anticipate and overcome supporters of the status quo who will insist that progress of this sort is not possible in *our* company.

Enterprise Information Technologies presents an approach for applying today's information technologies to power the operations of tomorrow's high-performance companies.

THE PLAN OF THE BOOK

The book is structured into five parts or sections. Parts I, II, and III present the nature of the untapped information opportunity and a design to seize it. Parts IV and V provide the integration and implementation strategies needed to establish those capabilities and to receive the full benefits. The five parts comprise an integral whole.

Exploiting a Valuable Business Asset (**Part I**) introduces the opportunities and obstacles involved in tapping the hidden powers of information. It presents a comprehensive vision for employing Enterprise Information Technologies (EIT) to transform data into competitive advantage, along with an enabling framework for establishing the needed capabilities. The three chapters provide an overview of the major themes of the book, and Chapter 3 presents a summary of the following four parts.

Identifying the Information Opportunities (**Part II**) demonstrates, primarily by the use of examples, how a company can exploit information to enhance critical competitive programs, accomplish organizational redesign strategies, strengthen responsiveness to unexpected threats and opportunities, and enhance the overall management of the enterprise. These chapters provide the basis to identify the expected business payoffs for each information opportunity area, and to help articulate a general information strategy for the company.

Designing the General Information Solution (**Part III**) examines some of the ground-breaking efforts undertaken by innovative companies that have been most successful in wresting advantage from their information asset. Two detailed examples serve as EIT Design prototypes, along with the criteria for determining their suitability to other companies. The EIT Design describes the set of capabilities needed to transform production data into useful business information, and the underlying infrastructure needed to support expansion and changes in a company's information environment. Each capability is illustrated by examples.

Integrating the Information Technologies (**Part IV**) offers an approach for integrating essential information technologies to enable the functions of the EIT Design. This includes an EIT Integration Model for configuring a coherent information environment, and a dozen criteria for evaluating technological products and capabilities. It reviews more than 20 general classes of technology, and presents archetypal and alternative examples for each. This section of the book also provides a review of the most promising information visions and architectures being offered by the major technology vendors: IBM, NCR, DEC, Computer Associates, and Oracle.

Implementing the General Information Solution (**Part V**) provides a roadmap for implementing the general EIT Vision, based on the most attractive information opportunities and guided by the EIT Design and Integration Model. It identifies the activities for getting started, for selecting and prototyping the first application, for justifying the investment, for charting the major implementation vectors, and for constructing a phased and incremental approach to moving forward on several implementation fronts. A strong case is made for starting immediately down the "yellow brick road" to a companywide information capability.

Enterprise Information Technologies is intended for computer technology executives, such as Management Information Systems (MIS) directors and Chief Information Officers (CIOs), and those technology managers and information users who must grapple with design, implementation, and support of mission-critical information systems for large companies. Read selectively, the book can also help non-technical business executives and professionals understand, shape, and manage the "information agenda" of their organization.

For readers pressed for time and for those without a great amount of interest in or knowledge of information technology issues, considerable value can be gained by reading the three chapters in Part I and selecting particular topics of interest in Parts II and V. These sections of the book describe information technology at a more general level and are capable of being understood by any business professional or manager with a need to learn more about the general topic.

Part III is required reading for the information executive and professional and may also be of value to the determined information user and business professional. Part IV is intended squarely for the information technology professional and for those technology executives and "power users" with a strong interest in specific vendor architectures, products, and solutions. For all readers, the Recommended Readings section allows a deeper look into the sources and inspirations of the book's themes and examples.

Finally, a caveat is in order. *Enterprise Information Technologies* is not the final word on this rich, shifting subject. The hope is that the book raises the visibility of information as a mostly unexploited business asset and provokes a dialogue that results in greater innovation and benefit. Since many of the book's themes and approaches are anchored in real-world experiences, diverse company settings, and fast-emerging technologies—all dynamic, rapidly changing environments—it minimizes the discussion of specific information solutions, technologies, and products.

Instead, *Enterprise Information Technologies* paints information's "portrait" in large brushstrokes. This is especially important because of the far greater need today for technology and business executives to possess common concepts, goals, and visions for harnessing information's power. They need to share the same language. With communications established, the specific and appropriate solutions will quickly emerge for each company.

Acknowledgments

Most of all, I want to acknowledge the support of the Teradata Corporation and to thank them for their graciousness in allowing me to use some of the concepts I first articulated when I was a member of the company. In particular, I want to thank Ken Simonds, the past Chairman and CEO, for his enthusiastic and unflagging support.

Jill Dyche was one of those "Teradatans," and the first truly data-oriented computer professional I ever trusted. She is an expert at looking at the world of business through the "information mirror," and one of the few people capable of wrestling to the ground the world's largest and toughest databases. She has been extremely helpful in the writing of this book, and like all the others who have helped me grapple with this fascinating topic, she bears no responsibility for any errors or flaws that may have resulted.

Several others stand out from that time at Teradata—people who helped articulate or shape many of the ideas that led to the creation of this book. Foremost of these are Larry Scroggins, Bill Nowacki, Dave Clements, Bob Flynn, Mike Ehrensberger, Rob Klopp, Miles Coverdale, Nick Johantgen, Jon Gausman, Hugh McDonald, and Thom Blishock.

Beyond that unique group were the pioneers in such technology-using companies as American Airlines, the Bank of America, Wal-Mart, Transamerica, Bell Atlantic, Procter & Gamble, American President Companies, AT&T, Kraft, Mervyn's, U.S. West, Liberty Mutual, Citicorp, K mart, and others—companies that were quick to see the potential in information and were busy blazing new trails. Some of the innovators include people like Cecil Jones, Glenna Taylor, Jean Rowe, Coby Dunn, Fred Young, and Jeff Hardigan. Ken Sloan (now with Perot Systems), in particular, stands out as having one of the truly seminal voices.

Others who have helped a great deal, especially in the research of ideas and materials, include: Jnan Dash (previously with IBM and now with Oracle); Al Atherton, Barbara Piquet, and Steve Griffin of IBM; Michael David of Compuaid; Jennifer Nance and Ralph Kimbell of Red Brick Systems; Kamran Parsaye of IntelligenceWare; Robert G. Brown of The Database Design Group; Jim Brown of Ultimate Resources; Katherine Hammer of Evolutionary Technologies; Mary Vargo; Evan Levy; Irwin Konopolsky; Ken Orr, founder of the Ken Orr Institute; and Phil Neches of NCR.

I also owe a large debt to the information technology and management gurus. This group includes Michael Treacy, Chuck Gibson, John Donovan, Warren McFarland, Shoshana Zuboff, Peter Keen, David De Long, John Rockart, and Michael Hammer. Their contributions, along with those of many others, are noted in the Recommended Readings section.

Finally, I want to thank Laurie Harper, Carrie Vendrame, and Jeannine Drew for their invaluable assistance, insightful suggestions, and unflagging support during the shaping and completion of the book. Most of all, I want to acknowledge the endless encouragement I've received from Jo Sletten, a woman whose compassion, sense of humor, and insight into the things truly important have made so much possible.

part I

EXPLOITING A VALUABLE BUSINESS ASSET

---

*From being organized around the flow
of things and the flow of money, [the
economy] is being organized around the
flow of information.*

—Peter Drucker

1

The Hidden Power of Information

- Citibank has long been a leading innovator in the banking industry, especially in the aggressive use of information technology. The first bank to implement automatic teller machines (ATMs) on a large scale, Citibank used this technological advantage to triple market share in the first few years of operation, offering a much-needed banking service to both current and prospective customers. Because other banks had yet to offer such capabilities, Citibank achieved a significant competitive advantage over those slow to adopt the new technology. This not only took customers away from competitors, Citibank ATMs also led to an increase in the number of banking transactions (and related ATM usage fees), reduced teller costs, and more accurate and timely transaction postings.

- K mart was one of the first large retailers to see the benefits in installing point-of-sale (POS) devices in its 2,200 discount stores. The ambitious use of this technology enabled K mart to improve its store operations dramatically, taking advantage of more timely and accurate sales, inventory, and product reordering information. With this greater visibility, shelf and inventory space was more effectively used, turnover rates improved, and shifting shopper preferences were more quickly spotted. While many of its competitors were still replenishing goods on a mostly visual and infrequent batch-processing basis, K mart used POS technology for pinpoint real-time control of its sales data to keep goods moving as customer demand dictated.

Building on such successful use of technology, K mart is moving into new areas, such as testing radar-like systems that track store traffic. By knowing how many customers are in what sections of the store, the system will alert salespeople to cover crowded departments and open more checkout lanes before long lines form.

▪ American Airlines was early in adopting technology to automate the customer reservation process. Its Sabre system led competitors in the use of on-line, real-time ticket reservation and purchasing, linking travel agencies and customers nationwide to its computers. Being the first with this strategic capability allowed American Airlines a major advantage with travel agents, making it easier for American to handle flight bookings, with the airline often receiving reservations that in the past might have gone to a competitor. In addition, the more timely and accurate information improved American's ability to manage its airport terminal and flight operations, providing a more flexible and accurate process that got passengers on board quicker, with fewer sold-out or half-empty flights. Needless to say, the system revolutionized the airline business (and eventually the travel industry), and gave American a major advantage over its competitors for a number of years.

▪ McKesson Corporation achieved significant competitive advantage by using an information-based strategy to upgrade its links with its many pharmacy customers. McKesson was the first company in its industry to develop an on-line ordering system that resulted in substantial time and cost savings, primarily by eliminating or reducing paperwork, errors, and delays. It allowed the company to reduce significantly the sales and clerical staff that was needed to support this process prior to the introduction of the new technology.

A GLIMPSE OF INFORMATION'S POTENTIAL

These innovative companies and others like them quickly saw the advantages of using technology for creating competitive advantage. Bold and insightful, they extended the limits of automation, reaping impressive benefits and important competitive leverage. The enormous successes of these systems demonstrate the power of preemptive strategies when based on the creative use of information technologies.

As companies wield their new technology programs, competitors respond with matching or more advanced initiatives. The initial competitive edge, as impressive as it might be, is generally not sustainable. The stakes are raised, as each company seeks to capitalize on what has gone before. Competitive leapfrogging takes on new meaning with the availability of more powerful technologies.

The examples above demonstrate the possibilities of using information technologies creatively and boldly for automating the *operational processes* of the organization, i.e., its business operations. Such Business Automation is typically concerned with improving internal operations, such as inventory management or order processing, or in bringing benefits to operations that link the company to its customers, suppliers, and distributors.

There is another dimension of automation, however, that extends the boundaries of opportunity beyond the realm of Business Automation. It is an area where the astute company can raise the bar a couple of notches higher, using information technologies to achieve sustainable competitive advantage. Each of the breakthrough applications of technology described earlier has, in one way or another, opened the door to the hidden power of information—a corporate asset widely available and still mostly untapped.

TRANSFORMING DATA INTO VALUABLE BUSINESS INFORMATION

▪ Citibank was quick to parlay its ATM advantage into a number of leading-edge customer and marketing programs, greatly benefiting from the detailed data collected by the new technology. The bank was one of the first to achieve sophisticated relationship banking, using the new sources of data for driving programs to, for example, encourage single-account customers to elect additional services (important not only to increase business, but also because customers with two or more services are less likely to change banks than those with only one service). Information about loans, deposits, credit cards, and other banking services for a customer could be, for the first time, easily and quickly analyzed against the bank's existing and planned products and services. By creatively combining this new source of data with other information, Citibank launched focused programs to define new market segments, increase the level of existing customer business, and snare customers away from its competitors.

▪ By linking its stores' POS scanners to roof-top microwave transmitters and sending sales activity information to their central offices each night, K mart went well beyond the benefits of improved in-store operation. The use of that detailed data allowed K mart much greater control of product movement based on sales levels, providing the means for better corporate merchandising and purchasing capabilities. The ambitious use of this rich source of information enabled K mart to improve operations across its regional logistics and inventory networks and in the overall management of product and customer demand. Products that unexpectedly fizzle can be carefully marked down as their short and sensitive life cycle progresses. Products that are surprise winners can be spotted and replenished quickly while the demand lasts. Items that sell in only certain regions and stores can be moved from those places where business is poor—all quickly and electronically. The frequency of store POS transmissions is increasing as K mart fine-tunes its complex and powerful system.

So, too, will the radar-like system that tracks in-store traffic help well beyond its expected operational benefits. Such technology can produce data to quickly determine what percentage of shoppers actually make purchases (often as little as 30 percent in the discount store business), thus helping store managers identify opportunities to convert browsers into buyers. Which areas of the store have the greatest traffic? Which areas have the greatest sales per traffic flow? Are sales of products helped by their placement and if so, which products benefit the most? What routes do customers typically take and how long are they in the store? What changes in merchandising mix and store layout will keep customers in the store longer? Answers to these types of questions can provide the important clues to improving sales overall and per square foot.

▪ In addition to the impressive operational advantages it gained from Sabre, the booking data from American Airlines' on-line reservation system is used extensively to support other critical business needs: to operate its complex and highly successful frequent flyer programs (including joint marketing programs such as those that credit free miles based on credit card purchases); to schedule flights, aircraft, and crews, using an almost real-time yield management system that balances those resources with changing customer demand, fare strategies, weather patterns, and other factors affecting flight seating; to stock food and beverages for dynamically changing flights; to manage optimally its extensive equipment inventory; to plan new maintenance and airport facilities; and, in general, to track closely the profitability of its entire operations while watching specific trouble spots. Imagine the impact on American (or any large carrier) of an unexpected, sudden, and major fuel price increase (or worse, the unexpected loss of a major fuel supply). The reservation data in Sabre makes it possible for the airline to respond as intelligently as possible to these kinds of challenges. Without that data, they would be literally flying blind.

▪ Seeing further potential in the detailed data it was collecting, McKesson linked the on-line pharmacy orders directly to its internal distribution and inventory control systems. This enabled pharmacies to order items directly and have them automatically scheduled and shipped. The information was also used to help pharmacies restock their shelves more rapidly and efficiently, which in turn greatly simplified in-store reordering and record-keeping. These automatic reordering mechanisms helped relieve pharmacy workload, further tightening McKesson's grip on its retail store customers. Finally, having leveraged its "automation competence" in these critical areas, McKesson began handling payment and claims processing work for its customers. This not only resulted in faster payments but spawned an entirely new business—insurance claims processing. The ability to exploit its information asset creatively opened an entirely new source of revenue for McKesson.

HARNESSING THE POWER OF INFORMATION

These examples show how innovative companies can build on their initial information advantage—how they can recognize and seize the aftermarket value of raw, detailed data that is being collected in such volume today. These examples also demonstrate how companies have moved beyond the world of Business Automation into a new territory—automating the transformation of data into valuable business information, or using Information Automation to create new sources of competitive advantage.

(*Note:* Information Automation is a term used throughout this book to denote a general class of information processing that in the past has gone by many different names. The term seeks to embrace such seemingly diverse information solutions as decision support systems, executive information systems, data extraction and conditioning systems, simulation models, data analysis and inquiry systems, statistical analysis, and several others. IBM has called it "informational systems." Shoshana Zuboff, in her book, *In the Age of the Smart Machine,* refers to a similar idea as "informating" (see Appendix). Information Automation is not being offered as yet another term to complicate an already complicated world, but to reduce such confusion by seeking to consolidate this broad array of capabilities into one, interrelated category of automation. The term itself is not nearly as important as the underlying concept.)

Information, the basis of knowledge, is power. Innovative companies treat their computer data as a vital, valued asset of the organization (and not just as a means to an end, i.e., for booking an order, posting a checking account, or adding to inventory levels). But computer data, no matter how timely and detailed, is not alone a source of power. Data must first be endowed with relevance and purpose. The transformation of data into information requires a rigorous yet flexible process that encourages a company's information users to exploit fully the quantity and diversity of its information resource.

With a few exceptions, all large organizations have abundant quantities of detailed operational data, the raw material of business knowledge. But until they can transform that raw, untreated data into a meaningful and accurate form; until they can interpret and share it rapidly and consistently in an understandable manner; until information is fully available for analyzing and strategizing within the context of a tangible problem, that rising mountain of facts represents nothing more than an unexploited opportunity.

POSSIBILITIES FOR EXPLOITING INFORMATION FOR COMPETITIVE ADVANTAGE

What are the information opportunities and matching technological capabilities that, when linked together, will be the basis for the next breakthroughs in achieving major business benefits? What specific technologies will prove to be the greatest sources of advantage for those who learn how to squeeze business knowledge from those massive quantities of operational data?

While these questions cannot be answered with complete certainty, it seems likely that the successful organizations of the future will be those that are most flexible and responsive to market shifts, technology developments, competitor moves, shareholder demands, employee needs, and customer desires. Information and the technologies to exploit it will be a critical means for achieving that flexibility and responsiveness and for gaining and maintaining a competitive edge.

One of the most attractive aspects of information technology is that it can be directed towards very different ends. The swift rate of progress and innovation in hardware, software, methodologies, and applications is continually widening the territories of its use and value. That, in turn, creates new opportunities for exploitation and development.

When used creatively, information technologies can meet challenges and create opportunities not possible using conventional automation strategies. Consider some recent examples of new technologies and their possibilities for competitive breakthroughs:

- Pen-based digital input devices for handwritten or manual data collection
- Electronic data interchange (EDI) for instantaneous ordering and payments
- Multimedia hardware and software capabilities
- Hand-held computers with wireless radio transmission
- On-line, real-time and worldwide customer reservation systems
- Powerful workstations with graphic user interfaces (GUIs)
- Computer-aided design (CAD) software for engineering and architecture
- The use of on-board computers in trucks and ships
- High-throughput enterprisewide voice and data networks
- Nightly satellite transmission for regional, next-day newspapers.

Some of these technologies have resulted in major improvement; others have yet to realize, and may never realize, success as a tool for competitive advantage. Today's technologies, both existing and emerging, hold untold possibilities for exploiting the information asset to maximum advantage. Following is an overview of the more promising Information Automation possibilities, those areas where companies can creatively use the most attractive information technologies for transforming data into competitive advantage.

Uncovering Vital Relationships in Massive Databases

Recent developments in software have opened opportunities for companies to augment the standard inquiry and analysis capabilities of their computer systems. Derived from extensive work in areas such as expert systems, artificial intelligence, and neural networks, powerful machine learning and reasoning capabilities are becoming more readily available, which would allow companies to "methodically stumble" upon potentially important and hidden conditions, subtle relationships, and unknown facts about the business that are buried away in large databases.

As technology offers ever more powerful capabilities for storing and manipulating vast quantities of detailed information (*trillions* of bytes, or terabytes, of data), automated means for tapping the meaning of that information become essential. Software capabilities are available that automatically create and test hypotheses about the facts and figures of the business based on the contents of databases, i.e., they generate opinions from the information. Once discovered, these hidden patterns and relationships can solve problems before they grow too large, seek out potential areas of improvement, and provide the basis for new or enhanced policies and strategies.

A recent example: A high-quality European retail clothing company was concerned that its advertising for petite women's fashions in their slick color catalogs was not as effective as it expected—that it looked as though the fashions weren't appealing to buyers. Having previously built a large collection of information to manage its inventory and sales programs, the company was able to run a series of "automated discovery" analyses, looking at the sales of petite women's clothing and relating it to the names on the catalog mailing list, a process far too massive and complex for conventional analysis technologies.

The software discovered that a large number of women who requested the catalogs didn't buy petite-sized dresses at all; in fact, many of them were larger-sized women who apparently ordered the catalogs to follow the smaller women's fashions. As a result, the company redirected its color catalogs to women who had previously ordered petite apparel. It produces a tremendous response and made a major success of the program.

"We would never have suspected, much less discovered, this relationship between the two groups [of customers] without having access to the right kind of information," an operations manager commented. "One of our analysts was using a program that looks for hidden patterns in massive quantities of data and it came up with this hypothesis. No one believed it as first. A few hours later, she completed an extensive series of standard statistical comparisons. That gave us a very high level of confidence to pinpoint the source of our previous misunderstanding. It appears we had been looking in all the wrong places."

The potential of "automated discovery" adds a totally new dimension for using information for improving the operation of the enterprise.

Opening New Windows for Management

The ability of advanced technologies to economically capture and maniulate huge volumes of information makes it feasible for managers to be informed about almost every aspect and nuance of the company's operations. Excellent information can help management understand that:

- Responding to a competitor's move to lower prices in one product group is a poor decision (because the competitor is not a player in that area and cannot sustain its thrust).
- Errors in manufacturing are really due to poor training (and not to inadequate supervision as was commonly suspected).
- A major new product offering is meeting lukewarm response and carefully orchestrated price markdowns must be enacted immediately (rather than increasing promotion efforts).
- A major line of business has been losing ground steadily for 10 years and requires major changes to keep it alive (and the past six month's "surge" of revenues is not a valid indicator of a turnaround).

These and other examples are presented in greater detail in Part II.

The ability to guide a company based on exact and instantly available information offers management an incredible opportunity—to make decisions with great precision, deep insight, and reliability. Powerful information capabilities can provide new windows into every corner of the enterprise: to help management spot critical business patterns and dynamics; to anticipate and head off major problems; and to make and monitor finely-tuned adjustments or the most sweeping and radical of changes.

Reshaping the Basics of the Business Organization

The application of information technologies reshapes the business organization. When they are first introduced, the interconnected web of relationships, procedures, communications, expertise, and even the culture of an organization, are irrevocably altered. Much of this reshaping is an unintended byproduct of automation; however, a company can apply information technologies to purposefully redesign the operating dynamics of the enterprise. This is a more sophisticated approach than simply increasing the efficiency of existing processes and their supporting systems.

For example, properly designed information capabilities can be employed by the company engaged in acquisitions to quickly assimilate new companies, plugging their data into a common information structure. Or these capabilities can be applied to alter the management and control dynamics of the enterprise, enabling greater centralization of strategic decisions, increasing decentralization of tactical decisions, expanding the range of control, and ultimately creating a flatter, more effective organization.

Using cutting-edge information approaches for restructuring an organization goes well beyond simply optimizing individual business operations or providing management mechanisms to assure conformity with business goals. When used intelligently, it has the power to alter the basic processes of planning, design, development, and delivery, and even the very nature of the company's flagship products and services. Information that transcends the confining boundaries of existing organizational arrangements can be a great leveler and magnifier for helping management redesign the fundamentals of the business enterprise.

Liberating Information Users and Empowering Employees

Liberating the information user is one of the most attractive ways of realizing the most promising of Information Automation possibilities. For still untapped is the wealth of creativity and resourcefulness of the many users of information—those business professionals, managers, analysts, planners, staff, and other specialists and executives who regularly access and manipulate computer information.

To maximize productivity, these "knowledge workers" must be liberated from the straightjacket of unresponsive systems and inadequate information. They must be given access to the most sophisticated and powerful tools and the highest-quality, most detailed, and far-ranging information. These are the new computer-literates, those people who can expertly employ powerful technologies such as graphical user interfaces (GUIs) and expert systems for managing a dynamic information environment. Even the design of new information capabilities will be handled by this new breed of user, with the assistance of a few technical specialists. Information users will then be where they belong—at the top of the information food chain.

Further, as the products of information technology become ever more ubiquitous and powerful (e.g., cheap and portable mainframe-powered workstations for everyone), and as the information resource grows to astronomical size (thousands of terabytes), the business organization will have the unique opportunity to significantly increase the involvement and productivity of *everyone* on the work force, not just the regular users of information. All employees will be connected to the company's information resource, tapping into knowledge that had previously been available to only a designated few.

Empowering every employee with the means to access information can result in an increase in morale and commitment, as each person better understands the company's bigger picture and his or her part in it. Immediate and local problems are more likely to be solved by those who are closest to them, and who first discover them—salespeople on the front lines, production employees in the trenches, buyers and operations personnel working with distributors and suppliers—eliminating unnecessary layers of involvement and facilitating dialogues that generate deeper insights. Information empowerment provides the basis for bypassing ineffective authority and organizational structures, and enables self-forming, autonomous teams that are going to focus on the company's most pressing problems.

All this can occur because widely available information will have unleashed the unmeasured productivity and creativity of every employee capable of using it, and of putting it fully to use. While difficult to measure, such effects will filter down rapidly to the company's bottom line.

Transforming Operational Data into a Strategic Resource

Some of information technologies' greatest possibilities are just beginning to be fully understood. One is the transformation of vast quantities of operational data (captured by ATMs, POS scanners, on-line terminals and workstations, optical page scanners, hand-held computing appliances, dial-up home computers, telephonic billing, and other means) into competitively strategic information. For example, the incredible growth in the amount of information being collected by these data collection sources has resulted in an expanding array of marketing strategies such as Frequent Shopper and Frequent Flyer programs. The success of these programs is leading to an ever greater expansion of customers' appetites for them, making the automation and manipulation of information one of the most exciting competitive possibilities for a growing number of corporations.

This ability is being further expanded as new *enterprise information technologies* make it increasingly feasible for companies to extend the range of information strategies beyond narrowly focused marketing programs. Some companies have already moved from this first generation of Information Automation to employing technologies that encompass companywide information, support all of a company's competitive strategies, provide powerful and precise tactical responsiveness to outside challenges, and support executives in their most critical planning, decision-making, monitoring, and control functions.

INFORMATION AS A BUSINESS STRATEGY

Recently, a "non-standard" property and casualty insurer in the western United States sought to increase its market share by identifying very small but profitable segments of the high-risk driver business. The company created a massive information capability with enough depth and power to it such that the insurer could readily identify potentially profitable "marginal business" that other carriers would not handle.

By conducting finely-tuned analyses, the company was able to move into California, a neighboring state that had voted car insurance premium rollbacks. Because this change was expected to produce a large fallout of marginal-risk drivers, the insurer saw an opportunity to carve out a significant chunk of this overlooked market segment. One executive of the firm recalls:

> We wanted virtually an electron microscope to look at our business, where all of our competitors are looking at it with a magnifying glass . . . to be flexible in rapidly identifying profit and loss elements (for) staying ahead of the competition by moving swiftly. Since we reject no more than 3 percent of the business that comes to us, where others might reject as much as 50 percent, we see the key to our profitability resting on being able to analyze these segments differently and in finer and finer subsets, so we can find a way to write a policy and make money. We are more than willing to take what others leave on the table.

Extensive information capabilities like the one above are increasingly supporting, if not actually driving, major business strategies. Executives are more readily accepting the notion that major competitive advantage is possible from early and innovative uses of Information Automation (in some cases because they have been victims of such strategies themselves). Such information capabilities can be used by a company for preemptive competitive advantage, as a value-added component of a product offering, or as part of an ongoing program to leverage its most basic corporate strengths.

Here's another example of how information can be strategically applied, in this case to take advantage of a fleeting opportunity. A major U.S. freight transportation company was recently offered an opportunity to buy a large number of shipping containers at a favorable price. But there was a catch: It had to make the deal in 24 hours.

The firm had just recently established a companywide information database containing detailed and historical information about their business operations. With it, they immediately initiated a number of sophisticated projection models to determine if the current plans for expansion could take advantage of the types and volumes of shipping containers being offered.

By tweaking a sizable number of complex factors (a capability made possible by their powerful new technologies), the company was able to determine with a high degree of confidence that it could indeed make full use of the added capacity. In fact, executives concluded they could accelerate their planned expansion without taxing existing budget or operational plans. This was accomplished on top of the discount realized on the shipping containers, worth several million dollars by itself. "We probably would not have done that deal if we didn't have our fingertips on the kind of information we did," a senior executive asserted. "It was the critical difference between a whopping success and a missed opportunity."

Many of the potential strategic applications of Information Automation have yet to be exploited. As will be seen in Chapter 2, one reason for this is the lack of an adequate guiding vision. But there is another, perhaps more fundamental, phenomenon at work. Most companies are experiencing the maturation of the first generation of programs for applying technology to their business operations. Though the tools and techniques of automation sprout as fast as ever, the major high-payback automation opportunities have diminished in both number and impact.

With fewer rich targets, companies are left with more subtle and difficult issues to address. For example, information technology can be applied to:

- Increase the level of repeat business
- Snare new customers from competitors
- Generate more innovative and cost-effective products
- Develop new products quickly in response to customer input
- Understand and surpass competitive offerings
- Anticipate competitive moves with preemptive product promotions
- Continuously alter product mix to favor high-margin items
- Identify and exploit ways to enhance existing revenue sources
- Upgrade distribution and retail delivery channels
- Improve general decision-making abilities, i.e., work smarter
- Eliminate competition within the company's own product lines
- Motivate employees by providing more local decision-making authority

Some of these opportunities carry with them significant technical challenges, but for organizations willing to pursue them, they also offer some of the highest payoffs.

Information for Survival

The ability to exploit information is an increasingly critical factor in gaining a competitive edge. The anecdotes at the beginning of this chapter clearly show that an important advantage is achieved when information-based strategies are bold, innovative, preemptive, well-implemented, and well-timed. McKesson, K mart, American Airlines, and the rest of the classic success stories deployed information capabilities that produced substantial competitive advantage for the enterprises in question.

But can such advantage be sustained? There is evidence that suggests that most competitive advantage (including information-based advantage) is not sustainable, however beneficial it may be at the time. Many who have achieved pre-emptive advantage have either been unable to hold onto it, or have not been able to leverage it for greater use. (Consider IBM, which lost its long-time advantage in mainframes to the humble microprocessor chip and its cheap desktop mani-festations.)

Any advance, however sophisticated, is likely to be matched or exceeded by one or more competitors. Such initiatives are inevitable, made possible by the relent-less advance of technology and made mandatory by the urgent forces of competi-tion. These is good reason to believe that the kinds of strategic moves highlighted in the opening anecdotes are more a matter of long-term survival than of advan-tage.

The Secret of Lasting Competitive Advantage

While sustainable information-based competitive advantage is not possible in many cases, it may be possible if the company's key technological and information components are: (1) based on unduplicatable capabilities that are kept secret or patented; (2) used to leverage other fundamental and unique corporate strengths and assets; or (3) turned into a general-purpose "information utility" that can take advantage of accumulating more powerful capabilities.

While the first two circumstances are the ones most frequently found as motives among those companies seeking information-based competitive advan-tage, it is the utility aspect of information that promises to be the most effective of all. Because it involves building on and creatively using a common information resource, one that is continuously evolving and expanding, this aspect represents one of the few remaining sources of lasting competitive advantage for corpora-tions operating in today's whirlwind global economy.

The more comprehensive the information, the more a company knows about its own operations and the marketplace, which gives the company more leverage over its inherent strengths and control over its greatest exposures and weaknesses.

Here's another example that was mentioned earlier: Retail store scanners pro-vide an immediate source of competitive advantage by improving checkout per-formance and store-level inventory control. But it is the additional application of that technology—its utility aspect—that holds the real potential for sustainable advantage. The byproduct scanner data allows companywide, just-in-time inven-tory management and detailed tracking of trends and preferences. This, in turn, permits finely-tuned purchasing and shipping actions—which raises profit mar-gins, expands market penetration, increases advertising effectiveness, and attracts new customers. And so on and so on.

By improving the organization's capabilities and performance levels on an ongoing and ever-accelerating basis, Information Automation can be used to achieve lasting competitive advantage. This advantage is achieved, not by using technologies to do the same job incrementally better (faster and more efficient customer checkout in a grocery store), but by realizing entirely new possibilities of a greater order of magnitude (using scanner data to provide real-time reaction to customer buying patterns, as when local tastes in soft drinks stubbornly defy nationwide trends).

It is impossible to anticipate all the specific competitive possibilities that lie ahead; no one can predict with any real accuracy which additional capabilities will be spawned by more immediate ones. The "secret" for the organization seeking a lasting competitive edge is to capture all the essential information of the business and to establish a process for continuously exploring opportunities of that ever-expanding and more valuable information resource.

THE VITAL ROLE OF MANAGEMENT

Information technologies, once loosed on an organization, do not remain neutral. While companies consciously choose their information strategies, approaches, and tools, they are, in turn, altered by them as the elements take root in the soil of the organization. These enablers are a potent shaping force that can dramatically affect the organization's range of choice and possibility. Their very application precludes and includes, and may do so without the participation of those most strongly affected.

If chosen and directed well, information technologies are capable of bringing immense improvements to the corporation. If chosen or applied poorly, however, information technologies can be a serious limiter for achieving important business results, or even harmful to the basic goals of the enterprise. Information technologies can be used for unrealistic or inappropriate projects; they can lock the company into inadequate processes and rigid systems that become rapidly obsolete and almost impossible to change; or they can be subject to poorly chosen approaches and projects that drain corporate resources and produce low returns on the company's investment.

Senior company executives must own the responsibility for deciding the company's basic information strategies. While CIOs and MIS Directors can usually provide the optimum designs and enabling mechanisms for accomplishing strategic information objectives (although not always; see Chapter 2), ultimate accountability for choosing information strategies, the technologies to support them, and their expected business outcomes, must rest with the senior executives of the company.

Senior management officers need not be technical experts; but they must know enough to separate the true promise from the bloated hype, the real opportunities from the probable dead-ends, and the serious proposals from the self-serving agendas. They must understand how many and what kinds of information technologies to adopt, to be applied toward which ends. They must know what it will take to succeed at building innovative information capabilities, and who are the best people to lead the charge. They must determine the incentives, policies, and controls that need to be put in place.

Most of all, the company's senior executives must themselves strongly believe in the ability of information to improve the business and to strengthen the company's competitive stance. That belief, once manifested, will spread rapidly throughout the organization. For the modern corporation in an increasingly competitive world economy, a determination to harness the power of its information asset can spell the difference between the thriving and barely surviving.

2

Obstacles to Exploiting the Information Asset

Information's promise, introduced in Chapter 1, reflects a seemingly unlimited potential for solving complex problems, making smarter decisions, initiating more effective programs, responding insightfully to change and threatening situations, and achieving important competitive advantage. But before the true value of information can be realized, a number of significant obstacles must be overcome.

This chapter discusses three major obstacles. The prevailing limits and visions of information and its supporting technologies are two hindrances that stand in the way of most companies anxious to seize information's full value. But the foremost obstacle is with information itself—its basic nature, its sheer size, volatility, and difficulty in management. Information is often the single, largest barrier to successfully exploiting its intrinsic value.

INFORMATION'S OBSTACLES

Information's problematic aspects are reflected in its ubiquitous and protean nature, along with its shifting and vague sense of usability and value. Infinitely replicable, resistant to consistent interpretation, difficult to organize, even more difficult to synchronize, easy to lose, susceptible to being altered—these and other troubling manifestations demonstrate the nature of the challenge for those who would seek to benefit from information's potential value.

The vast array of databases in a large company can be seen as constituting a huge warehouse of data. Unfortunately, most data warehouses contain information that is erroneous, unorganized, unmanaged, hard to locate, and practically impossible to change. They are filled to overflowing by daily additions, and choked with rapidly aging information that, except for the most determined of efforts, seems incapable of being effectively used. Nonetheless, a great many people rummage daily through the nooks and crannies of these dimly lit warehouses, hoping to stumble on the Rosetta stone that will open this storehouse of knowledge to greater use.

For most companies, the only people who know how to find the information tucked away in these hermetically sealed rooms of silently spinning disk drives and long rows of hanging tape reels are a handful of specialized technologists. These few experts always seem harassed, frantically working to keep things orderly according to arcane procedures. Even if they wanted to share their knowledge, no one has the time to learn it. Driven by the urgent demands of business, today's information users are impatient and demanding seekers of knowledge, expecting instant access to the most wide-ranging information to manage an increasingly complex world. The last thing they need is to take on the mastery of yet another world of complexity and frustration.

Figure 2-1 sketches how information typically works in today's typical business enterprise. Access is to active production databases or extract files created by individual and uncoordinated programs. Information is stored locally at a workstation or a department or local area network (LAN) file server for subsequent analysis and manipulation. While this is a great improvement over older processes (where access was possible only by using "dumb" terminals linked to unresponsive and expensive mainframes), there are a number of major drawbacks to this environment:

Large numbers of uncoordinated procedures and files—The great numbers of independently developed extract programs and shadow files result in massive information confusion, extra costs, and wasted computing resources.

Extensive information redundancy—This endemic condition necessitates a major effort to manage the many duplicate information copies. (The author has seen internal company studies that estimate this can be as high as 25 copies, on average, for *every* item of computer information. This amazingly high level of duplication seems more believable when one recognizes how many people at desktop machines are pulling information from a mainframe or minicomputer for special analysis). This duplication necessitates extra computer storage and processing costs, and leads to inconsistent and unreliable business decisions and actions.

Unsynchronized copies of information—Even when justified, duplicate information copies require complex and costly synchronization capabilities.

Lack of information relatability—The difficulty of relating information from disparate systems of automation means that each user must seek out or reinvent the rules and processing needed for combining multiple sources of information, and for keeping them updated as conditions change.

Information residing on diverse hardware platforms—Lack of information relatability is further compounded by the many computer hardware and software platforms that exist in most companies, making access and integration more complex and subject to change.

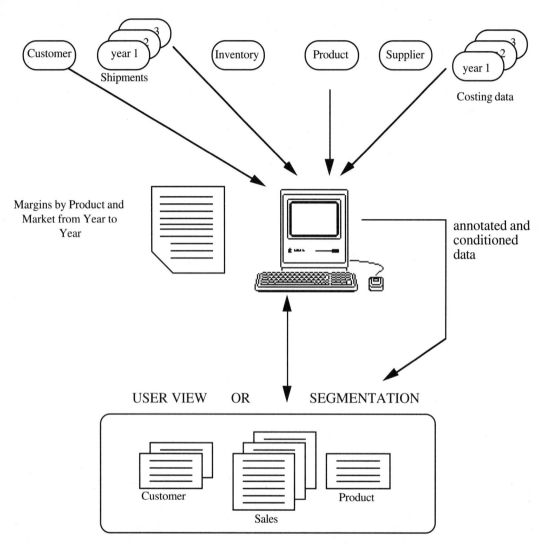

Figure 2-1. How Information Works In Today's Typical Business Enterprise

Poor quality information—The basic information contents themselves are often wrong, inaccurate, out-of-date, or inconsistent. Using inaccurate or old information as a base for business decisions is a recipe for disaster.

Information volatility—In addition to suspect information content, constant changes in the business mean that information is subject to constantly changing definitions, structures, and usage. This makes it necessary to alter inflexible, sensitive, and often unfamiliar computer programs and their data definitions (or risk depending on incompatible and shifting information meanings).

Information overload—The sheer volume of information grows at a rate that out-strips most companies' abilities to control and exploit it. Lost in that flood tide are the critical clues and indicators for spotting the fundamental problems and fleeting business opportunities.

Untimely information—This problem includes the time it takes for information to move from initial capture to availability, the length of time information is retained in usable form once captured, and the response time needed for satisfying a request for information. Inadequacy in any of these three time dimensions greatly reduces the value of information for a business.

Unavailable information—Information that is purged, summarized, archived, temporarily generated, or never captured reduces a company's opportunities to detect problems, analyze prospects, and accurately model future scenarios of action. A simple example is a critical calculation based on changing information values that is immediately lost because there is no mechanism for conveniently saving the temporary results for future use.

Inadequate information access—Not having free and ready access to information when and where needed (because of limited computer resources or other constraints) results in delays, dangerous short-cuts, and inadequate processing, which in turn leads to suboptimal business payoffs.

Information hoarding—Either through restrictive policy, poor systems, or personal practice, many companies do not get the greatest payoff from information because its users deny access to those who need it. Unshared information is a loss of business opportunity.

Companies have addressed some of these problems, usually one at a time and almost always while satisfying a particular demand for information. Collectively, the problems are numerous and major—daunting, to say the least. With the proper capabilities and a more general approach, however, it is possible to make significant headway in addressing several problem areas at once. And as each problem moves towards resolution or elimination under a general solution, it tends to resolve or limit the negative effects of the other problems.

THE PREVAILING LIMITS OF INFORMATION TECHNOLOGY

In addition to information itself, powerful and pervasive obstacles to effective information use lurk in the general field of the information technology profession and its industry, and in the practices and approaches that have evolved over the past 30 years. Some of these are problems of perception; others reflect self-serving political and philosophical agendas; still others reflect true limits for an organization wishing to fully utilize its information asset.

Conventional Automation's Diminishing Returns

In every large enterprise, all major business operations and functions have been automated at least once. Much of the value and benefit from Business Automation, be it cost reduction, efficiency, or increases in speed or accuracy, have been achieved. As pointed out in Chapter 1, there remain increasingly fewer areas to be automated. The business applications that remain, with a few exceptions, are not going to have the same high levels of return as the areas already automated.

Further Business Automation, by remodeling or upgrading functions currently automated or by converting older systems to newer technology (because changes in the business or in technology obsoleted the system), also keeps in play the effects of diminishing returns. While these efforts may be desirable, even mandatory, and the newer systems rich and powerful, they simply do not carry the kind of payoffs present in the first rounds of automation. In most cases, renovations of existing systems basically amount to doing the same job in a marginally better way.

In fact, as each new application is added to the inventory of existing systems, there is the added burden of having to integrate it with the portfolio of current systems. Therefore, each new system becomes ever more expensive, given that there is no general systems architecture in place to begin with, a situation still true for most enterprises.

The Unresponsiveness and Rigidity of Conventional Designs

The conventional automation design paradigm—moving from a specific problem to a specific solution—can be a masterful exercise in definition, analysis, and implementation. Bright people carefully define the desired capabilities, costs, and benefits, then design and implement the proposed solution. Nothing is quite as impressive as a well-designed information system tackling an endlessly complex and important business problem.

Unfortunately, this wonderful state of affairs is short-lived, since the problem and its associated solution often have a very short "half-life" in the business world. Business Automation, when based on matching fixed solutions to fixed problems, may actually impede an enterprise's ability to react to changing demands. Conventional approaches for developing systems are not at all adequate when competitive and operational pressures demand quick, dependable results. This can happen for two reasons: when a company cannot build or adjust its information systems quickly enough to respond to a rapidly changing marketplace and other conditions, and when its information systems, based on automating existing procedures and methods, cement the existing process, rendering the business process useless or difficult to alter when faced with these new and changing demands.

Conventional automation approaches can have great value to a company. In fact, the fundamental concept of Information Automation—of transforming raw computer data into business knowledge—wouldn't even be possible without these core production systems. But this orientation is intrinsically limiting, if not fatal. Developed in this fashion, conventional systems reinforce current practices, structures, biases, and views. And by restricting their capabilities to only known requirements, these systems encourage operational stagnation and marginal operating performance. For these "classical automation approaches" do not address the unanticipated and unstructured information requirements that will arrive on the manager's desk tomorrow.

By designing systems around the many fixed and linked aspects of the business, the gestalt of Business Automation locks an organization into a frozen process that grows progressively out-of-date. Worse, the systems are not put into the hands of the very people who know best when and how to change them: the information user who is first and foremost a business professional, not a computing engineer or programmer.

The Inaccessibility of Conventional Systems

Classic Business Automation also limits the information user to working within confined information structures and views based on the scope and nature of the system itself. This reduces the user's reach for grabbing larger and differing information areas as conditions and requirements demand. Further, typical Business Automation restricts access to the mechanisms and structures provided by the system itself.

While these may be sufficient for transaction processing, i.e., for placing customer orders, for controlling inventory movement, or for posting accounts payables, they are not well-suited to ad hoc reporting, executive information systems (EIS), and intensely analytical information requirements, not to mention handling incredibly complex "what-if" modeling scenarios, or massaging massive quantities of information for large-scale mission-critical decision support applications.

The Crippling Myth of Information Linkage

Although computing technologists have the skills and knowledge to help a company meet its information needs, because of no-longer relevant or no-longer correct premises, they find themselves not addressing the highest priority information opportunities. One such critical limitation springs from the misguided belief that they are the stewards of the company's information resource, an attitude that in some companies borders on bald-faced arrogance.

These technologists have perpetuated the myth that information is inherently a part of and captive to the system that creates it. This misconception argues that to use information from a production business system requires using the system itself, with all the problems and dangers associated with an exercise of that sort. This "misunderstanding" keeps MIS departments in power and, in an ironic way, causes them their biggest headache. It saddles them with the essentially impossible task of meeting the overwhelming needs of information users with the wrong set of tools, designs, and approaches.

Too many technology professionals have refused to admit that information can not only be freed from its sensitive parent systems, but that it should be completely liberated from them, opening the way to numerous creative solutions for exploiting the information asset. Liberating information from the clutches of unresponsive, and often mission-critical, business systems allows the enterprise the means and the power to use information in new and more substantial ways.

The Same Tired Old Approaches . . .

These are some of the realities that characterize the information systems milieu in many organizations today. Other constraints include the slowness and difficulty in dealing with a large MIS bureaucracy, and the even greater difficulty in getting access to relevant, accurate, rich, and cross-functional information.

Even with the availability of new and more powerful information technologies, most organizations do not adopt approaches that emphasize autonomous user access and development. Nor do they devote sufficient attention to designing systems that can quickly satisfy unanticipated and unstructured requirements. For many information professionals, the idea itself sounds contradictory, despite the fact that business always has to deal with unforeseen and sudden requirements.

As a result, efforts to implement new information technology solutions have not concentrated on providing effective ways for getting fast and accurate answers to problems and requirements not yet visible, or to enhancing the unstructured, creative process where people invent new uses of information. Instead, most of these efforts continue to be deployed in the interest of building conventional systems better and faster. While there is nothing wrong with that objective, it overlooks the truly major information needs and opportunities of the organization. Business organizations are crying for help, and the high priests of information technology continue to offer the same old tired approaches and solutions.

The Revenge of the Frustrated User

In reaction, disaffection sets in, causing users to go off on their own to find ways to get their information requirements met. Stand-alone capabilities result, duplicate capabilities spring into existence, and information hoarding tends to prevail. Hundreds of databases spring into existence. What was unpleasant but manageable chaos before, now threatens to overwhelm the enterprise with conflicting answers, contradictory facts, and irreconcilable conclusions.

THE PREVAILING VISIONS OF INFORMATION

The limiting aspects of information and information technologies discussed above are holding back enterprises from exploiting their greatest information possibilities. However, for some of them, the single greatest obstacle is that no adequate enabling vision has been articulated, no bold and sweeping strategy has taken hold within the company. Lacking the right kind of strategy and framework, enterprises cannot address information's true promise and the challenge of taming information's problems, thereby reducing its many difficulties and transforming it for major business advantage.

To better appreciate the need for such a vision, it is first necessary to under-stand the current state of information use in most business enterprises and the several guiding philosophies.

Information Chaos

There are some companies that have no overall vision for utilizing information or its attendant technologies. Their MIS departments are apparently content to apply information technologies on an individual and limited basis as needs, funds, and priorities dictate. These companies buy or build stand-alone, special-purpose systems that, while perhaps individually less expensive and more effi-cient than general-purpose solutions, quickly grow to resemble a complex, broken web of relationships—one that may best be described as *information chaos* (see Figure 2-2, Prevailing Visions). Unlike their desktop counterparts, i.e., desktop information users (whose development activities are far more limited in impact), the company's professional technologists build large, complex, costly, mission-critical systems without much concern for the future.

Such organizations pay dearly for those quick, cheap solutions, as they are increasingly required to produce ever more complex and interrelated capabilities to compete in a tougher, faster-changing, and hungrier business world. Their lack of a common information architecture hampers their flexibility, responsiveness, innovation, and intelligence-gathering. Complex and expensive integrating mechanisms have to be laid over this mess to meet even a small portion of their strategic needs. At some point, someone will realize that the entire systems and database portfolio has to be replaced *en masse,* a prospect unlikely to meet with any real success.

Information Central

Other companies, typically as an extension of general centrist organization prac-tices, have embraced a vision of *information central,* a vast wheel of connected hardware and communication equipment tied to one or more massive central mainframes in the corporate "glass house." This central complex protects and dishes out information from a variety of databases according to complex and hard-to-understand rules.

This environment has all the disadvantages of any tightly managed hierarchi-cal or central command arrangement, including poor responsiveness, lack of flex-ibility, and great expense. While there may be a well-thought-out hardware and software structure behind it, there is just as much chaos and lack of coordination, with regard to its information asset, as in organizations with no vision at all.

Information Scatterplots

Still other enterprises have adopted a vision possibly best described as *informa-tion scatterplots.* This consists of an imposing array of heterogeneous systems and platforms tied loosely together in a network that passes information back and forth via established links and protocols. The companies taking this direc-

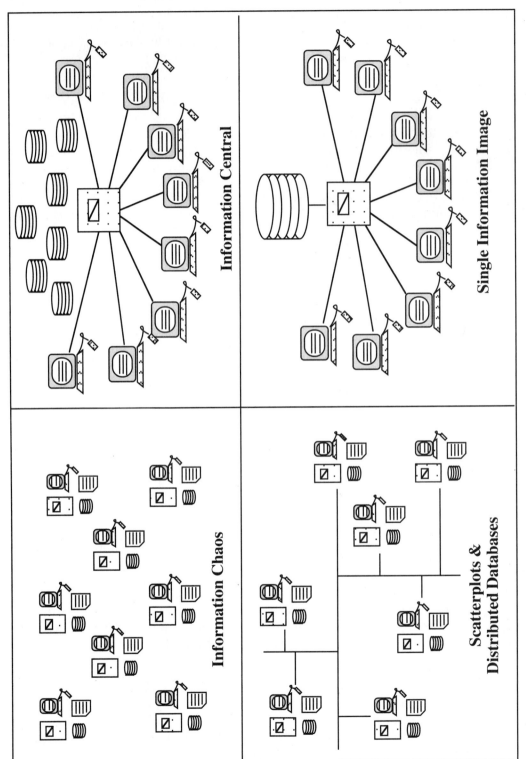

Figure 2-2. Prevailing Visions of Information

tion have typically been the first to seize the benefits of technology downsizing, first with minicomputers and later with local networks of workstations and microcomputers.

Despite its attractive price-performance (at least as compared to "information central"), from an information perspective, this collection of dots and lines fails to provide a coherent vision of information.

Distributed Databases

A variant of the "information scatterplot" environment is one in which that same network of scattered systems maintains selected portions (or copies) of the information resource at designated locations. This arrangement is often referred to as distributed information or *distributed databases,* and relies on elaborate routing and synchronization mechanisms for connecting the requesting user with the desired information.

Despite the advantages of a generally more cost-effective computing environment, this vision introduces enormous complexity and cost into the management and utilization of information. Nonetheless, it has great potential, and depending on the particular enterprise, may represent the preferred strategy despite its current disadvantages. It will be seen in Chapter 12 that most of the major computer vendors are working towards some form of this vision.

Single Information Image

Single data store or *single information image* is a vision that calls for information to be resident in one physical location—there is only one copy of an information element. It demands that this one copy be managed by a single database system, and that it be under one enterprisewide information structure. All information requests take place against this single image.

This is the most extreme of information visions. The benefits for achieving it would be immense: uniformity, consistency, integration, timeliness, simplicity, and lack of redundancy. But while this vision is bold, sweeping, and broad, it is not practical. Reducing 25 copies of every information element in the enterprise to one seems unlikely. For example, "single information image" would require the sharing of one image of information between mission-critical ATM systems and large-scale management decision support requirements, two largely incompatible processing environments.

Today's information technologies simply cannot handle that demand in truly large-scale information environments. And even if such shared processing could be handled, getting companywide agreement on the security, form, retention, and level of detail of that poor, overworked single information copy would be unlikely, given the many different computing needs, processing environments, user styles, and physical requirements of a large company.

A company embracing "single information image" would also have to deal with having all of its users rely on an information capability modeled according to a single information blueprint or design. This might be possible if the business could stop operating for a year and everyone could agree on a common design, both obviously impossible.

Even if a company surmounted all these problems, there would be the all-important matter of implementation. How does an enterprise go about replacing all the information managed by its dozens and dozens of information systems by a single structure? This would require converting or replacing every system in the company. Such an ambitious endeavor is well beyond the capabilities of most enterprises, and if it were doable, would cost far more than could be justified. Besides, such a feat would take too long, running the very strong risk of being obsolete when finished.

One large enterprise has recently embarked on a five-year, $50 million program for doing exactly that, laying out their ambitious program in several company pronouncements and internal newsletters. Systems personnel are diligently trying to convert the old systems under this umbrella vision. While the general ambition is laudable, the strategy for accomplishing it is misguided. The extraordinary investment in this impossible dream assures that the company will have little money left over to spend on projects that would yield far greater benefit, such as transforming data to help gain competitive advantage.

What is needed is a far better way to get at the benefits of *single information image,* a more pragmatic yet still bold and sweeping approach to employing information technologies for harnessing the power of information.

3

A New Vision: Enterprise Information Technologies (EIT)

This chapter presents a response to the opportunity to seize competitive advantage by exploiting the power of information, and addresses the problems and obstacles involved in doing so. This response takes the form of a general information architecture or vision made up of closely related objectives, components, and levels, along with a framework for enabling that vision in an adopting company. It is general enough in nature to avoid becoming obsolete due to technological and methodological developments, yet specific enough to allow an implementing organization to make significant progress without having to reinvent the wheel. This vision is called *Enterprise Information Technologies,* and its major elements are highlighted in Table 3-1.

THE UNDERLYING EIT PHILOSOPHY

Enterprise Information Technologies (or EIT) incorporates a pragmatic attitude for exploiting a company's information asset. It is results-oriented and it provides an effective way to meet immediate information needs while constantly moving closer to larger, longer-term business and information goals. EIT is a coherent set of workable ideas and integrating concepts derived from leading-edge experiences.

EIT is also flexible. While it contains a core set of standard components, they are meant to be adapted to the unique conditions of the individual enterprise.

The EIT vision is grounded in a reversal of the traditional problem–solution paradigm, the notion that there is always a straight and clear line between a

TABLE 3-1   HIGHLIGHTS OF THE EIT VISION

The Underlying Philosophy
Pragmatic Flexible General in nature The Crucial Premise—Separate Information Automation and Business Automation
The Key Objectives
Transform data into competitive advantage Sustain competitive advantage by building on what exists Empower the information user Use information for guiding information technologies
The Central Components
General information strategy Central information resource General-purpose information capability Common information utility
The Major Development Levels
Level 1: Replicated central information resource Level 2: Official system of record Level 3: Single information image
The Enabling Framework
Identify the information opportunities Design the general information solution Integrate the information technologies Implement the general information solution

defined problem and a designed solution. Enterprise Information Technologies is, instead, a general solution designed to meet specific but not fully defined (or even known) information needs. This general capability makes it far more powerful than conventional solutions, for it encourages information uses that promise to stretch the limits of the possible and that can bring overwhelming benefit to the originating organization.

The Crucial EIT Premise

The basic premise underlying the Enterprise Information Technologies vision is that, in order to exploit the information asset to the fullest extent possible, the automation of information must be sharply separated from the automation of business operations.

The reason is simple: The needs of those who use information to meet production objectives (i.e., Business Automation users) are different from those who use information to achieve strategic, tactical, and managerial objectives (i.e., Information Automation users). Standard approaches to Business Automation, designed to support the everyday operations of the business, are process-oriented, work in real-time (or the just-past), and are concerned with speed and efficiency. Business Automation does not provide the information capabilities required by analysts, project team members, planners, marketers, operations managers, and senior executives who are concerned with global perspectives rather than specific processes, the future rather than the past, and with precision and insight over speed and efficiency.

Two sets of users, two sets of requirements—yet, most Business Automation efforts attempt to meet both sets of requirements. For example, in addition to processing orders, matching them to finished goods inventory, and preparing items for shipping, an order entry and inventory control system might produce summary booking and billing reports for management and provide on-line access to a limited amount of detailed data (perhaps a month's worth) on customer orders and shipment information.

To enhance these modest "Information Automation" attempts, companies turn to new tools and approaches, such as fourth-generation languages (4GLs) and graphical user interfaces (GUIs), to allow users to meet information requirements beyond those provided by the system itself. These are important advances, but still part of an approach dependent on the production system.

Despite greater awareness of the importance of providing information for these purposes, most capabilities are "tacked on" to Business Automation systems almost as an after-thought, and limited to whatever information capabilities are available. Critically important, user access is restricted to those segments of information collected for the core users of the production system.

Attempts at simultaneously serving the needs of Business and Information Automation users are destined to be limited in their effectiveness. Basic production systems simply cannot hope to serve two sets of disparate needs. Information must be released from the confinement of a company's basic production systems.

Separating Information Automation and Business Automation

Separating Information Automation from Business Automation does not mean that new methods for collecting information must be created. Nor does it mean that existing capabilities, infrastructures, and plans must be tossed out and an all-new environment built from scratch. What it does mean is that Information Automation capabilities are implemented "on top of" what has been done so far, that they fit in with the hardware, systems, and information developed and improved over many years and at great expense.

What is really implied by the act of separating the different requirements is the notion that, *not only is it possible* to address the needs of information users separately and still take advantage of what has gone on before, but *it is far better to do so.* Neither class of automation user must be prevented from achieving the advantages so important to the welfare of the company. Each side can seek out its own most effective methods and tools and its own most appropriate practices and approaches, linked by the central energy of the enterprise—information.

Freed from its operational function, information becomes the sole object of a separate class of automation, with its own set of rules, functions, and objectives (rather than being seen primarily as a means for supporting a business function—handling a sales order, preparing a financial statement, planning a manu-facturing process). It can then be managed by a dedicated, user-based capability that seeks to eliminate the many problems that exist with information and make it available for an increasingly larger set of purposes and users. Information, once the captive of production systems, is freed to be exploited for maximum business advantage. With all that information available at the flick of a switch and in whatever form users choose, it is likely that knowledge and uses never antici-pated or believed possible will be discovered by the company's most innovative employees.

THE KEY EIT OBJECTIVES

The Enterprise Information Technologies vision is based on closely related infor-mation objectives. These objectives provide the *raison d' etre* for its existence and the fundamental motivation that moves a company towards the needed policies, mechanisms, and capabilities. The objectives are ranked in order of importance:

- Transform data into competitive advantage
- Sustain competitive advantage by building on what exists
- Empower the information user
- Use information for guiding information technologies

Transform Data into Competitive Advantage

The prime EIT objective is to transform raw production data into usable business information for competitive advantage. This objective takes advantage of the already collected data in a company's basic production systems, as well as data available from other, usually external, sources. This objective is attained by pro-viding information that is:

- Intelligible, timely, consistent, reliable, and available
- Stored at the lowest possible level of detail
- Maintained for the longest possible period of time
- Part of a coherent image that accurately reflects the state of the company
- Organized in ways most natural for information users
- Easy and quick to access and handle
- Shared fully with all users in the company

Sustain Competitive Advantage by Building on what Exists

In addition to the benefits gained by building information capabilities on top of existing production systems and their data, once that portion of raw data is trans-formed for competitive advantage, another objective of the EIT vision is to lever-age that capability for further advantage by keeping it available and improving on it. This is done by the:

- Addition and integration of new areas, types, and sources of information
- Enhancement of existing information contents

- Reuse of existing Information Automation capabilities
- Accumulation of a body of knowledge about the company's information resource
- Sharing of the information, artifacts, and results with a maximum number of users

Empower the Information User

Essential to achieving these objectives is the ability of users to determine how to plan, design, and manage needed information capabilities on their own, rather than their being forced into using rigid and predetermined technologies, intermediaries, or procedures. Another key EIT objective would provide users with the capabilities for satisfying imprecise, poorly understood, and unanticipated information requirements—the way most problems and opportunities arrive.

Information and the other end products of Information Automation should be as readily available to and adaptable for users as the end products of any common utility such as electricity, telephone, or water, are available to consumers. Information users' purposes, formats, and approaches are not constrained, nor their capabilities limited, in order to permit the widest use.

EIT capabilities empower users by giving them control over the access and manipulation of information. With such power, preoccupation with mechanics quickly gives way to solving problems and seizing opportunities.

Use Information for Guiding Information Technologies

Another critical EIT objective is to make information itself, rather than hardware, communications, or software, the central element that guides the application of information technologies within the company. Thus, information technologies are applied primarily to serve the information needs of the company and its body of users, rather than the latter conforming to the dictates and restrictions of technology, its plans, or its architectures. This objective is achieved gradually, as the components and dimensions of the EIT vision are implemented in subsequent stages and levels of sophistication.

THE CENTRAL EIT COMPONENTS

EIT's central components have been derived and generalized from concrete and specific real-world experiences, specifically from a handful of innovative companies who have been singularly successful in exploiting data for competitive advantage. As the common threads of these breakthrough efforts, these major components serve as the core of a conceptual structure that allows other companies to benefit from these often painful experiences. The components are:

- A general information strategy
- A central information resource

- A general-purpose information capability
- A common information utility

These are *conceptual components,* i.e., they do not describe the *physical solutions* that underlie them, and they may be enabled by more than one set of specific technologies. However, while not physical in nature, these components have been made possible by a class of technologies loosely labeled *enterprise information technologies.* (The real-world experiences are discussed mostly in Parts II and III. Specific solutions, concrete technologies, and recommended processing arrangements are dealt with primarily in Part IV.)

General Information Strategy

One of the EIT's central components is a *general information strategy* that states the company's broad information goals, values, and directions. It identifies, justifies, and prioritizes the major opportunity areas. Such a strategy establishes guidelines for moving forward in a coherent and managed manner, and helps to shape an information environment with a reasonable degree of order and focus. It is the basis for choosing the mechanisms for coordinating information, computing, and people resources.

As will be seen in Part II, companies have numerous areas of opportunity for exploiting information. Seen collectively, these areas connect and overlap. To embrace a general information strategy means understanding and believing in the fundamental value of the company's *collective information opportunity,* and in articulating a strategy for seizing that collective opportunity.

A general information strategy provides the basis for supporting policies, incentives, controls, and responsibilities (these are discussed in Part V). Once in place, these management pronouncements keep things on track and moving in the right direction, helping to level-set the opinions and purposes of all members of the company, and establishing a common base for communications and coordination.

EIT capabilities bring greatest benefits for the company whose general information strategy supports a multitrack, open development environment, and where information capabilities are implemented under a gradual approach driven by critical business needs. Adapting the core elements of the EIT vision is an effective way to articulate a company's general information strategy, tailoring its underlying philosophy, premises, objectives, central components, levels, and enabling framework to the needs of the organization.

Central Information Resource

At the dead center of the EIT vision is a *central information resource* that is designed to accurately and fully reflect the detailed and complete state of the business. This "computerized information picture" is made up of all relevant data about the company and its operations—both internal and external. It is organized in a way that corresponds to the shared mental model of the corporation: how its managers see things working and how the fundamental functions and goals of the company relate to one another.

The single view or image of the enterprise contained in this central information resource is carefully organized to reflect basic and enduring business characteristics. At the same time, it is capable of responding immediately and precisely to the actual changes in the business environment and to the changing ideas about the business. This resource is capable of expanding to assimilate new information and to create new arrangements of existing information.

This is not an "information depot" or "data warehouse" where people check information in and out as they need it, or some massive data storage facility where information is placed and everyone hopes for the best. This is a highly organized, dynamic, almost organic, electronic library of facts, figures, and annotations made accessible to the savvy and novice user by a comprehensive index or directory.

Data flows in from source systems and is sifted and enhanced (or conditioned) according to tightly managed processes (see Figure 3-1 for how information works with a central information resource under the EIT's vision of information). But while the conditioned contents of the EIT's central information resource is designed *only* to meet users' needs for information, this core component is not based *exclusively* on those requirements, because doing so would make it quickly obsolete as new problems, opportunities, organizations, and people came and went. Instead, the organizing structures for information are fundamental to the business. They go beyond the people, procedures, and organizational structures in place, beyond even the current profit-and-loss territories. These structures conform to the basics about the customer, about the company's products and services, and about the fundamental operations and functions of the business.

This unbiased (or neutral) information design leaves people free to ask questions in any form they want. It allows the CEO (this one, the next one, the one after) to have his or her finger on the pulse of the company, regardless how the company is organized today (centralized), tomorrow (decentralized), or the day after (some American version of Japan's vertical industry *zaibatsu*). The central information resource allows users anywhere in the organization to access reliable information about any area or function of the business, no matter the computing, organizational, communications, or logistical arrangements in place.

General-Purpose Information Capability

To effectively maintain and use an EIT's central information resource requires a *general-purpose information capability*. This broader type of information capability standardizes on a wide range of critical Information Automation functions, especially those used repeatedly, and allows the company's users to easily change and customize functions to meet unique and changing needs, styles, and conditions.

A general-purpose information capability supports the modeling and definition of new and changing information, the extracting of data from source systems for placement in the central information resource, and the critically important "scrubbing" or conditioning that makes information suitable for analysis, manip-

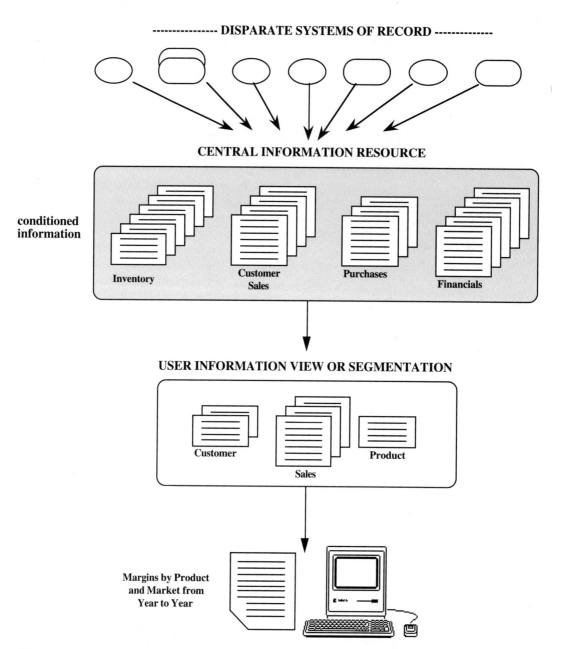

Figure 3-1. How Information Works With a Central Information Resource under the EIT Vision

ulation, presentation, and action. This general capability also provides a rich user directory (containing information about information), a constantly updated set of tutorial, navigational, and explanation aids, facilities for automatically integrating different types of information, and procedures for "embedding intelligence" in the ongoing automation of information.

An EIT's general-purpose information capability contains an institutional memory that resurrects previous solutions and results for maximum reuse and modification, and provides users with powerful analysis capabilities, such as those that automatically discover patterns and relationships about the company's operations that are buried in large collections of information.

While general-purpose and common, this information capability does not unnecessarily constrain users in their handling of information. Information is made usable for a variety of people and purposes, some unknown, others expected, such as:

- The manager seeking specific and detailed information on a current problem
- The executive who only wants a one-line summary every quarter
- The computer-literate recent college graduate using power software
- The senior manager who has her staff operate the workstation for her
- The sales rep querying his customer's purchases for the past three years
- The planning analyst working on a complex financial projection model

Most important, a general-purpose information capability gives control of the information process to those who best understand the business context, the relevant needs and motivations, and the important connections that exist in information—the users themselves. With the *right kind* of general-purpose information capability, users—from the entry-level order entry clerk to the seasoned top executive—are free to select, filter, and shape the facts at hand without technical middlemen, placing them at the true center of the EIT vision.

Common Information Utility

General-purpose capabilities are more expensive and difficult to establish than a one-time, focused system, even though the former's payoff is greater over the long haul. To justify a general-purpose information capability and the infrastructure to support a central information resource requires that a company look at information in a new way—as if it were the product of a *common information utility*. This perspective not only changes the company's attitudes about information; it creates a basis for making choices and for committing funds in a rational, business-like manner.

Take the telephone or electric power: Who would run a business without them? Yet, the initial investments in their "taming" infrastructures were immense. Information has greater potential for differentiating competing companies, as industry-standard information technologies for creating an "information infrastructure" within every company exist today. Information should be as readily available and convenient to use as making a telephone call or switching on a light.

The difficulty is not so much in figuring out how to design and implement these general capabilities (although that is by no means easy), but in settling on an approach that insures that each further investment, each additional application, and each new use improves the return on the company's information investment. Such an approach leverages technology, people, business needs, and information itself.

A common information utility *leverages technology* by employing the most attractive computing platforms, software, connectivity, and information processing arrangements. It takes advantage of proven and appropriate technological solutions that not only eliminate the need for custom development, but add important new value by encouraging creative information uses and applications.

There is a rich base of diverse technologies "out there" that, when integrated under the EIT's guiding vision, can provide powerful general information capabilities at relatively low cost. Flexible technology integration not only works with the company's existing hardware and systems infrastructure and processing arrangements; it allows future expansion to take place without costly replacement or expensive renovation.

A common information utility also *leverages people*, especially in the important areas of motivation and reward. An environment built around the EIT vision emphasizes innovative uses of information, and encourages each organization to seek out business opportunities using a common information capability. People and business units are free to make their own information plans and generate their own information solutions, subject only to normal business conventions (such as justifying the cost in advance and being held accountable for the results) and to using the company's general information capabilities.

With this approach, there is no competition for scarce skills or resources. Each group moves at its own pace, having its own skills, access to information capabilities, and funds to pursue its highest priority opportunities. In this setting, every user is helping to create and expand the information utility for the entire company. With each successive use, information's quality and usability improves yet another notch.

A companywide information utility *leverages business needs* as well. While several information applications may be worked on simultaneously, all information opportunities are not going to be accomplished at the same time. Different opportunity areas have different levels of importance which change over time. The full extent of the information utility (and opportunity) is achieved gradually, with incremental expansion along several fronts.

But how does a company get started? How does it first erect the infrastructure and core general-purpose capabilities? Under the EIT vision, a company identifies its most strategic or critical opportunity areas and moves on from there. The first opportunity is highly significant to the business: its expected benefits, *on its own*, justifies the initial investment. Once built, that same capability becomes more and more cost-effective as implementation proceeds in other areas of the company.

For example, the first area might be a critical customer satisfaction program that tracks customer purchase activity. By adding further information, several marketing programs are put into effect, leveraging further that original base of information. With product marketing in the information picture, other areas are included—product costing, for example—further expanding its usefulness. At this point, the company's information utility is being used to support a number of decision support and executive information systems, all helping management better monitor performance. As each new need comes into being, it further leverages the value of a common information utility.

Finally, a common information utility *leverages the actual information resource itself*. Shared use of information makes its value or return higher. General-purpose processing reduces net new invention and improves consistency of result, which in turn increases the usefulness of information for different purposes and organizations. Reusable facilities further improve the cost-effectiveness of an information utility.

All these factors tend to improve the economies of scale of a common information utility, as the level of information use increases throughout the company. Once collected, good information may be used over and over again, with no further cost except for the minor processing expense. In this fashion, good information becomes better information, as each user adds value with their increasing knowledge. And as the uses of an information utility expand in several directions at once, they begin to tie together the most fundamental areas of business opportunities, further leveraging the central information resource.

THE MAJOR EIT DEVELOPMENT LEVELS

How should these components take shape as a company delivers information to meet ever-changing business needs? While each company evolves EIT capabilities according to its unique and prevailing plans and needs, there are three "levels" of development that may be used to guide expansion to its ultimate goals. Reaching these levels or plateaus assures a company that adequate progress is being made in achieving the company's most critical business and information objectives. The three levels are:

- Level 1: Replicated central information resource
- Level 2: Official system of record
- Level 3: Single information image

As was true of the central EIT components, these levels do not specify physical or implementation arrangements—they, too, are conceptual in nature. How a company achieves them and what they use in the way of concrete products, detailed designs, and actual configurations is a subject reserved for Parts III, IV, and V.

Level 1: Replicated Central Information Resource

EIT Level 1 calls for separating the two classes of automation and linking them by a replicated central information resource. A general-purpose information capability is created that transforms operational data into information for storage in the company's Information Database, a key component of the central information resource. The other major component is the Information Directory, which contains the rules and processing for transformation, and the definitions and structures for managing the information in the Information Database. The Business Information Model is the "information map" that organizes information according to the boundaries and relations that make up the shared mental model of the corporation (see Figure 3-}2, EIT Level 1).

At this level, the central information resource contains only information needed by the first application. This is a business opportunity area that has been carefully chosen with the dual objective of meeting urgent business needs and providing sufficient "information critical mass" (i.e., information of the range and interest to seed future expansion). While first applications vary by company and by industry (and whose identification and selection is the major subject of Part II), there are several areas considered excellent starting places. These are highlighted in Table 3-}2, Ideal First EIT Applications.

After information critical mass is established, Level 1 is characterized by expansion of the central information resource, continually fed more conditioned information as new Information Automation applications are developed. Gradually, older, independent "Information Automation" systems are eliminated (and their information copies with them) by new applications using the central information resource.

This continues until all Information Automation needs are being met by EIT general-purpose information capabilities, and there is only *one copy* of every information element in the company in the Information Database. (This is a deliberate simplification. Other copies will no doubt continue to exist in Business

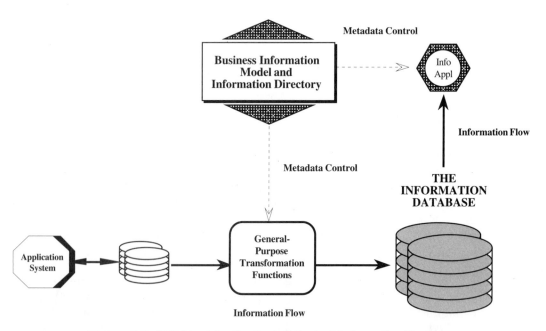

Figure 3-2. EIT Level 1   Replicated Central Information Resource

TABLE 3-2   IDEAL FIRST EIT APPLICATIONS

Customer Areas

Information to help customers be more effective and profitable
Information to help tailor products and services to particular customer needs
Any and all information links between the company and its customers

Marketing Areas

Information that facilitates integration of products and services
Information capabilities to lock in the customer by raising "switching" costs
Information capabilities that increase the cost or "barrier for entry" for competitors
Any and all information about market, competitor, and industry activities
Information capabilities for innovations in sales, marketing, distribution, or service
Information capabilities for finely focused promotion and advertising

Product Areas

Information capabilities for greater product functionality, reliability, training, and use
Information capabilities to help develop and deliver new products and services

Management Areas

Information for improved business performance tracking
Information to improve margins, market share, earnings, and customer satisfaction
Information to raise the company's ability to compete in the marketplace
Information for innovative organizational or cultural "reshaping" efforts
Information capabilities to help integrate acquisitions, mergers, and partnerships
Information links with vendors and distributors
Information capabilities to foster business expansion and growth

Information Areas

Information that is captured close to the source, especially by the customer
New and potentially useful detailed information areas
New and potentially useful historical information areas
Information that transcends organizational and functional boundaries
Information capabilities that can help discover important aspects of the business
Information capabilities that handle massive amounts of information
Information for meeting complex ad hoc needs for executives

Automation systems, perhaps many. And the Information Database will certain ly not contain *every* information element in the company, only those items designated as important).

Level 2: Official System of Record

When there is only one copy of replicated information, the second level is reached (see Figure 3-}3, EIT Level 2), and the central information resource, by policy and use, becomes the *official system of record* of the enterprise, the one official representation of information accepted without question throughout the company.

At this point, the transformation links between the central information resource and the company's Business Automation systems are expanded to

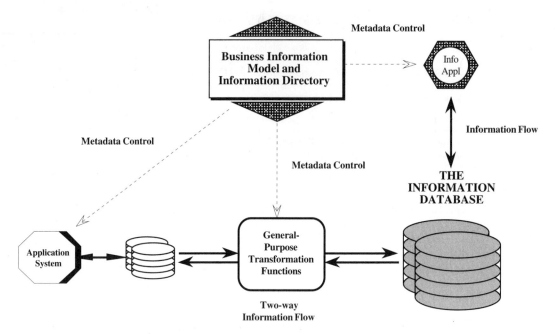

Figure 3-3. EIT Level 2   Official System of Record

ensure that changes to information copies on either side of the "automation
boundary" are reflected in both environments, i.e., that two-way synchronization
exists. (At the first EIT level, except for information coming from external
sources, or annotations made directly to the Information Database, information
moved one-way only, from Business Automation systems to the central information resource.)

This new synchronization suggests that the Information Database is no longer
a "replica," however enhanced and independent, of the data in a company's production systems. Although the major movement of information continues to flow
from Business Automation databases to the Information Database, both information copies have separate and distinct processes that maintain their own structures and contents.

At EIT Level 2, Information Automation applications continue to be developed.
New areas and types of information are integrated into the central information
resource, gradually filling out the information picture of the company. More users
come on-line, further expanding the use and scope of EIT capabilities. The general power and speed of information analysis and interpretation increases, as the
collective knowledge of the business expands to include more organizations and
users. Powerful new applications emerge that take in wider swaths of information, as people seek to understand the more fundamental operations and
widespread issues of the company.

In the meantime, as Business Automation systems are continually developed
or renovated, the information definitions and processing rules resident in the
Information Directory are made part of their specifications. Hence, the informa-

tion formats and functions used by EIT capabilities slowly manifest in production systems. This reduces the complexity of the transformation process, as both sets of information gradually come to resemble each other. While Business Automation applications are designed with the idea of moving towards smaller numbers of information copies—reaching ultimately one copy—each class of automation continues to use its own information.

Level 3: Single Information Image

When the information definitions and rules used by applications on both side of the "automation boundary" are essentially the same, the third EIT level is reached (see Figure 3-}4, EIT Level 3). From this point on, a single information image comes into existence, as new and revised Business Automation systems shift over to using the central information resource directly, rather than their own separate databases.

(Note: Use of a truly common information resource requires improvement equal to several levels of magnitude in both the power and price-performance of today's information technologies. Based on the rapid advance in hardware and software technologies, however, those improvements are expected to be available well before most companies are ready for them.)

As the two copies of information are reduced to one, the central information resource jointly serves the two separate classes of information needs, making the corporate system of record also the single information image of the enterprise. What was seen in Chapter 2 as virtually impossible to accomplish as a single con-centrated effort has occurred gradually over time and at a fraction of the cost under the EIT vision.

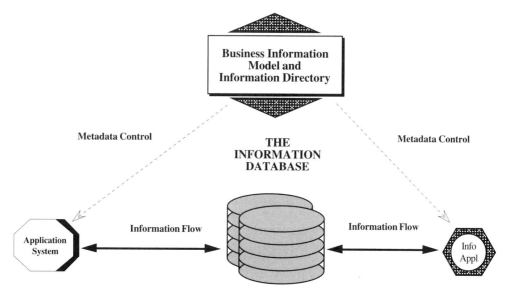

Figure 3-4. EIT Level 3   Single Information Image

THE EIT ENABLING FRAMEWORK

The EIT vision also provides an *Enabling Framework* that a company can use to plan and manage the tasks needed to make that information vision a reality. This framework concentrates on those crucial activities needed to:

- Identify the information opportunities
- Design the general information solution
- Integrate the information technologies
- Implement the general information solution

Such a framework, like the rest of EIT, must be comprehensive enough to bring sizable value to the adopting company, and flexible enough to be able to be adapted to the major differences of each company without losing its basic cohesiveness. Presented below is that framework; it also serves as a summary of the remainder of the book.

Identifying the Information Opportunities

The first part of the overall enabling process looks at the information opportunities of the business enterprise, that is at the portions of its overall information opportunity terrain. These broad opportunity areas are the most likely places for a company to exploit information for addressing its most critical goals, problems, and operations.

Strategic information opportunities advance a company's most fundamental goals and needs, either with head-on competitive strategies or enhanced organizational abilities. For most companies, especially in highly competitive industries, the key business strategy is understanding customer behavior. Another important source of information advantage lies in organizational redesigning, in which a company strategically employs information to reshape its organizational structures and processes to increase operational effectiveness, or to reduce costs of operations, or both.

Tactical information opportunities are best addressed by a high-level capability using information collected from the strategic programs mentioned above, especially to respond to unexpected and fast-moving events. Successful but isolated tactical responses based on the information resource are institutionalized under the EIT approach, thereby helping to protect a company from surprises and unexpected problems.

Management information opportunities to improve leadership effectiveness exist in all companies. This is an especially important area for enterprises with a management style best characterized as long-range in orientation, offense-minded, strategic, participatory in nature, and risk-oriented. As the range and depth of the central information resource grows, managers determined to operate by the facts find their ability vastly improved, whether to plan, manage, make decisions, or motivate employees.

Designing the General Information Solution

This is the synthesizing process that creates a design for a general information solution. This solution is the "engine" of the EIT vision and is primarily concerned with establishing a general-purpose information capability and central information resource. The EIT Design includes an underlying information infrastructure that, forming the basis of a common information utility, is used for systematically exploiting all of a company's information opportunities. The mechanism for doing this is a consistent user-based process for transforming raw data into useful business information.

EIT precursors and prototypes provide useful models for designing a general information solution. Such a design builds on the past experiences of companies who have pushed the limits of technology in using information for meeting pressing business needs. More recent experiences serve as concrete prototypes that help companies move ahead while skipping the more painful interim stages. The applicability of these prototypes for an individual enterprise is determined by comparing the common factors that make it possible to transfer these prototype approaches and solutions.

The EIT Design takes the most successful elements from these prototypes and weaves them into a flexible yet concrete set of functions and features. The *EIT Information Infrastructure* includes the Information Desktop, the Information Directory, and the Information Database, respectively the eyes, brain, and heart of a company's information solution.

EIT Information Transformation is grouped into four functions: (1) Information Design helps users understand and enhance the usefulness of information; (2) Information Acquisition makes the bridge to production systems, where source data is extracted and placed in an accessible central information resource; (3) Information Analysis is concerned with navigating this resource, testing it against prevailing opinions, and generating new hypotheses; (4) Information Delivery addresses interpretation and presentation of the results, and feeds business outcomes into the next cycles of information transformation.

Integrating the Information Technologies

This is the partly scientific, partly artistic process of integrating essential technologies for bringing EIT capabilities into existence. This approach incrementally creates a general information capability by employing proven technologies and eliminating custom or "net new" development.

An *EIT Technology Integration Model* helps companies configure a coherent information processing environment and employ a flexible structure by which technologies can be selected and integrated. The ideal processing environment is based on *Large-Scale Client Server Architecture*, which offers the ability to access terabytes of information anywhere in the company. Included in this model is a comprehensive set of criteria that helps companies select technologies that meet the requirements of their EIT vision. They are critically important from a number of standpoints, such as performance, connectivity, capacity, price-performance, functionality, and sharability.

Attractive *enterprise information technologies* must then be matched against the features and criteria of the EIT Design and Integration Model. Generic technologies include the microprocessor, object, and expert reasoning technologies. Infrastructure technologies include the central database server, linked local database servers, enterprisewide connectivity, intelligent client workstations, industrial-strength relational databases, information directories, and industry-standard interfaces. Transformation technologies include capabilities for information design, re-engineering, extraction, conditioning, analysis, discovery, and delivery.

The implementing company must also examine the most promising of the *vendor information visions*, those packaged information architectures, and compare them to the EIT Design and Integration Model. These architectures include IBM's Information Warehouse, NCR's Open Cooperative Computing Architecture (along with Teradata's Database Computer), DEC's Information Network, Computer Associates' CA90s, and Oracle's Parallel Server.

Implementing the General Information Solution

This is the actual implementation process, where selected information technologies are incrementally deployed to meet business requirements according to the company's general information strategy. A company needs an *EIT implementation roadma*p for realizing the goals and objectives of the overall EIT vision.

Getting an implementation program started requires *establishing a favorable information environment*. This includes using the EIT vision, its objectives, staging, design, etc., as an initial base for the program, then finding a powerful champion and enlisting the help of the true information users. It is also necessary to establish a general information strategy, with policies, planning mechanisms, incentives, expectations, controls, and clearly defined responsibilities. Organizations must further plan to head off the expected blockers of the program, especially those people who will see the program as a threat to the status quo.

Once started, it is important for a company to *select and prototype the first application, and justify the entire EIT program.* Selecting the first opportunity area is critical to overall success. Prototyping provides a cheap insurance policy that the target selection and general approach is correct. Justifying the overall investment requires a rational business case that takes qualitative and organizational enabling benefits into account without ignoring ROI and cost/benefit considerations. This expanded business case blends strategic, economic, and alternatives analysis, while fully accounting for expected benefits, costs, and risks.

*Implementing the Solutio*n requires charting the *EIT implementation vector*s that describe the information opportunities, the information areas involved, the affected organizational units, the needed capabilities and functions, and the required technologies, for the different stages and levels of implementation. Each vector contains priorities, sequences, and considerations that are an integral part of the implementation program. The company follows a phased, incremental approach to implementation, bringing significant benefits into existence while working toward the successful establishment of a companywide EIT capability.

part II

IDENTIFYING THE INFORMATION OPPORTUNITIES

4

Information for Critical Business Strategies

This chapter begins a survey of the information opportunity terrain within a company and is the first component of the EIT Enabling Framework. It provides executives with a systematic approach to estimating the importance of and level of payoff for exploiting information in different areas, and is the basis for articulating a general information strategy. Examples accompany each of the major information opportunities.

This chapter focuses on the use of information to support or drive critical competitive and organizational redesign strategies. Together with the tactical information opportunities described in Chapter 5 and the management information areas in Chapter 6, they make up a company's collective information opportunity.

Each information area, while important on its own and varying in value from company to company, is related to the other areas and is part of a coherent whole. Viewing these opportunities within a larger context opens a company to the possibility of exploiting each opportunity according to prevailing priorities and goals and under a general information solution.

CHALLENGES FACING THE BUSINESS ENTERPRISE

There is a host of challenges facing the senior executive of the large corporation. Understanding the nature of these challenges is vital to developing effective responses to them, including the use of information technologies. Many of these challenges are external to the organization. The world of business is changing rapidly, putting pressure on corporations to explore more effective and creative ways of conducting their business.

Some of the external forces are: dynamic economic fluctuations; increasing competition from overseas firms; corporate restructuring due to mergers, divestitures, and acquisitions; more sophisticated customer demand for quality, options, and alternatives; pressures for downsizing to adjust to lower demand; closer relations with critical distributors and suppliers; and increasing demands from shareholders for greater accountability, higher revenues, and earnings.

The large corporation is also subject to a host of internal conflicts. The company's most central goals may be at the mercy of fierce organizational struggles. Critical objectives may not be met because the people being asked to achieve them may perceive (perhaps rightly) that doing so would threaten their status or jobs. Other challenges include poor communication channels, a less-educated work force, hierarchical structures that inhibit employees from performing at their peak, and ineffective or outdated policies and procedures.

These internal problems may manifest themselves more slowly than the more dramatic external challenges. They may be so subtle that they may be seen only when the enterprise is faced with an immediate threat or opportunity—as for example, when a competitor launches a new product and the organization cannot adequately respond, or when a compelling business opportunity presents itself and the organization is incapable of moving swiftly enough to seize it. Or a company may find itself in the throes of rapid growth and then suddenly discover its processes and policies are incapable of managing its expansion effectively.

CRITICAL COMPETITIVE STRATEGIES

There are many responses to these challenges. One of them is using information to power critical business strategies. The first, and possibly most important, business strategy is concerned with drastically improving the company's competitive abilities.

While the discussion below addresses one specific type of competitive strategy—a company's customer strategy—there are other, perhaps more important competitive strategies, depending on the company and industry. Some of these were identified in Table 3-2, Ideal First EIT Applications, and include greater product functionality, reliability, training, and use; the development and delivery of new products and services; improving business performance tracking; and increasing margins, market share, earnings, and customer satisfaction.

Regardless of the area of greatest strategic importance, the general approach is the same: aggressively using information to support or drive that business strategy. What will vary most is the relative size of the payoff and risk, and how large a role information can play in enabling that business initiative.

The Customer is King

At the heart of any business lay its basic competitive strategies. And at the very center of a company's competitive strategies is the fundamental relationship with its customers. For most companies, the most attractive use of information for achieving substantial, continuing competitive advantage is centered around this essential relationship. With a firm foundation of information about the behavior of the customer in place, an enterprise can safely and rapidly build up and out to meet other strategies, needs, and opportunities (see Figure 4-1, Information for Powering the High-Performance Company), secure that the core structure will withstand change.

Chapter 1 gave examples of companies that used creative applications of information technology to achieve impressive competitive advantage: Citibank with ATMs, K mart with POS devices and microwave transmissions, American Airlines with its real-time terminal links to travel agents, and McKesson with its tightly connected pharmacy ordering capabilities. In doing these things, companies like these not only raised the bar for others to use technology to operate more effectively; they created an immense source of leverage, for the detailed information they had to collect for these breakthrough capabilities could be used for more critically important purposes.

With the range of possibility for acquiring advantage from Business Automation dwindling, yesterday's sources of competitive *advantage* become issues of *survival*. Therefore, new competitive advantage must come from new places and novel approaches. Systems like the ones mentioned above offered such a possibility—driving powerful competitive marketing strategies by the exploitation of customer information.

Competitive Marketing Strategies

The implementation of capabilities such as on-line reservation systems, bank ATMs, and retail POS scanners generated data that was fed into standard reporting systems, with computers working overtime to collect, segment, and summarize the massive details flooding in by the hour. With a lot of computer processing, a company could provide its operations and marketing managers with highly summarized information on weekly sales in the Midwest, or what products had fallen in market share in the past month, or what customers were buying in a big way, and who was giving discounts to whom. Good information, but not much different from what was available before.

Most of that rich information was being ignored or even lost. Once it had served its primary purpose—debiting an account, posting a payment, computing a total—it was stored away in some dusty tape vault, never to be seen again. *Companies were letting a valuable asset slip through their fingers.*

But not for long. The more astute ones recognized the aftermarket value of this detailed information. Here, for the first time, was the real possibility of understanding the consuming habits of individual customers and prospects, of plotting their motives and means from cradle to grave, of being in the position to take advantage of those small windows of opportunity to promote the right products to the right people at the right time.

Individually targeted marketing would replace niche and zip-code marketing, just as the latter was replacing costly and ineffective mass marketing. The marketers were given rifles to replace shotguns. With that greater accuracy, they

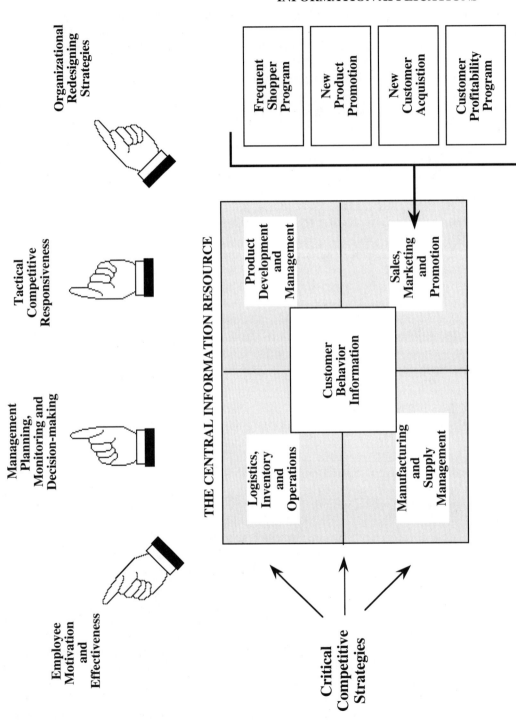

Figure 4-1. Information For Powering the High-Performance Company

quickly envisioned highly targeted catalogs, advertising flyers, newsletters, magazines, coupons—all customized and delivered to an individual customer (or household) based on an up-to-date profile. Here, almost for free, was a vast gold mine of information that could be used for a number of critical sales, marketing, and promotion capabilities for:

- Nurturing repeat business through "frequent customer" programs
- Gathering new customers through industry-wide "customer acquisition" programs
- Expanding current customer business via finely targeted "new product promotions"
- Improving the margins of new business by means of "customer profitability" programs

The more nimble and imaginative organizations wasted little time in seeking further advantage from their newly-acquired asset. Companies built powerful capabilities for managing these huge volumes of detailed customer information. They moved quickly to supplement this data with information from outside sources about important demographic, financial, and lifestyle data (see the Huck Fizz examples in Part III for one organization's creative use of externally derived competitive information).

Two examples of such efforts are presented below. They show how a leading-edge company can employ this type of information to increase customer acquisition, improve customer retention, upgrade customer profitability, expand penetration of products and services to existing customers, and raise purchasing, distribution, and merchandising effectiveness.

(Note: From this point, most of the examples are not identified because of the proprietary and competitive nature of the capabilities. In some cases, the facts are altered slightly to purposely disguise the identity of the example without robbing the illustration of its intended value. The information about these efforts comes from first-hand experience, internal company reports, or computer vendor papers and studies. The companies used as examples are consistently recognized as leaders in their innovative use of information technologies, either in statements by their peers and competitors, in cross-industry studies, or in technology leadership award programs.)

Banking on the Customer

A major bank sought competitive advantage by providing information-based capabilities to help its business units dynamically define market segments for new products and promotions. It also wanted to lessen the costs of operating these programs, and to reduce loan losses. This highly successful strategy was made possible by exploiting a massive marketing database (more than 120 billion bytes) made up of one year's detail history of all the bank's accounts.

On an ongoing basis, information is collected monthly from more than 20 bank operating systems. It involves extracting and loading 12 million records, with more than 300,000 additional updates throughout the month. The information consists of credit card history and balances, loan history and balances, current account balances and activity, indicators about the type of customer, key financial summary and snapshot information from credit agencies such as TRW, and line-of-credit information for their commercial accounts.

The marketing database is heavily used in credit card and other retail marketing areas of the bank. For example, if a group is interested in promoting home equity loans, the system determines who in a geographic area is likely to need one by identifying people who had taken out mortgages in the past five years but who didn't have a home loan already. Or, if car loans were being pushed, users analyze prospects based on the number and type of old or existing car loans, the type and age of the cars, the age of the customer and of any children, as well as whether that person is likely to afford a new loan based on an analysis of his or her bank balances, other outstanding loans, previous payment and credit history, and so on.

This finely targeted information is carefully monitored against results to determine its effectiveness, which in turn, is used for improving future campaigns. Was the free checking offer successful? Did a bonus incentive program to increase use of customer credit cards have the results intended? Did the car loan program meet its objectives? For example: 2,275 targeted mailings produced 250 loans, with the estimated yield of that finely-honed approach pegged at $36 per loan. Using previous promotion techniques, 98,000 mailings had produced 150 loans, at an estimated cost to produce a loan of about $500.

The marketing database is also used to discover new market segments. For example, management asked if it is worthwhile to market new credit card offerings to out-of-state customers. A detailed analysis of past performance suggested that 17 states were excellent candidates for such solicitations. Other examples involved programs for convincing convenience card users to convert to revolving accounts (not so easily done, as it turned out), and generating $25 million in new business by reducing the minimum payment charge on a credit card balance by half.

The use of the bank marketing database helped enormously in bringing in new business and in expanding the penetration of existing markets and segments. One estimate pegged it as being responsible for 200,000 new accounts over the initial two-year period. The bank's information strategy had other payoffs as well.

By using the power of its rich database, one official estimated the bank saved between $160 and $350 million in a two-year period in loan loss avoidance. This was accomplished by having the ability to monitor customer behavior closely for critical factors and trends (for example, over-limit accounts) and to highlight changing delinquency patterns that would identify potential bankruptcies long before they happened. With this greater insight, the bank was able to strengthen its credit policies significantly. These capabilities allowed the bank to be more effective in avoiding loans with unacceptable degrees of risk.

These soft benefits were augmented by hard ones, such as those that resulted from better target marketing capabilities, which saved the bank between $30,000 to $40,000 in postage alone for the average campaign, primarily by not targeting unattractive prospects. No dollar figure has been placed on the cost savings of eliminating the hundreds of systems whose functions are now handled by a single marketing database, nor the value of eliminating the delays experienced from relying on inadequate technologies.

In fact, delays were once the bank's biggest problem. The new marketing database means that users get information within a week of the close of the month. Prior to that, they had to wait up to 90 days to get summary reports that were all but useless by the time they arrived. For many of these users, because of the huge volumes involved, they simply could not get the data, no matter what the level of urgency. Traditional technology had forced them into data summarization approaches that were inflexible and limited in their ability to answer important and unanticipated questions. Reports were rigidly constructed and would take months, sometimes years, to get produced.

One of the senior bank managers instrumental in establishing the new capability said that the biggest user of the system ". . . is angry because, now that they know the power of it, they want to put everything imaginable on there. They want it all—now. They're pushing like crazy because they know what the power is."

Nurturing the Frequent Customer

An information and financial services company launched a program to help grocers and suppliers attract new business and increase revenues from existing customers. The general strategy is to collect scanner data from grocery store chains around the country, organize and store the data at the lowest possible level of detail (by product codes and household information), and provide access to individual grocery stores, consumer packaged goods and other manufacturers (paper products, foods, drugs), and independent discount, distribution, and wholesale companies.

Under the program, incentives are offered to frequent shoppers who, using a plastic checkout card, are automatically given discounts. For example, a regular beer buyer is given discounts on a particular brand of beer he regularly buys, and special prices on related products such as pretzels and popcorn. A cat owner is targeted for specials on her favorite brand of cat food. Or, a customer who is a frequent buyer of many products in the store other than meat is enticed back to the store's meat department by a special offer of high-grade, low-priced hamburger. Each month, shoppers receive a detailed statement describing their purchases, credits, and discounts. Included in the package are targeted promotions for products the customer buys regularly, and in some cases, payments from manufacturers for being a frequent buyer of their products.

The marketing database includes all grocery stores in a given region, so that every participating company knows which customer bought which items from what stores. Individual stores can use the data to determine which competitors pose the greatest threat to their business and in what product areas, targeting advertising and promotional efforts accordingly. Manufacturers and food growers can monitor stores to determine which are the most effective in promoting their products.

Further benefits include targeted promotions that eliminate costly and ineffective mass advertising (newspapers, direct mail, coupons, and flyers). The system also improves the ability of retailers and manufacturers to manage inventories and promote their products, benefits expected to increase enormously as the system catches on.

Initial customer reaction, driven by attractive financial incentives and the promise of eliminating unwanted mass advertising, is positive and expected to grow. With results from the first stores in, the company believes that most consumers are willing to lose some privacy, if in return they get cheaper prices without clipping coupons or doing extensive comparison shopping. If this is found to be true on a large scale as well, and combined with the overwhelming economies of finely-tuned marketing, such information-based strategies as this one will increasingly find favor over mass marketing approaches.

This *frequent shopper* ability for groceries is similar to the *frequent flyer* programs for airlines, except that it is much larger (the size of the database is expected to exceed a trillion bytes when completed, making it the largest on-line commercial database in the world). With the introduction of more customer-based information applications and powerful database technologies, a host of focused marketing programs will spring up, perhaps best characterized as *frequent customer* programs. Many of these efforts are either underway or in place in companies where innovators have seen the need and technologists have understood how to deliver the results.

Frequent customer capabilities are based on a standard paradigm—leveraging detailed customer information to track and reward frequent purchasers with incentives such as discounts or free purchases. As discussed above, this can be applied to the shopper, flier, lodger, traveler, reader, credit card user, and many other types of consumers. This basic paradigm can also be extended to "wise consumers" who make effective use of scarce resources such as water, energy and fuel; to "good citizens" who qualify as safe drivers, good taxpayers, and good voters; and to those "poor citizens" who are persistent traffic violators, polluters, and scofflaws.

CRITICAL ORGANIZATIONAL STRATEGIES

- A car company takes an order for a custom car on Monday and delivers it by Friday.
- A manufacturer wins market share by cutting its product development cycle by 75 percent.
- An electronics company cuts it order-to-ship time from three weeks to three hours.
- Another car manufacturer cuts administrative staff in a department by 80 percent.
- Computers track failure rates and notify the manufacturer before maintenance is needed.

Redesigning the Organization

Advanced and creative use of information is making possible radical improvements similar to the examples above. Tinkering with the formal structures and processes of a company produce only marginal improvements, not these drastic kinds of results. Radical changes include reworking functional groupings and responsibilities, recasting lines of authority and accountability, realigning communication channels, renovating procedures and processes, remaking personnel practices and incentives, and reordering the flow of information and decisions.

In a world where time frames for response are ever shortened, where more and more sectors of a company must work more closely together, and where powerful automation tools are increasingly distributed and interconnected, conventional approaches to organization improvement are less sufficient for competing effectively. But confronted by these business and marketplace demands, many companies find themselves saddled with ineffective arrangements that put them at a serious disadvantage in an increasingly aggressive economy.

Carrying Excess Organizational Baggage

Most organizational structures and procedures are erected when the enterprise is small. They gradually evolve to meet the needs of a larger, more complex business. Conventional Business Automation allows this expansion to continue well beyond its natural limits, primarily by speeding up mundane and definable functions. A vast complex of systems, procedures, programs, structures, and rules come into being. Operating with this excess baggage from past eras, companies can barely succeed at meeting their primary charters, much less respond athletically to rapidly changing demands. The example following shows how one company was able to overcome this weighty inheritance with the creative use of information.

Performing Operational Open-Heart Surgery

In the face of very stiff overseas competition and a much softer economy, a major U.S. industrial manufacturer needed to dramatically reduce expenses. It planned for these improvements by seeking significantly higher levels of performance. The first target: the heart of its aging administrative operations.

The current purchasing, receiving, and payables functions were fragmented among many people and places, and done according to an out-of-date process that was costly, error-prone, paper-ridden, subject to delay, and fundamentally unresponsive to exceptions or special orders. A much-heralded competitor was alleged to be performing the same functions with *one-fifth* the number of people.

The company replaced the step-by-step process with an on-line companywide information capability. Purchasing now places an order electronically. When the goods arrive, they are checked immediately against the database and registered as received (if not, the goods are simply returned). The system matches the receipt to the order, kicks out a check, and Accounts Payable verifies and sends it to the vendor. In this arrangement, there are no written purchase orders or invoices.

The results? The company now operates with the same size staff as its competition, has greater control over receiving, and a much higher level of accuracy in its financial information. Exceptions and specials have been easily accommodated, allowing greater flexibility with vendors and with its own geographically dispersed plants. And more attractive terms have been negotiated with vendors as a result of reduced paperwork and easier business procedures.

Driving the Need for Organizational Redesign

The redesign of the business enterprise is concerned with changing formal structures and patterns of work to bring about large-scale improvement. One source of motivation for these changes comes with *mergers and acquisitions,* especially for those done for strategic reasons, as when extending a critical product line or market, or seeking improved earnings growth in times of relatively slow economic growth.

Effective integration of the many parts of a newly merged entity must be as successful as the synergism of the primary business factors that drove the deal. If this process can happen over a weekend, as with the British Airways takeover of British Caledonia, the chances for success are great. If the process bogs down, as was true for Univac and Burroughs, valuable time and momentum are lost, hurting the chances of the merged entity.

Another driving factor for organizational redesign is *divestiture.* For spinoffs or selloffs, an organization must quickly downsize by stripping away unneeded functions, while retaining the assets most relevant and valuable to the remaining organization. Some sales are ruthless and strictly for profit, like Beatrice Foods and Borg Warner, or driven by burdensome debt reduction. But the bulk are based on issues of business vitality and profitability, i.e., for enhancing assets, not just for selling them. For them, the need for radical and precision surgery is critical to achieving the results sought.

However, *changes in business conditions* are the forces that most often demand organization redesigning, whether due to the effects of growth or decline, governmental, cultural, economic, competitive, or technological forces. A rapidly growing company such as Wal-Mart must constantly reshape its organization to absorb the next round of growth, to handle additional volumes, new complexities, unexpected problems, revised issues of scale and range, and novel matters of conformance and diversity.

When companies such as IBM see unstoppable technological pressures obsolete their big, profitable computer business, the need for organizational redesign becomes critical for survival, whether for radical downsizing, for responding to new and tougher customer demands, for creating more innovative products and services, or for creating effective organizational arrangements in a world of smaller machines and smaller margins.

Tightening procedures, instituting quality programs, re-automating the order entry system—these kinds of actions are not going to help much in satisfying these greater demands. Only major organizational surgery can make a big enough difference when an organization is faced with pressures and challenges like these.

The Fine Art of Buying Banks

A major regional bank, noted for its rapid growth and aggressive business tactics, created an information architecture to serve as a backbone into which the information systems of newly acquired local banks could be readily absorbed. Since each new bank brought with it its own set of demand deposit and other operational systems, and since the cost of converting those systems significantly reduced the financial incentive of the acquisitions themselves, this company took the position that it was smarter to simply "plug in" the information from the acquired banks' systems.

That was made possible by an information capability that allowed for differences in local banks' information by adjusting it for incorporation into a composite database. What might take six months or a year to integrate by conventional means, now takes a few weeks or a month at most. "It's a lot like having a layer of cement poured over many separate bricks and flagstones," said a member of the executive staff. "It makes a smooth surface, yet builds upon the work done before.

"Our system is like that, only more adaptable. The people at the local bank get to keep their old way of doing business, and we get what we need to manage the entire bank. The daily information comes across these 'data bridges' where it's stored at a very fine level of detail. Almost any question an executive has about any of the subordinate entities—or all of them for that matter—can be answered quickly without asking the local bank or disturbing their operations.

"For some people, it's a little like magic. But not for us. It's allowed us to grow to the size we're at. At this rate, we plan to be the biggest regional bank in the country. After that, who knows?"

Bridging Organizational Islands

Another organizational redesign example is a recently merged regional communications company that wanted to market interrelated products and services among its five regulated and six diversified business units. However, it found itself unable to cross the boundary lines of these previously distinct operating entities. Spread over more than a dozen states, these organizations were supported by scores of uncoordinated groups, systems, and procedures that had been built up over decades and were tightly bound to their geographic areas.

Here was a multi-billion dollar company with a split personality. It seemed impossible to perform the most basic product management or market analysis functions. With the deregulated marketplace breeding tough, agile competitors, the company needed some way to bridge these isolated worlds. Management was able to make this happen by creating an information capability built around its customers, products, and networks.

For example, if the product manager for Custom Calling Services is seeking new revenues by selling additional product features, in the past he would get a random list of names, produce a mass-mailer asking the sample of customers what products they currently have, compile the results, perform another mass mailing to determine how many of the Call Waiting customers would respond to a campaign offering Call Forwarding as a second feature, and so on.

This took months to complete and had to be repeated for each operating company. With the new information capability, however, that same manager queries the integrated database of all customer accounts to see how many have more than one service. This might show, say, that 75% percent of all accounts have one service and 15 percent have two. Encouraged, the manager then asks how single-feature products are spread among single-feature users. This might indicate that Call Waiting is the most popular single-feature services.

This type of information suggests there's an excellent opportunity to market Call Forwarding services to single-service Call Waiting customers. But before producing the mailing, the manager tests the validity of that idea by analyzing the current makeup of two-feature packages. This might show that Call Waiting and Call Forwarding are popular combinations, making up over 50 percent of two-service packages. With his hypothesis validated, a precise target marketing campaign is launched to specific customers.

The results from programs like these have been very successful. The program mentioned above helped the company increase revenues by selling existing single-feature Call Waiting customers on Call Forwarding and vice versa. This was just one of the many promotion programs launched once the "bridging power" of the company's information capability was in place.

Information for Redesigning the Company's Structures and Processes

Management's use of information plays a major role in creating effective and rational organizational processes and structures. Redesigning the business organization requires that managers rethink the company's basic strategies and processes, that they look hard at the painful realities, challenging everything that has been done so far. They must determine why things are the way they are.

Redesigning an organization is not concerned only with doing things better, but with doing things in the very best way possible. This invariably requires gutting existing procedures and structures and replacing them with novel arrangements based on new operational paradigms. Any change that does not radically reinvent an operation or recreate a practice from the ground up is likely to be cosmetic. Such change is not going to result in the enormous improvements needed, such as drastic reductions in delivery times, overnight inventory replenishment, or 10-fold reductions in overhead.

Applying information's capabilities for these purposes means going beyond satisfying users' information needs (as critical as that is). It calls for new uses that impact the basics of the company and its customers, margins, earnings, and shareholder value. With the larger business relationships understood, information can be used to bypass or supersede current organizations, operations, structures, processes, and constraints. It can be part of a new organizational order that allows managers to reorient, span, flatten, and integrate the disparate parts of the enterprise. In this way, information helps neutralize the legacy of marginally effective practices.

Turning Applications Into Revenue

For example, a nationwide insurance company fundamentally changed its application process. The operation, involving several departments and dozens of people performing specialized, serial tasks, meant the average application took a week or more to complete, and the fastest any application could be turned around was no less than 24 hours. The excessive cost and resulting poor service was harming the company's ability to compete.

By recasting this process outside the boundaries of existing arrangements (credit checking, quoting, rating, underwriting, etc.) and by viewing it from the standpoint of the customer, the fundamental process was recognized for what it is: getting applications turned into revenue-producing policies. With that basic understanding, it was possible to see that with the use of an integrated and on-line information capability, one person could handle the entire application from beginning to end. In this new arrangement, there would be no inefficient paper shuffling, no costly inter-office checking procedures, no cumbersome and unnecessary signature authorizations, and no embarrassing losses of the application itself.

True accountability was established along with greater employee autonomy. Specialized knowledge came from either the information system itself, or if that was insufficient, from experts called in when needed. The results? Three days to handle the average application; the same staff handles twice the volume of applications; a hot application can be completed in four hours; and 100 field positions have been eliminated.

Information to Revitalize the Heart of the Business

Rather than seeing the business in narrow "vertical" slices, such as operating divisions or departmental functions, managers must see it in more fundamental terms, such as its success or failure with customers, products, market segments, or shareholders. With this "horizontal" perspective, it is easier to recognize that practices in one part of the enterprise may create limitations in another, or that attempts to improve matters within a single organization may miss the larger opportunities.

As the above insurance company example illustrates, effective information capabilities can eliminate organizational limitations. No longer valid information workarounds are targeted for extinction. Organizations chartered to pass along problems and information are naturally removed, freeing them for more dynamic roles. People whose job it is to answer questions about customer orders are put to work doing more useful functions, leaving that task to an interconnected information capability.

Managers can use the right kinds of information to streamline or integrate separated business processes, redesign organizations with more simultaneity of operations, and upgrade departments to operate at greater speeds and higher response levels. It can help people on the front lines make more informed decisions with customers, and automatically initiate operations when a transaction is received.

Information can also improve connections with the outside world. It helps management, for example, adjust relationships between product development and customer service, when market-driven products are linked with highly customized offerings. It supports executives in changing the relationship between product development and delivery, when very short product life cycles and complex manufacturing issues are involved. And information can help executives alter the dynamics between product delivery and customer service operations, when short order cycles and high volume relationships are driving the market.

Information can even help a company long accustomed to doing business in a certain way change to a radically different emphasis, as seen in the following example.

Shifting the Emphasis From Products to Customers

A very large U.S. consumer goods manufacturer decided that it was essential to move from an exclusive brand-manager to a customer-based orientation. This meant that, instead of a sales executive managing one product brand for all retail customers in a region, they would handle sales of all company brands for one retail customer. The change was nothing less than massive, not only because of the sheer number of people involved, but because of the incredibly interwoven systems and procedures in place. Capabilities fine-tuned for years would have to be changed overnight.

But the marketplace demanded this change. For one thing, it would help sales executives match the retail buyers' knowledge of what the retailer was doing as a total entity, enabling the manufacturer's sales executive to better negotiate prices and volumes for products, for an entire brand, or for all products. This would help balance the retailer's inherent advantage, because with their widespread scanner capabilities, the retailer can always know how a particular product is doing in the stores. Retail buyers were using that knowledge to get unfair price concessions.

With a new information capability in place, the sales executive will watch all of a retailer's purchases and restocking patterns, while getting product or brand information about other retailers. For example, if XYZ Stores is moving a product at a higher price and volume than ABC Stores in the same area, then ABC Stores won't get lower prices when they ask for them. They may even get a push to promote the company's product more effectively.

"To make this massive reorganization happen required on-line access to all order and shipment information by individual retailer and brands," said one of the company's marketing managers. "In the past we didn't keep detailed data, [and] instead we produced reports weekly for each product or brand manager. A smart retailer would hit up one brand manager for lower prices while sitting on other brands. He was always a week ahead of us. Or he would simply refuse to match requested sales levels and promotion efforts because he was, *he said,* pushing our other brands hard.

"How could we know he was putting us on?" the manager added. "None of the brand managers shared that kind of information with each other. In fact, no one had the time to even ask! Now we track brand level activity as well as product lines, so we can watch daily activities for all products for the complete retailer, by region, and store. That access has leveled the playing field."

5

Information for Tactical Response

TACTICS: THE MIRROR IMAGE OF STRATEGY

For every planned strategic objective, there are dozens of unplanned (and often just as major) problems and opportunities that arise from the complex interplay of marketplace forces. And as companies deploy ever more powerful information-based strategies for competitive advantage (such as frequent customer programs), the rules and limits of the game are kept in constant flux, forcing players to maneuver ever more quickly while under enemy fire.

Information for tactical needs is just as critical as is information for well-planned and carefully positioned strategic purposes. In fact, acquiring the right information to respond to tactical pressures requires a clear strategy of its own. As will be seen in the discussion below, strategic and tactical information needs are closely related, making it possible for a company to address tactical needs by using a much broader approach.

TURKEYS FOR CHRISTMAS

K mart was handed a "turkey" on Thanksgiving. Shoppers were not buying its top-of-the-line Christmas toy, and it looked like its chain of nationwide stores might not move enough of the product overflowing its warehouses. But it was able to deploy a carefully coordinated series of daily price markdowns, based on sophisticated information analysis that tracked very small changes in purchase and inventory activity, and turn that turkey into a big Christmas present.

Armed with knowledge from an extensive marketing database, K mart management was able to take extremely precise pricing actions to encourage the needed customer purchase levels. If a price drop did not produce adequate sales increases, the price was immediately lowered further. If a drop raised sales levels more than expected, it was held steady until erosion of demand took over again. In this way, the company sold all the endangered toys by Christmas and at reasonable margins. Similar penetrating analysis spotted an unexpectedly hot-selling item in time to stock up for the short season. The combined result: an increase of $250,000 on the bottom line.

Acting this quickly at this level of exactness made it possible to do things that just weren't possible before. Their tactical response capabilities had become irreplaceable and were helping to produce profits that a senior executive claimed were "significantly improved" over previous years.

BUILDING STRATEGIES ON A FOUNDATION OF TACTICS

Tactical solutions can become strategic once they are proven successful and the concept institutionalized. For example, Domino's Pizza initially embraced the idea of home delivery as a tactical response to intense competition. But the company took it well beyond a tactic, making it into a key strategy that revolutionized not only Domino's, but the entire pizza industry. Domino's became synonymous with pizza home delivery.

In a similar manner, to transform ad hoc, information-based tactical response into an ongoing capability requires a broad and detailed base of information for unknown and unplanned business needs. While such a capability can be fashioned from scratch, it is far better to implement it using the information collected to support strategic programs, such as the banking and grocery store examples in Chapter 4. Once underway, that core set of information can be used (and expanded) for meeting unexpected tactical needs.

For example, suppose a company decided on an information strategy targeted at increasing revenues and margins through the use of frequent customer incentives. But suppose further that the realities of the marketplace rewarded companies adept at snaring new customers, because there was an inherently low level of maximum purchase activity for the average customer. While the same information would be used in pursuing the new opportunity, there would also be the need to add competitive information from outside information providers in order to seek out those prospective new customers.

The ability to change competitive emphasis quickly while building on a core information capability represents an information strategy flexible enough to accommodate unplanned tactical realities. Put another way, the tactical uses of this information alter the company's originating strategy, at the same time that the original strategy begets tactical uses that in turn alter and drive the general information process forward.

COLOR ME GREEN

A major U.S. beauty products company implemented an extensive database to track product sales in stores throughout the country. The company competes fiercely on price, promotion, packaging, and availability, and management used their extensive database to closely monitor revenue and profit trends. In addition to discovering interesting insights about their customers (e.g., women in the Southeast use more hair spray), management became aware of an *especially* interesting piece of news: there appeared to be very definite price breakpoints that were clearly affecting the demand for shampoos with certain combinations of ingredients.

This was extremely important because the company's products were in a market where there was little in the way of dramatic new product or technology breakthroughs. Progress was generally made in small increments over long periods of time. The researchers in the laboratories would take months working out the optimum balance of costs and ingredients, only to find that the market had moved ahead of them and stubbornly disagreed with their price-formula models.

Using information gleaned from a long history of detailed product purchases, company researchers were able to take what people were saying with their wallets and quickly create new product models. Coming up with new product-ingredient-price-combinations *in a few hours,* they were able to take advantage of the changing market's preferences, and in a few cases, accurately anticipate shifts as well.

INFORMATION FOR TACTICAL PURPOSES

Tactical users require information quickly, usually on-line and real-time, with access to differing levels of detail, segmentation, and summarization. They typically require information covering short time periods but in great detail, with an almost telescopic ability for zeroing in on a particular aspect of a problem. Subsets of information are dynamically defined for browsing, analysis, what-if modeling, critical success factor monitoring, and other advanced processing.

As in the example above, the information must be quickly analyzed and verified. While information for tactical use is almost always found in a company's production systems, this does not mean that the information is necessarily adequate. The effort to transform operational data into useful form may be considerable. Worse than the efforts and costs involved, it may take more time than the problem permits. There is very little time to locate and clean up information from production systems, much less to develop complex analysis scenarios from scratch each time a new demand or opportunity appears. The information must be waiting and ready for use when the demand arrives.

RACING THE HURRICANE

A United Kingdom property and casualty insurance company had been using a detailed customer information capability to track new clients and product offerings for only a few months when it got word that the south coast of the country was in danger from a freak storm. Most people laughed—there hadn't been a serious storm in that part of the world in more than a hundred years. Nonetheless, they ran a series of analyses to determine the extent of the company's exposure. They sliced and diced the information to produce a range of interpretations from best to worst-case. The results: there was much greater risk than anyone imagined.

Company executives decided to play it safe. They made standard arrangements for funds to cover an expected short-fall that might occur in the worst case scenario. They then made plans for a quick-to-deploy loss adjustment services program.

The storm hit, and caused far more damage than expected. The company responded efficiently, using the cheaper capital they had acquired. Their competitors fared less well—they were slower to respond and had great difficulty finding funds at any interest rate. The company's strategic information capability allowed it to respond to a completely unexpected situation, and to improve its control over specific risk categories.

MAKING THE AD HOC REPEATABLE

Typically, companies handle unpredictable, or ad hoc, needs for information one at a time and as they occur. They eschew any general approach for delivering consistent and common responses to tactical needs, continuing to build unique solutions in a variety of ways with no overall plan or structure. These organizations reinvent the wheel every time they face a new threat or opportunity. There is no significant carryover of residual artifacts or technology, no human knowledge still available, no software that may be used again.

Tactical users of information are engaged in a highly creative process. They are inventing new functions, exploring different angles, and generating new perspectives not found in conventional data reporting and analysis. Unfortunately, their creative insights are likely to be lost after the problem is solved. If the enterprise is to transform information tactics into strategies, it must retain as much as possible of the process and the results of those actions. In addition to the information extracted, conditioned, and organized, each response to an ad hoc requirement can contribute to a common electronic library that may be used for future needs.

Repeatable ad hoc solutions (as contradictory as that sounds) occur under an accumulating information capability, helping a company meet each new need a little bit better and a little bit faster than if it were done under the standard one-at-a-time approach. It also provides the company an extra edge: future tactical needs will be somewhat more anticipatible as the collective knowledge of the enterprise accumulates.

6

Information for Effective Management

THE INFORMED MANAGER

A major U.S. shipping company got word from one of its sales offices that a competitor was suddenly offering drastically lower rates for its primary transportation routes. The marketing people were very concerned that if the company didn't follow suit quickly, "they were going to lose a lot of very important business," at least according to one senior sales executive. The pressure on senior executives to respond immediately was intense.

This was an area in which the company was a major player, and lowering prices would have a devastating effect on margins and profits. Just as bad, it would create a snowball effect on prices for its other routes. Cutting prices to keep step, as the sales people were urging, would be costly, estimated at well over $8 million on the bottom line for the first year alone. The total impact might go as high as $50 million.

Management turned to its information resource. After extensive analysis, it determined that the competitor, while a major threat in other areas of the company's market, had almost no presence in the sector under siege. The predators were simply trying to buy their way into a new (for them) market segment with give-away prices, a move they could well afford to make. Executives decided to do nothing.

Immediate access to the right information—in this case, detailed customer shipping information and monthly government import-export information—and the right tools and attitudes to arrive at the correct interpretation made the critical difference between succumbing to the threat and making the smarter decision to do nothing. The results? The competitor dropped out of the market area after a few months of losing money.

Information holds within it the potential for dramatically improving the intelligence of the business. As the example above shows, information can make a large and positive impact on supporting managers who understand its value and use it to excellent effect. On the other hand, information can be a largely undervalued, distorted, or abused asset.

This chapter focuses on the value of using information to support the management of the company. It looks at how the value of information varies with managers' operating styles and with the major functions they are called upon to perform: to monitor the business, to make effective decisions, and to raise the level of employee effectiveness.

INFORMATION AND MANAGEMENT STYLES

Information reaches its fullest potential in the executive suite, where it has the power to influence plans and decisions of the highest order. At this level, executives need information that is clear and brief, identifies deep causes and relationships, and answers clearly articulated needs. It must be extensively filtered to shed light on complex issues and point the way to strong action. For many reasons, computer information has had a small but growing importance in this realm.

Information's value tends to be higher with middle and line managers who regularly confront challenges where time-frames are shorter, issues more concrete, and people less a factor, than in top executive issues. These managers value information highly when it supports their business operations, and helps them manage more effectively. Compared to top executives, they require information that is more quantitative and timely, and capable of greater manipulation.

But information's value is affected far more by a manager's style than by his or her level of responsibility. While managers may vary their styles to suit the current situation, most tend to lean to one style or another. And although all management styles benefit from information, some have greater impact on an executive's capacity for utilizing information. These are contrasted below and in Figure 6-1, Management Styles Versus Information's Potential Value.

Offensive versus Defensive—The precision and power of information tends to favor the offense-oriented manager, especially when creative ways to enlist it in a strategic program are employed. For example, an initiative that seeks to capture market share by aggressive pricing has a much better chance of succeeding if based on exact knowledge of customer price sensitivity levels and past competitor reactions. More exacting prediction models may be constructed before committing to a particular offensive strategy, especially one that has the potential for surprise, as in carefully crafted preemptive actions.

Strategic versus Tactical—The strategic style gets the greater value from information, for these managers apply information to the most basic areas, problems, and opportunities of the company. The strategic need to cross or link organizations, understand patterns that affect the company's critical success

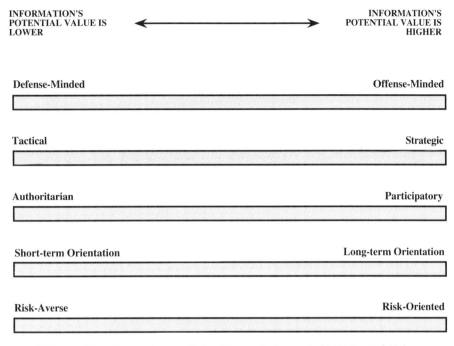

INFORMATION'S POTENTIAL VALUE IS LOWER ← → **INFORMATION'S POTENTIAL VALUE IS HIGHER**

Defense-Minded — Offense-Minded

Tactical — Strategic

Authoritarian — Participatory

Short-term Orientation — Long-term Orientation

Risk-Averse — Risk-Oriented

Figure 6-1. Management Styles Versus Information's Potential Value

factors, and shape the major factors connecting objectives with marketplace realities are well served by information. An example: finely-tuned actions will have a greater effect when strategically directed at products and stores with the highest unit sales and margins than when applied to all products and stores of the company.

Long-Term versus Short-Term Orientation—The long-term management style benefits more from high-quality information. With greater volumes of detailed, historical information, short-term fluctuations can be properly evaluated to get at the deeper and more complex trends and directions. Extremely granular and longitudinal information can be used to make more accurate projections, such as determining who are the company's best customers overall, not just those who did the most business in the last quarter. Being able to tune programs to keep those kinds of customers coming back for more is much more likely to help the company succeed than being a hero on that last big deal.

Participatory versus Authoritarian—More authoritarian styles tend to filter information, to impart a "spin" that fits the views of its leaders. Hence, a good deal of the informing power of information is lost or ignored. A more participatory style of management finds greater value in information, using it to open the enterprise to the creativity of employees. By making information more readily available, it allows more people to get in the game.

Risk-Oriented versus Risk-Averse—Risk-taking managers benefit greatly from information. This was seen in the initial examples in Chapter 1 and in the strategic examples in Chapter 4, where companies willing to take sizable risks to gain significant competitive advantage successfully used information as a weapon to gain customers, market share, and profits.

NO EXCUSES, PLEASE!

Cypress Semiconductor Corporation is a rapidly growing electronics company that has oriented its entire work culture around a companywide information capability. Driven by a detail-oriented CEO, the company relies heavily on this ability to manage performance at every level of the business. The information systems capabilities track corporate, departmental, and individual performance. It gives executives the capacity to monitor what's happening at all levels of the organization, to anticipate problems, to intervene when appropriate, and to identify the best practices, all without creating layers of bureaucracy that bog down decisions and sap morale.

The capability is designed to encourage fresh thinking and to force everyone in the company to deal with the hard facts of the business. This information window creates a sense of openness, which in turn works against infighting and bureaucracy. There is always room for disagreement, but it must be about substance. Information transparency motivates people to perform effectively and helps to allocate resources more productively across the entire company.

One part of the system tracks people's goals. All work is organized by project and designed to emphasize speed and agility. Yet the process makes for a clearer sense of reality, resulting in less burnout and fewer reasons for failing to execute. The information is also used to provide positive feedback to employees and is a key part of performance evaluations. Raises are granted that reflect this performance and as ranked against other employees and relevant factors.

This information is most critically used by executives to manage the business and look for problems and patterns. What's going wrong? How should it be fixed? Who's losing control of an operation? The information is used to hold people accountable, to identify problems before they become crises, and to provide the help needed to correct them. It helps management cut through to the truth, whether of falling productivity, a late shipment, or suddenly superior results. Weekly information includes:

- Revenues by employee, organization unit, and product line
- Revenue and other comparisons with the competition
- Average quality level per product line
- Number of delinquent orders
- Rankings of senior executives in terms of performance of their units
- Insight into departments' fundamental strengths and weaknesses
- The yields, costs, and cycle times of every operation

With this kind of ability, performance has been excellent. The company meets sales projections within a percentage point or two every quarter. Management doesn't go over budget. While they plan for the long-term, they expect the plan to be obsolete quickly, so they treat quarterly revenue and profit targets as sacred (e.g., they track shipments and revenues on a daily basis and adjust the plan accordingly). The prime indicator of performance is reacting instantly to unforeseen competitive development.

The bottom line? Annual revenue increases of 40 percent per year for the past eight years, consistent quarter-to-quarter profitability, ever-increasing ratios of revenues per employee and fixed assets, and ever lower expense ratios. Top management is intent on building a billion-dollar company without the waste, bureaucracy, and complacency that afflict so many large organizations. To do that means getting the utmost performance, creativity, and cooperation from its people.

INFORMATION FOR MONITORING THE BUSINESS

As in the example above, information's value is great when supporting executives who constantly monitor the state of the business, who are trying to make sense of what is happening. Much of this value comes from helping deal with the ambiguity in any large organization, and in magnifying managers' finely honed judgment abilities.

For information to make this kind of contribution, it must support the executive's mental model of the business. (Experienced executives simplify the management process by making intuitive certain facts and relationships. They know which variables have the greatest impact, and how they may be altered for the greatest benefit.) Information helps an executive to corroborate this model, or, when it doesn't, to identify new variables or circumstances by understanding the patterns and relationships at work. This helps to create more accurate reflections of business reality, replacing or reducing the tendency to use information primarily to confirm prevailing opinions.

Information can be used to focus on important issues, especially by identifying the questions that management would most like answered and that, if answered with accuracy and insight, would have great potential for improving things. Hidden in these seemingly simple questions—Who are our best customers? Which are our best products? Which are our most productive sales offices?—are relationships and issues that open up new avenues of information use and analysis. (An approach to articulating these questions is presented in Part III.)

Monitoring is best supported when it is based on information covering long swaths of time and is capable of being manipulated by powerful analytical capabilities. Such support includes general scanning capabilities and tools to "drill down" into the details when something interesting or out of the ordinary is spotted. Also important is information that shows the status of various situations quickly and easily, and that automatically triggers red flags when designated thresholds are exceeded. Access to critical external information and highly valued softer information (e.g., predictions, appraisals, explanations) helps managers monitor the true state of the company.

CALL CHURNING

While one of the biggest U.S. communications companies was losing customers at an alarming rate, its executives were busy disagreeing among themselves about the causes of the defection. Deadlocked, one manager asked about a new system the company had just installed: "Doesn't it contain call data that could be used for understanding what's going on?"

A team was formed to look into this massive database, containing millions of telephone calls made over the past six months. To better understand this irksome customer behavior, they ran a complex series of models and analyses (referred to as churn analysis) to determine the patterns of calls of customers who had discontinued service. Making comparisons to customers who did not make the switch, it might be possible to develop different use profiles: the satisfied, the already dissatisfied, and the potentially dissatisfied.

It was this last category management most wanted to identify, so they could spot potential customer fall-off before it occurred and offer incentives to keep these customers on. But going through hundreds of millions of records to create hypotheses to explain this dissatisfaction was a far-from-certain prospect. Not only would immense computing power be needed, but incredibly sophisticated techniques would be required to make the many necessary comparisons.

With the right combination of information and technology, the company isolated a small number of patterns. Using precision marketing prototypes coupled with qualitative findings from marketing focus groups, they identified the major reasons customers were switching. All were addressable, and they found to their delight that most dissatisfied customers were more than willing to stay on board if their concerns were addressed.

With this information and a continuous tracking capability that updated potential dissatisfaction profiles, the company was able to head off a sizable number of would-be defectees. The new knowledge also provided them with valuable insight into how to go about tapping the susceptibility of their competitor's customers. As it turned out, they were able to get a good number of them to switch over, since many of the causes of customer unhappiness were not unique to their company.

THE SLOWLY SAGGING LINE OF BUSINESS

When a large and profitable U.S. insurance company performed a standard statistical analysis of claim expenses for one of its major product lines using three years of data, it was encouraged: losses had declined slightly for the first time. Management was pleased that their long-standing concerns about the product line were not as serious as they feared.

However, when they introduced more powerful information technologies that allowed them to run the same analysis with 10 years worth of information, it revealed the line of business was indeed losing ground badly. The "good news" from the three-year study turned out to be a blip in a generally long-term decline in profitability. Short-term fluctuations in profitability were masking deeper trends that were slowly squeezing the bottom line.

Armed with this information, the company revised its premium and renewal rates and restored the line to profitability. A senior executive of the firm commented: "We were able to spot that long-term trend because we were able to slice the information in enough ways that we could not be fooled by statistics. The insight we gained enabled us to improve profitability a great deal. The sad part is we probably wouldn't have known we had such a loser if we hadn't massaged that massive information the way we did."

INFORMATION FOR EFFECTIVE DECISIONS

Information helped the two companies in the examples above address subtle but important business problems. It allowed their managers to look more closely at a suspect situation that resisted a correct interpretation. Perhaps these executives even knew the truth before the hard facts were massaged with enough power and information range to finally yield the obvious message. This illustrates the illusive nature of the decision-making process, and how it can be improved by the availability of information.

For highly structured decision-making, reliable and detailed information is essential for supporting repetitive or iterative operations. These areas are often focused on individual functions such as marketing, finance, production, or distribution, or even smaller, more concise areas, such as product pricing simulation or profit margin projection models.

For all types of decision-making, important benefits accrue from having information with a great deal of detail, history, and range. This greater scope not only provides the basis for generating results with greater precision and insight, it can unleash new and more fruitful approaches for analyzing situations in uniquely creative ways. As managers apply powerful analytical capabilities to information that spans the entire company, they uncover important and fundamental relationships that exist throughout the organization (see Figure 6-2, The Bigger Information Picture).

For example, subtle but critical connections between promotion, inventory movement, and competitor pricing for a particular product in a specific part of the country may come to light only when analyzing information that originates in different organizational units and outside sources. Or, persistent but illogical correlations between perceived and actual demand may surface and provide a convincing explanation only when management subjects information to a magnifying lens that crosses the artificial boundaries of individual functions and organizations.

To dramatically improve the intelligence of the company's decision-making requires nothing less than an information resource capable of describing every detail of its operation and its business dealings with outside entities stretched over long and meaningful periods of time.

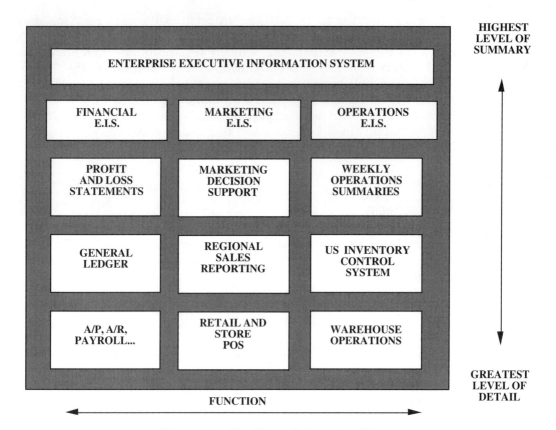

Figure 6-2. The Bigger Information Picture

INFORMATION EMPOWERMENT

The plant personnel of a large national manufacturing company stood by helplessly as it watched demand for its products gradually drop. Particularly painful was seeing their loyal dealers and distributors cut back or discontinue purchases altogether, shifting to competitors who were selling the same product at lower prices. Plant management requested help from headquarters. But nothing came back except complaints and tighter monitoring. In quick succession, a division executive was transferred, the plant manager retired early, and an audit team came in, studied production operations and left. But the problem grew worse. Local management decided to act.

Working closely with employees, they created an environment where workers shared responsibility for all decisions on schedules, quality, controls, costs, hiring, firing, raises, even pricing. They designed a complete information capability that allowed employees to regularly review production results and make changes to correct inadequate quality or erroneous production procedures. Within a short time, every employee was spending time looking at production and quality information to further improve operations.

The results? Productivity and performance rose, enabling the plant to start selling its goods at more competitive prices. Over the following months, the plant recaptured most of its lost business and began to gain market share. Empowerment worked for these people and the use of information was a key factor in helping the operation raise productivity and improve performance. Even with the extra responsibility, people were more satisfied with their work environment than with the old way of doing business.

INFORMATION FOR EMPLOYEE EFFECTIVENESS

The above example shows that the information opportunity for business management extends to the very culture of work itself, especially when used in conjunction with drastic changes in management styles and worker attitudes. Used boldly for these kinds of purposes, information enhances the effectiveness and productivity of employees. And when used creatively by those same employees, it helps to create an active concern for the quality of the company's products, a commitment to its goals, and a willingness to work as a full-fledged member of the team.

To *involve people* in the life of the business means they must truly feel part of a collective desire for success. Management helps create that involvement by increasing the sharing of information. Freely circulating information creates new scenarios of action.

Executives can use information to *share responsibility* by allowing people to "cross the boundaries" inside the enterprise and see the business as a whole. Unproductive turf battles, misguided personal loyalties, and general myopia to core objectives give way as employees see the true relationships between themselves and the different parts of the organization. Broad access to information lessens the hierarchical implications that so often squelch initiative.

Opening the valves of a company's information resource creates *new sources of creativity*—by generating powerful suggestions, new angles on a problem, new uses of existing assets, and overlooked opportunities.

In an open information environment, employees are put on-line *setting goals, objectives, and performance measures,* and using them for closely keeping track of performance. Information is used throughout the company to sustain momentum, ensure follow-through, resist distractions, improve responsiveness to change, and add important value to top-priority projects.

And, as was seen earlier, intensive use of information is essential in *identifying the best solutions to problems.* Throwing open a problem with the supporting information allows for a broader set of approaches and garners important additional viewpoints. Freely providing information opens wider the many sources of solution.

Finally, people are more effective when there is *a sense of fair play and an open management process.* Information sharing is a palpable expression of a company's philosophy of authority, since only an open and dynamic system of authority encourages the free circulation of information.

This completes Part II and the exploration of the major dimensions of the information opportunity terrain: for using information to meet fast-moving tactical needs, for supporting the competitive strategies so critical to any business enterprise, for providing the means to redesign an organization's structures and processes, and for meeting the needs of executives for monitoring, decision-making, and enhancing employee effectiveness.

Across this wide expanse, information's value changes with each part of the general terrain. So, too, does its payoff vary based on the individual enterprise, the problems blocking it from moving ahead, and the opportunities available. Executives of each company must identify and size the payoffs of each of these areas based on their particular conditions, needs, and goals.

These three chapters help business managers get a grip on this high-profile, elusive asset. The examples presented can be used as frames of reference to improve the understanding of information's potential and to articulate the areas of greatest benefits. These chapters also provide a perfect jumping-off point for a company wishing to establish an effective strategy for pulling those areas together and to create a general information solution that takes advantage of its collective information opportunity.

DESIGNING THE GENERAL INFORMATION SOLUTION

7

Prototypes for an EIT Design

Part III, Designing the General Information Solution, the second major component of the EIT Enabling Framework, presents a design for the EIT vision. Coupled with the right set of enabling technologies and implementation strategies (Parts IV and V), the design can be used to meet the Information Automation needs of the large, complex company. It is the conceptual basis for seizing the information opportunities described in Part II as part of a general information solution.

This chapter briefly discusses developments in Information Automation, two important design prototypes, and an overview of the EIT Design. Chapter 8 presents the design's underlying information infrastructure. Chapter 9 describes the capabilities needed to transform production data into useful business information.

EARLY INFORMATION AUTOMATION CAPABILITIES

The range of opportunities for finding and keeping information-based competitive advantage was seen in Part II to be wide and diverse. However, because of the obstacles pointed out in Chapter 2, there might seem to be little real hope of seizing the full range of benefits, much less of doing so in a single, coherent way. Yet progress towards that goal has been made, driven primarily by the large payoffs and rapidly improving base of information technologies.

This progress (see Figure 7-1, Major Developments in Information Automation) has discernible patterns for those seeking to build on the experiences of others, primarily the early information visionaries and innovators. It has led to the point

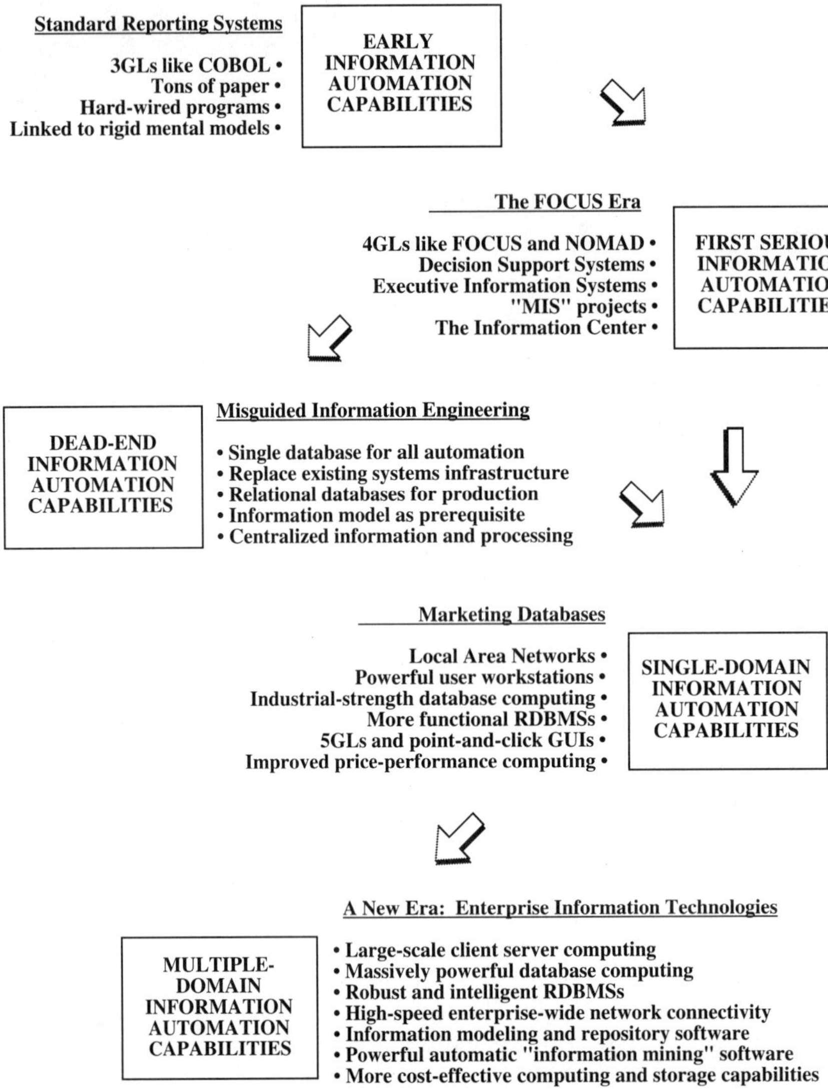

Standard Reporting Systems

3GLs like COBOL •
Tons of paper •
Hard-wired programs •
Linked to rigid mental models •

EARLY
INFORMATION
AUTOMATION
CAPABILITIES

The FOCUS Era

4GLs like FOCUS and NOMAD •
Decision Support Systems •
Executive Information Systems •
"MIS" projects •
The Information Center •

FIRST SERIOUS
INFORMATION
AUTOMATION
CAPABILITIES

Misguided Information Engineering

DEAD-END
INFORMATION
AUTOMATION
CAPABILITIES

• Single database for all automation
• Replace existing systems infrastructure
• Relational databases for production
• Information model as prerequisite
• Centralized information and processing

Marketing Databases

Local Area Networks •
Powerful user workstations •
Industrial-strength database computing •
More functional RDBMSs •
5GLs and point-and-click GUIs •
Improved price-performance computing •

SINGLE-DOMAIN
INFORMATION
AUTOMATION
CAPABILITIES

A New Era: Enterprise Information Technologies

MULTIPLE-
DOMAIN
INFORMATION
AUTOMATION
CAPABILITIES

• Large-scale client server computing
• Massively powerful database computing
• Robust and intelligent RDBMSs
• High-speed enterprise-wide network connectivity
• Information modeling and repository software
• Powerful automatic "information mining" software
• More cost-effective computing and storage capabilities

Figure 7-1. Major Developments in Information Automation

where it is now feasible to implement a companywide and general-purpose information capability. What was once considered impractical if not impossible to accomplish is being actively pursued in highly competitive companies today.

Precursors to Information Automation Capabilities

The most innovative uses of conventional automation revealed the hidden dimensions of information's power (examples were given in Chapter 1). Progress in all areas of automation continued to create opportunities for capturing and utilizing greater amounts of information. With more powerful mainframes and greater magnetic storage capacities, companies built standard reporting systems that ran overnight when the mainframe was mostly idle. Programmed in third generation languages (3GLs) like COBOL, these systems produced tons of paper for the waiting fork-lifts outside the computer room each morning.

These reporting systems proved costly, slow to build, and difficult to maintain. They were inflexible when changes were needed, their hard-wired software closely tied to momentary business needs, organizational structures, and operating styles. These early information capabilities simply weren't designed to hold onto the information advantage, to adapt easily and quickly when the business needed information for new purposes. They were frozen information balance-sheets, obsolete almost as soon as they were programmed.

First Serious Information Automation Capabilities

Awakened to the potential of their companies' information asset, technology practitioners sought to build on those early experiences. By raising the importance of information as a separate and distinct object of automation, they developed more effective capabilities for exploiting the information in operational systems.

The first Information Automation capabilities began to emerge, promising a new set of benefits for tighter management controls, better quality decisions, and finer exception tracking. While these benefits were generally softer than cutting order processing times in half, they were seen as being potentially more important. Using newer technologies, these innovators created the first elements of a new class of information capability:

- User-based systems with fourth generation languages (4GLs) like FOCUS
- Decision support systems for analyzing complex numerically driven situations
- Executive information systems that tracked the company's critical success factors

This stage ushered in the forerunner of more extensive Information Automation capabilities, the *Information Center.* Espoused by computer vendors like IBM, the information strategy attempted to create a separate computing environment dedicated to meeting the information needs of users. Relying heavily on prescheduled extracts of data from basic production systems, and using 4GL software to support users, the Information Center, while a step in the right direction, was only marginally successful for most companies.

This FOCUS Era created several important capabilities: systematic extraction of source data; rudimentary conditioning programs; reports containing information from multiple databases; more responsive access to databases. Users were getting information that wasn't possible to get before. But these developments also created problems (many of them described in Chapter 2), such as proliferating extract programs and unsynchronized copies of data. These systems perpetuated existing problems as well—users drowning in data, inflexible and costly processing, difficult-to-use programs, and limited information access.

Dead-End Information Automation Capabilities

The relentless advance of information technology continued to produce a stream of more powerful database management systems (DBMSs), enormous disk storage capacities with blinding speeds, widespread use of terminals connected to more powerful mainframes, and the first massive waves of data coming in from scanner and ATM technologies.

Computer-aided systems engineering (or CASE) became available, allowing organizations to partially automate the automation process itself. And with that technology came the ability to define and model complex information structures. Technologists saw the possibility of creating a single logical view of information that could be used to manage information for all automation needs. Visions of a single information image dazzled systems developers. They believed that it was necessary and possible to map the information contours of the entire company, and that to do so was a prerequisite for all new development.

They set out on multi-year information engineering projects that floundered. They built mission-critical production systems using relational database systems that were unable to handle the operational requirements. They linked to a single database system hundreds or even thousands of users with different needs and skills and watched as the mainframe went down, paralyzing the company's operations. The technology simply wasn't there to support these ambitious goals.

Single-Domain Information Automation Capabilities

Personal computers, workstations, local area networks, industrial-strength databases, natural languages, user-based query systems, intelligent GUIs—these and other powerful technologies opened wide the doors to greater information exploitation. Organizations began cobbling together more effective approaches to satisfying their information needs.

This was the stage of marketing databases, in which, for the first time, it was practical to use technology to achieve major strategic objectives of the business, to tame the toughest problems of information, and to dramatically improve the precision of in-depth analysis and projections.

Single-domain Information Automation capabilities were built that could handle information at the broad subject level, creating capabilities beyond the boundaries of a single application, organization, or set of users. They made possible customer databases for marketing, promotion, and product development; product databases for production planning, inventory management, logistics management, manufacturing control, and quality assurance; and supplies databases for demand forecasting, requisitioning, purchasing, vendor management, receiving, and accounts payable. The success of this approach was seen in examples presented earlier, in the cases of:

- The retailer that turned its high-priced Christmas toys program from disaster to profit
- The shipping company that saved $50 million by not responding to a price cut
- The insurance company that reduced its financial exposure by outracing a hurricane
- The grocery retailers that snared customers away from competitors

- The food manufacturers that rewarded its customers for frequent buying
- The bank that added 200,000 new customers while reducing bad loans by $350 million

But with the successes came problems. These solutions fell short in a number of areas: in sustaining the original competitive advantage; in turning tactical competitive response into ongoing strategic capabilities; in satisfying other information users that turned to this capability for help; in spreading the costs of operations; in creating a more general-purpose solution for transforming information; in integrating all information areas under a single, enterprisewide view; and in achieving greater economies of scale and reusability.

WIDENING THE INFORMATION PAYOFF

Single-domain Information Automation capabilities support one major strategic program—or at most, two or three tightly related ones—grouped around a common subject. But once a company satisfies its primary information-based strategies, it lacks the leverage to use that same information for moving into other areas. This is critically important because the competition is going to catch up, deploying similar or better capabilities.

New, broader competitive strategies that must cross several areas of the business cannot be supported by single-domain information capabilities. Unplanned, high-level tactical responsiveness cannot be extended very far when it is limited to one subject area. To be truly effective, key management functions for monitoring and decision-making cannot be constrained in any way. Organizational redesign, by definition, demands very broad-based information.

Although the cost of collecting the detailed information has been paid for as part of the Business Automation system (e.g., ATMs justified for corporate survival or market share growth), well-run companies are always seeking as much value from their investments as possible. Multiple use of the information resource helps pay the freight for the operation of this massive database, as each additional application and user reduces the average cost per use.

Finally, there is the issue of information complexity. For example, the rewarding of desirable purchasing behavior is based on the dynamic analyzing of massive quantities of information. Using conventional automation approaches to produce lists and labels of "frequent folks" is going to result in a nightmare of coordination and confusion. Standard extraction and merging may work adequately once or twice, but on an ongoing basis, especially as usage expands, a radically different solution is needed. A general-purpose information capability is essential for keeping up with demands and for providing the leading-edge combinations.

Once They Get that Extended Vision

A West Coast-based company runs more than 25 modeling and decision support applications for its property and casualty insurance businesses. The load on its mainframes was beginning to dim the lights of the city—it looked like they would have to buy more computing equipment and reduce user accessibility. Instead, all its important information was collected and placed in a central information resource under a general-purpose information capability. The advanced technologies they used allowed them to defer the purchase of another expensive computer while it greatly enhanced access by their users and analysts.

The uses of this new capability are highly strategic. The system provides information to managers to monitor daily premiums and claims, peruse vital financial signs, track claims and reserves, determine market penetration levels, determine the most profitable lines of business, develop a relationship ability for matching holders of various kinds of policies, and track producer or agency performance at a very fine level.

As important, this capability increased employee satisfaction because of the greater confidence in the content of the information. One of the system's designers noticed that as "users start exploring, they find other information they can use. Once they get that extended vision, they rely on it more and more. It makes them more effective. The general level of enthusiasm and work load has increased tremendously," she went on. "We are continually increasing the size of the database. They want more stuff everyday. All our energies are going into getting them that [information]. Once there, it's up to them."

EIT VISIONARIES

As newly emerging technologies were achieving unprecedented levels of performance and functionality, a few people advanced the idea of a general information capability for the entire company under which all Information Automation needs would be satisfied. They understood the limits of older approaches and began to employ the new technologies to achieve that sweeping goal.

Some of these efforts were failures, either because the guiding vision was beyond the reach of the designers' skills or because of other problems. But with the failures came successes, some truly outstanding. These companies and others are helping to blaze the trail to the EIT vision described in Chapter 3. Examples of companies presented in previous chapters with these kinds of capabilities include:

- The consumer products company that changed its fundamental orientation from brands to customers through the use of companywide information.
- The regional bank that absorbs acquired banks under its umbrella information system.
- The regional communications company that helped merge independent operating entities by bridging "organizational islands" with information.
- The transportation company that fielded information capabilities of such power that, not only could it resist ill-conceived pricing challenges, it could even predict balance-of-trade changes before the U.S. Bureau of Statistics.

Still other, more compelling examples of companies with general-purpose information capabilities have emerged. The two examples presented below provide a better idea of the many layered features and benefits of such general information strategies. One of them builds on the *frequent customer* capabilities described in Chapter 4; the other expands on the bank marketing database capabilities also described in that chapter (although they are not the same banks). Both are valid but different approaches to creating a general information solution, seeking to capitalize on the value of current, accurate, and comprehensive customer information.

As with most of the other examples in this book, the two prototype examples remain unidentified due to issues of competitive sensitivity. First-hand involvement, design materials, and reports have provided a look at their systems efforts and business outcomes. Similarly bold approaches have been embraced by a few others in their respective industries—banking and retail, both obviously intense users of information—so that similar examples might have been offered from other leading-edge companies. As mentioned earlier, some identifying characteristics have been slightly altered to disguise the source of the example without distorting the nature or impact of the companies' visions and their subsequent successes.

EIT DESIGN PROTOTYPE—INSTANT FINANCIAL EXPOSURE

A very large money-center bank (not the one cited in Chapter 4) understood the limits of single-domain information approaches, and the need for a more general information capability. Having successfully operated a marketing database with a customer population of 8 million accounts (each containing information for 18 months), they then embarked on an ambitious program to expand the range and power of those capabilities to ultimately meet all their key competitive strategies and programs.

Its management envisioned an environment containing information from all the major functions and operating systems of the bank. It quickly saw the benefits of pursuing promotion, profitability, and cost-control efforts as a single entity, and added information from accounting, branch operations, and product development to the already massive collection of customer information.

With that additional capability, they can conduct carefully orchestrated marketing programs based on real-time profitability considerations, improving the margins of its new promotion programs, and improving profitability by raising the quality of its credit portfolio. Since the bank firmly believes that marketing broad-based financial services is the key to profitability, it uses this information resource to create customer profitability profiles that allow management to clearly see the strengths and weaknesses of its general portfolio.

Who are the bank's most profitable customers? What products and services are most profitable? What are the connections between certain products that encourage customers to choose more profitable offerings? What marketing strategies and promotions help better target these profitability profiles? In addition to answering these critical questions, the bank combined its operations information on personnel, expense, and overhead with customer information, making it possible to generate instant branch performance profiles. How productive are the branches? Why does this branch with 3 people do the same volume (and at higher profit) than this other branch with 12 people?

Answers to these and similar questions have met with considerable revenue and profitability improvements, primarily as the result of growth in new accounts. So, too, has the overall quality of the bank's portfolio improved substantially. And by more easily crossing functional areas and applications, the bank can tap into unknown but competitively significant synergies, such as knowing what's going on in the mortgage and bank card areas. With these cross-functional capabilities taking root, it is poised to go even further.

The bank is actively working on a single shared database for the company, a capability it believes essential to competing effectively in the years ahead. Existing demand deposit, ATM, and other mission-critical operational systems are linked tightly with this central database, so that, for example, ATM transactions immediately update the customer's account both in the standard operational systems and in the central database at the same time.

With this capability, bank personnel can perform real-time relationship banking. When a customer comes to the window, the teller can ask what kinds of services and accounts the customer uses, what bank cards or mortgages or other products make up her total customer profile—with up-to-the-second status. Cashing a personal check, for example, the clerk may discover the customer is well over the limit on her credit card—again. Yes, but she's also the president of a large, prestigious commercial account.

This *instant financial exposure* (not the exposure at 3 P.M. as determined at 3 A.M. the previous day) helps the bank better advise its customers and be in the position to make rapid and precise changes of its own. Perhaps this particular customer wasn't aware her son at college is using the "extra" card again.

With this one timely and accurate record of information, the bank can treat any customer as a single, immediately recognizable entity, no matter at what branch or ATM he conducts business, in which state (and ultimately which country or continent) he is currently located, with which of the 11 banking entities he maintains active accounts, or how many accounts he currently has. It can offer that customer services like telling him all the transactions that have occurred for the past 90 days while he stands at an ATM a thousand miles from his home (and then mailing a copy of the statement to his home).

That single database also allows the bank to operate more effectively. It eliminates, for example, the internal rivalry that results from private ownership of information. No longer does a customer account belong to the bank card division or to the loan group. Accounts and customers belong to the bank. With that shared purpose come fewer conflicts in meaning and interpretation.

Another example: analysts do not have to go to great lengths to produce confirming balancing totals to prove they are using correct information. The information will be already correct because it was entered in the database correctly, because it already has been subjected to rigorous quality control procedures, because the bank has declared this information the official system of record—the truth. In fact, it had better be right, because literally everyone will be depending on it.

This general information capability is an integral part of the total automation process at the bank. Having experienced painfully the importance of thoroughly preparing and organizing information for use in its marketing database system, the bank has gone to great lengths to take what it has learned from that program and apply it to this next generation in Information Automation.

EIT DESIGN PROTOTYPE—THE SMARTER APPROACH

This example, more extensive than the one above, is a highly successful company in the retail industry. Nowhere is the issue of information and its untapped potential more urgent than in the retail business, where retail is synonymous with detail. Despite large cash volumes, retail is a low-margin business. Hence, a small increase in margin results in significant earnings per share improvement. For Smarter Stores (a fictional name), the unleashing of information's promise had gone from a matter of strategic advantage to one of simple survival. Smarter Stores is a nationwide discount merchant of name-brand merchandise with almost 100 "superstores" (each carrying over 20,000 items) and aggressive plans to grow to 1,000 stores in four years.

Management decided it needed a sweeping strategy to squeeze the maximum advantage from its major strengths as well as address the issues needed for such expansion to succeed. Driving this decision were growing pressures for higher margins, more effective response to rapid shifts in customer buying patterns, and the means for dealing with the aggressive actions of its hungriest competitors. The strategy would put in place capabilities for improving revenues, market share, and profits by store and by product, along with reducing the rate of growth in overhead. Further, Smarter Stores wished to strengthen its centralized merchandising function, while improving its ability to meet growing regional and local requirements.

At the same time, Smarter Stores was in the middle of a multi-year program of opening outlets for its SmarterBuy stores (also a fictional name). They had 15 of these specialty stores operating, with 200 more on the drawing board. They wanted to expand these operations and gradually shift their image from mass discounter to trend merchant, where they would stock new fashions and products as they emerged (trend products have their highest margins at introduction).

Executives saw that, in addition to improving business vitality in their main areas of discount merchandising, the SmarterBuy stores, physically located next to the discount buildings, would help deliver new customers. The challenge here was even more intense, for buyers needed to have the latest fashions available at a low price when the customer came in. If not, they went elsewhere. They had to establish the image that Smarter Stores was the place to go to find the hot products. This was a major change for the company. Management knew it would be necessary to undergo a fundamental overhaul of attitudes, objectives, and organizational effectiveness.

Seizing the Smarter Information Opportunity

A key ingredient to moving forward with these ambitious strategies was to exploit information, something considered the lifeblood of Smarter Stores. Some data was coming in through transmissions from stores with bar code scanners, recently installed to improve inventory management. But once that information hit the data center, it was lost in the bowels of the company's big computers. Buyers and operations people received summary reports on a monthly basis, with weekly exception reports.

Management saw this data as the leverage they needed for creating significant business advantage. Detailed POS data provided the opportunity for gaining insight into precise daily activities and the patterns and shifts that were occurring. With daily capture and immediate analysis, a precision monitoring process could be established. If, for example, sales stayed strong for a product, the retailer could sustain prices at current levels. If there was a fall-off in demand, and other information indicated it was part of a general declining trend, quick action to markdown pricing would help reduce or eliminate inventory while the item still had customer appeal. This was in sharp contrast to the current process of waiting until the system indicated an inventory excess, which then forced a special sale with resultant lower profit margins and unsalable remnants.

Equally important was the ability to forward POS information directly to major suppliers, converting that shifting customer demand into immediate product orders. Management believed that by using this capability to more closely link their operations with its vendors, they could reduce warehousing requirements significantly, in effect telling the manufacturer when, how, and where to ship. Since 20 to 30 percent of retail prices are made up of distribution and warehousing costs (Peter Drucker, "The Economy's Power Shift," *Wall Street Journal,* Sept. 24, 1992), Smarter Stores could pass those savings along to its customers.

This strenuous response was important to the discounting side of Smarter Stores and flat-out essential to the faster-paced SmarterBuy outlets. With the right intelligence about what the customer wants, when, and why, retail executives could be far smarter about their business, and be in a position to increase revenues, market share, and profit margins. While this has always been true, advances in information capabilities offered Smarter Stores a powerful and economical way to make that happen.

Discussions with buyers and operations managers revealed that if they were able to see sales the very next day (instead of 30 days later), they could initiate real-time buying actions, spot trends earlier, and carefully monitor the response by the public to products on sale. They said they needed detailed, current information by size, color, and style, what was selling where, and in what store. They were very clear about getting information to answer the most pressing and specific questions they had about their operations (see Table 7-1, Representative Questions).

TABLE 7-1   REPRESENTATIVE QUESTIONS

What were all departments' total sales by product for a three-day period at all store locations?

Which products returned the highest margin, at which store or group of stores in a particular region?

How much stock of which model of lawn sprinklers should be placed in the West coast warehouses during the summer months? How far do sales drop off during the winter? Should we maintain higher reserve levels in our central warehouse in Kansas?

What color swimsuits do people in Kentucky prefer?

Is the current hot weather affecting sales of particular items and do we have enough stock to support a continued heat wave of 10 days?

Which health and beauty supplier has the most shelf visibility in our Canadian and Northeast stores and what are its sales in proportion to other health and beauty suppliers?

Are there items in the audio/visual department that we're selling below cost? If so, what are the pressures causing this money-losing situation?

Is it true the Beverly Hills store will sell more deluxe dog collars than Cincinnati, or does the deluxe model repel mosquitoes, making it more desirable in the Midwest?

Historically, how much suntan lotion is sold in Hawaii between October and April?

This information, when compared to similarly detailed information from a month ago, 6 months ago, a year ago, and 15 months ago, would be used for longer-term merchandise planning. It would also provide solid indicators about where to concentrate their promotional efforts, as well as how to effectively merchandise individual stores by season from year to year.

Smarter Stores saw the full potential of its information, and fully intended to exploit that opportunity well beyond the boundaries of their immediate business objectives. The solution to their revenue, market share, and margin objectives was also the basis for achieving advantage in other areas—some planned, others not precisely definable, still others not even suspected. By choosing the information strategy they did, they kept available their options for addressing those areas when business conditions demanded.

Describing the Smarter Information Solution

To seize that general opportunity, Smarter Stores needed an information solution that provided immediate and on-line visibility of daily sales and shipping activities by the next day; similar accessibility to 65 days (2 months) of detailed information by store, product, price, and transaction; and overnight query to 65 weeks (or 5 quarters) of that same detailed information by store, product, and price. On-line access would be available to all buyers, financial analysts, store managers, central merchandising, and operations people. And they needed facilities for handling detailed customer information for a planned frequent shopper target marketing program. Further, they needed capabilities to track exceptions to inventory movement (unusual increases and decreases); to identify what inventory is selling the quickest in each store (to reduce out-of-stock conditions for hot-selling products); and to identify which items fell in sales in every department, store, region, and season for the entire year.

Their smarter information solution had to provide better management of products not selling (so they can be marked down at the proper time); pinpoint monitoring of buying patterns for optimum pricing and ordering (improve revenue, increase margins, and reduce markdowns and excess inventory); provide the ability to get higher-margin products on the shelves a day sooner (increasing revenue and margins), and lower-margin products cleared a day earlier (increasing shelf space effectiveness and reducing unsold inventory).

Extensive analysis of this information would provide immediate insight into the impact of advertising or special pricing, such as knowledge about which markets respond to which sale products and the form of advertising that gives the best return over a given period of time, e.g., was the new dog collar promotion a dud? In general, the capability would enable rapid and precise trend identification to take both immediate and long-term corrective actions.

Smarter Stores realized that summarized information had proved totally inadequate for meeting these kinds of needs. Maximizing merchandise location and projecting optimum product performance would require nothing less than access to the most detailed and historical information. Working with month-at-a-time summary levels by store, store group, and regional totals, as they had in the past, buyers were unable to detect problems before they became headaches, or pursue highly profitable opportunities that might suddenly appear.

For example, if a buyer was forced to work with one price for an item, much profit potential was lost, since some stores obviously commanded higher prices due to shopper demographics, community socioeconomic levels, weather, and other local factors. If priced too high, merchandise won't move; if marked too low and it sells out too fast, it sacrifices margin and dries up a healthy revenue stream prematurely. Detailed and historical data would help determine the precise price-sensitivity points and enable more exacting quantities of a product to be shipped to a given store location.

Executives determined that to radically improve current operations and make possible their aggressive growth plans, they needed to center on one major information goal: to store daily at the lowest possible level all sufficiently important information. They would keep this information for at least 15 months and possibly as long as 6 years to support historical comparisons and analyses.

For Smarter Stores, the lowest possible level was information captured at the checkout counter: item quantity and price by customer by checkout session. This one category of data alone was estimated to grow to enormous proportions. For 1,000 stores, it would be approximately 1 gigabyte (1 billion bytes) of information per day, 500 gigabytes for 15 months, and close to 2.5 terabytes (2,500 gigabytes) for 6 years.

Realizing the Smarter Information Payoff

Smarter Stores was saddled with systems that were busy all day updating much smaller databases while cranking out huge reports no one looked at. The technical people tried tinkering with the touchy systems, but they could not be changed fast enough to keep pace with the business. Meanwhile, users bought PCs and were downloading week-old summary sales data (the best they could get) into spreadsheets for analysis. It was painfully obvious that even if they could make these systems responsive, they would not be able to handle their plans for expansion.

A new capability was quickly needed without replacing current systems. Smarter Store's general information strategy was to install bar-code scanners in every one of its stores and nightly forward all data to a new central database that would quickly grow to contain 65 weeks of detailed sales data. They would tie that capability into state-of-the-art warehouse control systems, provide direct connection to vendors through electronic data interchange (EDI), and allow buyers to initiate buying plans and order changes through the company's existing production systems. The current systems would continue to poll stores for replenishment orders, and process and relay them to vendors and distribution centers.

All this was expected to greatly improve buying decisions, increase leverage over suppliers, optimize trend merchandising and inventory management, and provide close monitoring of item movements and warehouse operations. This would provide the basic framework for rapid, profitable, and sustainable growth.

Trying to put a dollar value on the worth of this capability, Smarter Stores believed that a certain percent of its revenue expansion could be attributed directly to the availability of the new information capabilities. Conservatively, this was pegged at 1 percent. With full implementation and annual revenues expected to be over $10 billion, this would come to approximately $100 million per year. They also estimated the new system would provide a five-to-one return on investment over a four-year payback period. Beyond the hard dollar payoff, Smarter Stores believed their approach was absolutely essential to achieving their very aggressive growth plans, an advantage whose value could not be estimated in dollars alone, but nevertheless was believed to be immense in its impact for the company's long-term survival.

The results? While the new capability is less than a year old (at the time of this writing), the company has exceeded all expected revenue and earnings growth targets. If that phenomenal rate continues, Smarter Stores will dominate their industry for years to come. They are also continuing to expand the functionality and power of their new information capability.

FROM PROTOTYPE TO DESIGN

How did the people at Smarter Stores do all this? What specifically did their smarter information solution look like? What functions and attributes did that capability provide their users? And how applicable is that experience to another company in a different situation and industry?

A company doesn't have to be in Smarter Store's situation—critically dependent on information to survive and faced with an almost impossible problem to fuel growth—to take advantage of a similar information strategy. Thanks to the boldness of this organization and others like it any company can capture compelling business advantages without the same threats hanging over them.

The Smarter Stores example demonstrates that a company can use information in bold and innovative ways to achieve major business advantage. It also illustrates that the technologies exist for solving "impossible" information problems (managing half a trillion bytes of information was until recently considered impossible in a commercial setting).

Applicability to Other Companies

There are certain factors that suggest that these early EIT visionary efforts and the more recent prototypes offer approaches that will produce similarly high benefits in other companies. The general business-related factors faced by Smarter Stores may be relevant, in different degrees, to other organizations that have the equivalent of the "detail of retail."

One common factor includes the sheer quantity or complexity of products and customers. This situation is found in companies in such diverse industries as transportation, banking and financial services, communications, health care, insurance, consumer packaged goods, pharmaceuticals, information services, food growers, packagers and wholesalers, government, education, and utilities. Other common business factors include those companies that are market-driven, competitively sensitive, heavily time-constrained, or who have to handle a large number of variables in their normal operations.

At a different level, there are factors that have to do with a company's information requirements—its processing demands and complexities. These range from supporting a clearly defined strategic mission (vividly illustrated in the prototypes), to having to handle "impossible" size problems (carrying the bill-of-materials for a 747 on each aircraft, for example), to extremely complex analysis (where the number of conditions and cycles are beyond any one person's ability to manage). These and other common business factors are briefly described in Table 7-2, Common Business and Information-related Factors.

There are also factors that have to do with the general nature of the industry (will the marketplace reward innovation in these areas?), and with where the enterprise fits overall in its industry (how much impact is possible given the rank the company holds in its industry?). Also critical are more company-specific factors such as how advanced the company is in operational automation (has the company adequately automated its core business operations?), the company's experience in launching bold initiatives that utilize technology (has it a successful record promoting programs that represent major new technologies?), and the degree of acceptability to new approaches (what is the anticipated reaction by leaders and employees of the company?).

Comparing these factors will help determine the applicability of the prototypes to individual companies. For example, a high-volume retail organization that adheres tenaciously to its stodgy founding image of a hundred years ago, and that claims no burning desire to alter it, is an unlikely candidate for embracing an EIT

TABLE 7-2 COMMON BUSINESS AND INFORMATION-RELATED FACTORS

Common business factors

Large numbers of customers
Large volumes and/or types of products or services
A great deal of product or service complexity
A market-driven business with rapid and complex shifts in customer behavior
A highly competitive business with rapid and serious competitor moves
An information-based business in which products use information or technology
A time-constrained business
A great many variables to track, analyze and manage
Leading-edge problems that require innovative and sophisticated solutions
Substantial impact from external changes

Common information-related factors

A defined strategic mission that can be supported by information
A defined "unsolvable" or "impossible" information problem
A need for information capabilities to run or expand the business
Demand for information to respond tactically to external threats
A need for using information for organizational redesigning
Very short information response requirements
Large information volume or throughput processing requirements
Large information storage requirements
Complex information analysis requirements
A demand for linking diverse populations of users by information
A demand for cross-functional or companywide information
A need for using information for ensuring conformance to goals and standards
Clear agreement about the value of information

approach, no matter how compelling its needs may be. Or, if an organization is not subjected to any of the factors described above, then obviously the level of need is low, the comfort level high, and the applicability of the approach limited in value. If, however, most of the factors do apply, if the comfort level is low and there is a high amount of "pain," then the company is a candidate for benefiting from these approaches, and for looking at information as a major opportunity for addressing its most critical problems.

On Constructing an EIT Design

From the first general extract programs to the more dramatic Smarter Stores' information solution, important concepts and lessons have emerged. Often with nothing to go on but the basic urgency of its business demands, these companies have created capabilities that range from impressive to simply staggering.

From these experiences it is possible to generalize further, to create a general vision of information that, with modifications, can be applied to every large business enterprise. That vision, described generally in Chapter 3, is made up of the conceptual and transferable aspects that these experiences have in common: their guiding premises and philosophies, their most ambitious objectives, their central components, their approaches to implementation. Most of all, these companies possessed a commitment to pragmatism that made certain that the success of all this effort and creativity was measured by its effects on the business and on the company's bottom line.

None of the companies mentioned above implemented all aspects of the EIT vision, although some of the more recent examples have come close. The EIT strategy was created by picking the areas in which each of these companies did especially well, and combining them in such a way that any organization might reliably use and benefit from. For all, it is the information aspect that is always uppermost, the one aspect that never varies, whatever the technologies used or business strategies involved.

The translation of a general concept like EIT into day-to-day reality is never clean and straightforward. *What* a company chooses as its design for a general information solution, i.e., what elements it regards as most critical, and what levels of sophistication and power it believes most realizable for its unique environment, will vary based on complex considerations. *How* a company makes that all-important shift from design to productive use varies even more.

However, everyone has to start somewhere, building a bridge that may be blown up after the crossing. Presented below and in the next two chapters is such a bridge, a design for implementing the EIT vision. The basis of this vision comes from business experiences, the EIT conceptual framework, and the most promising *enterprise information technologies*. It weaves them into a set of functions and relationships that, at a minimum, may be used as a strawman for a company that needs a general design to meet its information needs. While that design will undoubtedly be altered by existing business conditions and chosen technologies, the central features remain essential to the EIT vision.

Guiding the construction of this design is the desire to be truly useful, to provide both a general rendering as well as a working checklist. Like an architect's plans for a new home, the design must provide the adopting company with a basic yet flexible foundation that holds together the many functional and technological aspects while giving it a central focus and purpose. And like that architect's plan, the design must also allow the new owner the ability to tailor and adjust its framework to fit changing needs and budgets.

EIT Design Summary

The EIT Design creates an environment for separating the capabilities and needs of Information Automation from Business Automation. It serves as the basis for bringing into existence a common information utility that improves the return on the company's investment by leveraging technology, people, business needs, and information. The EIT Design is the key element in a company's general information strategy, making it both possible and desirable for the company to seize its collective information opportunity.

The EIT Design is made up of two core sets of capabilities: those concerned with the transformation of data into useful business information, and those that provide the infrastructure or foundation for that process (see Table 7-3,

TABLE 7-3   EIT DESIGN CAPABILITIES

The EIT Information Infrastructure

Information Desktop: Intelligent User Interface, Information Applications
Information Directory: Business Information Model, Complex Information Representation, User Information Profiles, User Information Views, Applications Repository
Information Database: Database Administration, Database Engine
Information Interfaces

EIT Information Transformation

Information Design: Information Definition, Organization, Incorporation, Enhancement
Information Acquisition: Information Extraction, Conditioning, Populating, Maintenance
Information Analysis: Information Navigating, Analysis, Discovery
Information Delivery: Information Interpretation, Presentation, Feedback

---

EIT Design Capabilities). Together, they establish a central information resource and general-purpose information capability. Once the components of this general solution are in place, they are placed under the control of information users.

EIT capabilities help users get what they need. They assist in managing information complexity, reducing information entanglement, and enhancing information's existing value. They provide a range of reliable information and the means for working through the information maze of complex definitions, structures, and meanings. With these capabilities, the user can separate the relevant from the genuinely unuseful.

The EIT Design provides a full range of standard and reusable capabilities typically needed in information applications. Rather than starting over each time, there is an Information Automation tool chest with commonly used functions that can be readily selected, customized, saved, and later recalled. This simplifies and reduces work, while accumulating Information Automation artifacts for the entire company.

The EIT Design includes *information transformation* functions that help users exploit existing data, no matter the original form or location. Fundamentally a continuous and iterative process, information transformation provides capabilities to define, organize, and incorporate segments of information under a single, companywide view or structure (or Business Information Model). Once accomplished, the user can create ongoing functions that extract (or replicate) the needed occurrences of that information from source systems, and condition and store it for later use.

Information transformation also provides the functions to navigate and "map" portions of that replicated information into pertinent sets or groupings for inquiry, analysis, and discovery processing. Finally, it contains capabilities to help users interpret the results of analysis and present findings in a way that ensures an insightful and receptive audience.

The EIT Design's *information infrastructure* is made up of components that provide a foundation for the transformation process, while offering critically important capabilities for an ongoing information solution. Its implemented form is heavily influenced by the technologies employed by the implementing organization.

The information infrastructure consists of an Information Database, which manages the replicated information; an Information Directory, which contains the Business Information Model and other intelligence about the information and user community; and the Information Desktop, the users' primary means for accessing and manipulating the contents of the company's information resource. Basic information interfaces connect the major information infrastructure components.

8

The EIT Information Infrastructure

This chapter discusses the information infrastructure components of the EIT Design, beginning with the primary link to users, the Information Desktop, then looks at the Information Directory, and closes with a description of the Information Database. Along with the necessary Information Interfaces that connect them, the components (see Figure 8-1, EIT Infrastructure Components) provide the underlying foundation for carrying out information transformation, and for supporting a company's general information capability.

While these components are *conceptual* in nature, it is difficult to completely divorce them from underlying technologies, either because the technologies help illustrate their functionality, or because they are essential in making possible that functionality. However, the EIT Design does not prescribe specific technology solutions or processing arrangements. It will be seen in Part IV that there are several alternatives for satisfying EIT information infrastructure capabilities.

THE INFORMATION DESKTOP

The Information Desktop is the integrated collection of capabilities that provides access and manipulation to the contents of the Information Directory and Database. It is a complete user information environment consisting of the necessary hardware, operating systems, interfaces, programs, and other facilities. It helps nudge along the first-time user, as well as satisfy the most demanding of power users. The Information Desktop is the portal to the company's central information resource.

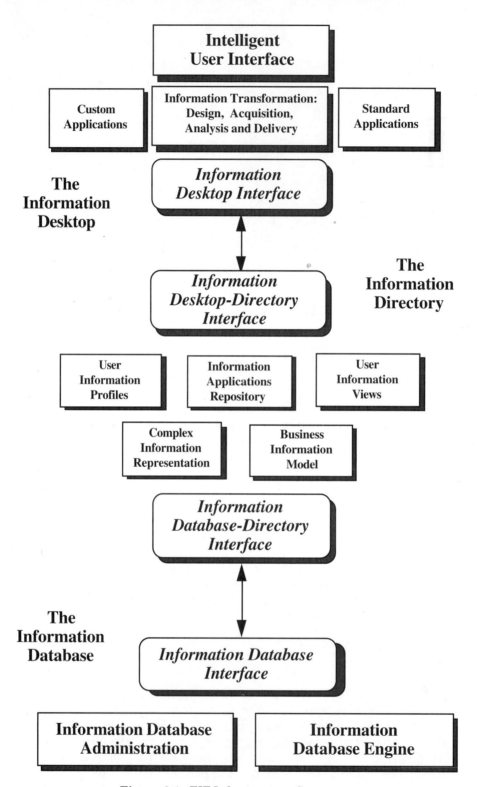

Figure 8-1. EIT Infrastructure Components

One of the EIT Design's objectives is to empower information users, to offer information in the form they need it, when they need it, wherever they happen to be. The Information Desktop helps satisfy that objective by providing capabilities for putting information under users' control, and for doing that in a way that is appropriate for each person. It provides standard capabilities that are adapted by both use and choice to satisfy a hierarchy of information needs.

Intelligent User Interface

The Information Desktop provides advanced information capabilities by adding intelligence to standard workstation operating systems and their graphical user interfaces (GUIs). GUIs are an essential component of the EIT Design, those desktop command systems that employ point-and-click selection of icons or encapsulated procedures. They allow users to interact with computing environments more naturally (popular examples are Windows, Motif, Presentation Manager, and the Macintosh).

An *intelligent user interface* builds on these capabilities by creating an information environment that closely resembles the relational and associative manner in which people think, make choices, compare results, and evaluate findings. It helps users easily group sets of facts and formulas, instructions, criteria, and information. For example, a dozen functions with hundreds of rules and criteria might make up a single, albeit sophisticated information task. These are organized around a certain process (or script) and then packaged in a graphic representation. Clicking on that icon triggers a complex set of choices, processing, and interactions. Similar high-level, high-density information units (or *information objects*) handle the complex information structures and rules of the Information Directory.

Both types of information usage are manipulated by users under the control of the intelligent user interface, and guided by a highly individualized *user information profile*. This capability helps users perform repetitive tasks in preferred ways and automatically monitor the Information Database for changing conditions of greatest interest. The intelligent user interface also makes extensive use of *expert systems* (onboard logical reasoning capabilities), greatly assisting users in complex tasks such as formulating complex queries or running large simulations.

Finally, the intelligent user interface helps an information user work intensively in an area without losing track of the bigger picture. This "zoom in and out" ability monitors the overall status of the Information Desktop, controls work-in-progress, links to custom and standard applications, automatically invokes requests, and connects the user to transformation and infrastructure capabilities.

Information Applications

The Information Desktop also helps to create a comprehensive user information environment by linking with and incorporating the needed *information applications*. These include the basic EIT transformation functions (discussed in detail in the next chapter); industry-standard applications such as spreadsheets and statistical programs; English-like languages and text retrieval systems; custom-built applications using 3GL, 4GL, and object-oriented languages; expert systems; and hypertext languages such as Hypercard.

These diverse capabilities are not only residents in common at the Information Desktop; they are also tightly integral to it as they share common methods of operation, information, and results. They access information in the Information Directory and Database without special effort on the part of users. This means that a user who, over the course of a morning, handles a complex simulation model, a detailed analysis using a graphical spreadsheet, the creation of a new design segment in an information modeling session, and the automatic receipt of weekly sales data from a previously defined request, can switch gears between these diverse applications with a minimum of effort. It means that users have a common language for working with information and can share results with less communication and effort and fewer mistakes.

These applications are stored in the Information Directory to allow widespread use and to make them available to a user at whatever Information Desktop he or she happens to be located. They are resident at the Information Desktop when in use and are "bounded" by the operating criteria and needs of the individual user. Hence, a new user may have a relatively small collection of applications with heavy use of tutorial and basic functions, while an "information veteran" may have hundreds of applications and thousands of rules for guiding their use and management.

The EIT Design takes this managed approach to facilitate the learning and transfer of skills and knowledge among all employees of the company. It also creates an orderly and standard, but adjustable, information management environment that can more readily accumulate sophisticated capabilities. None of this structure, however, inherently limits a user in either the access or use of the company's information resource, although an enterprise may elect to impose those constraints.

THE INFORMATION DIRECTORY

The *Information Directory* is the component that contains knowledge about the company's central information resource and the capabilities for managing that resource. It contains a Business Information Model (for handling standard information formats) and more complex information representations (image, text, etc.) that together describe all the information types in the Database with clear and up-to-date status about their contents. The Information Directory supports the access and manipulation of the Information Database by providing user information profiles, user information views, and an applications repository.

The Information Directory provides users with the means to understand the company's information and its uses. It serves as a lens or common viewing screen, and helps to improve the reusability of valuable information processing functions. Through it, users can more effectively enhance the meaning and value of production data. Finally, the Information Directory provides the mechanism for integrating different types of information.

Business Information Model

The *Business Information Model* contains the intelligence that governs the Information Database, and is the user's guide to that resource. It improves the utilization of information by providing the means to create greater meaning and understanding, manage the definitions, structures, relationships, procedures, and rules needed for transforming detailed production data into useful business information, and to help locate, segment, and cull those information areas that have the greatest potential "knowledge yield."

The Business Information Model uses *information objects* (the high-level, high-density information units mentioned above) to supplement the modeling capabilities of industry-standard database management systems, offering a direct and intuitive way to model the business—its operations, its basic entities, its explicit and implicit relations—through information. These are the building blocks that add a layer of meaning to the basic information elements in the Information Database. In doing so, they add an important layer of value as well.

With these rich information structures, it is possible to "charge" information with greater semantic content, to link the many strands of information territories into a companywide model, and to reconcile intersecting and conflicting designs. They also help provide directory and browsing capabilities, assist in construction of information views and mappings, and speed the development of new applications. Finally, these complex objects provide facilities for storing the needed rules and procedures used by a wide range of information users and applications.

The Business Information Model is used by many different areas in the company. Within an "information territory," users add, eliminate, or refine information to improve the representation of their portion of the business and the problem they're working on, with automatic reconciliation when they cross information borders. (For example, a marketing executive may need to include, and alter, product information that is normally part of the manufacturing function.) This highly effective user coexistence provides benefits not possible when working in separate and uncoordinated ways, such as having common and consistent information definitions and usage throughout the company.

Complex Information Representation

The EIT infrastructure represents, maintains, and integrates many diverse forms of information. As was seen above, the Business Information Model is primarily concerned with modeling and managing the more traditional forms of information, i.e., data stored as fixed and repeatable fields and records. While this type of information is critical for gaining competitive benefits, information users also need access to other, less standard types of information, and the ability to combine them when necessary.

The Information Directory supports this need by representing and managing complex information types. Using the same high-level, high-density information structures that the Business Information Model uses to model and manage conventional types of information, the Information Directory uses information objects to handle structured but unconventional types, such as expert knowledge, graphics, text information topics, and hypertext, as well as unstructured information such as text (free-form narrative), sounds, and images. A brief description follows for each major type of information.

Expert knowledge is complex information that contains the rules, algorithms, and logic for a wide range of EIT Design functions, and especially for use in expert systems. These functions benefit greatly from the availability of a common base of expert knowledge. Expert knowledge is carefully structured information that groups facts and relationships into highly complex and powerful concepts and arrangements. Over time, it provides the seat for accumulating a powerful intelligence about the company's information resource.

Text information is made up of the same numbers and letters as conventional information but is loosely structured or unstructured narrative made up of words, sentences, phrases, and mathematical expressions. Text information is usually accessed by designating values for chosen keywords and topics.

Information topics are more powerful than keywords. They allow a user to encapsulate several keywords and search arguments into a more sophisticated concept or schema. A concept can be subdivided into topics, and each given a different weighting factor. Documents with matching words of higher weighting values are given higher relevance, and the user is presented with selected documents according to their importance.

Hypertext is a more advanced form of information type that dynamically creates links between discrete pieces of information—generally textual or unstructured information. Every information item is capable of connecting with every other information item. Inquiry or analysis is performed on a lateral or associative basis, in which reasoning moves from one idea to another (i.e., from one hypertext node to another) as a concept "gives birth" to another.

Image information is made up of digital and spatially positioned bits arrayed in frames of two-dimensional space that are used to create visual objects. These are either images taken from photographs or actual drawings produced by computer software operating at the bit level. Sound and voice information may also be represented in this fashion, i.e., as extremely complex and massive bit strings arrayed in frames of time against two-dimensional space.

Graphic information is made up of two and three-dimensional geometric displays of form and space stored as standard numerical information. This information is displayed in spatial format by CAD-type systems that convert coordinates and vectors into the shape and dimensions of a graphical object.

User Information Views

Users don't work with the full (i.e., enterprisewide) information view in the Business Information Model. They instead focus on the most relevant or interesting parts of the company's information window. *User information views* provide that differentiating power as users work with these views extensively in information transformation activities. They help to bound and constrain the general information terrain to manageable cross-sections that increase the chances of getting excellent results.

One type of user information view is *culled information,* in which segments of information are physically copied from the Information Database and organized as a discrete information collection. The management of culled information is handled by the Information Directory. This not only ensures the availability of that information view to any user, it permits the synchronization of changes that take place in the Information Database with the culled information collection. Another type of view is a *virtual view.* Virtual views are logical views of information and do not affect the existing physical disposition of information. They are automatically synchronized with changes in the Information Database.

User Information Profiles

Each information user is different. Each has a particular style of working through problems, approaching complex issues, and analyzing conflicting results. At the same time, a good deal of an EIT's transformation capabilities can be satisfied by common and standard functions. As an individual becomes an intense (power) user of information, the need to expand and refine those baseline capabilities grows quickly.

User information profiles contain the full range of up-to-date user choices, interests, and working style parameters. Combined with expert systems capabilities, they help to model and guide user work sessions, seeking to reduce new work, reuse previous work, and increase the effectiveness of the effort expended. This can range from avoiding dead-end or unprofitable choices, to simplifying the selection and analysis process, to creating fully automatic capabilities that monitor information areas of interest for change.

User information profiles track the preferred styles and formats for handling information. These preferences are modified either by conscious change or by the accumulating effects of use. For example, if a user works with the same three functions every day, they will be waiting when the system is turned on. If a user has been working with a dozen information views over the past few weeks, those views are also waiting for him or her, presented in order either by the last ones used or by the ones used most frequently.

User information profiles are maintained in the Information Directory so that they are available at any Desktop and for making general changes to all profiles. They are capable of representing the full range of a company's users, from rank novice, where a great deal of Help facilities, on-line tutorials, and step-by-step menus are needed, to the power user, where techniques such as "fast paths" bypass unnecessary explanatory features and get directly at the desired information with a minimum of overhead.

Information Applications Repository

The Information Directory also contains a carefully organized repository of information applications, a library of Information Automation programs that will operate primarily at the Information Desktop. The *information applications repository* contains both baseline and custom versions of information transformation applications as well as industry-standard applications. Other applications, such as information security, synchronization and reconciliation functions, are not directly available to users.

Applications in the repository may be simple user requests, full-blown systems that contain complex information processing, stand-alone programs, or specifications for working with the Information Directory. They may be executed by user request, scheduled to operate at predetermined times, or run on internal detection, as when, for example, there is a change in an information condition.

THE INFORMATION DATABASE

At the structural core of the EIT Design is the *Information Database*, that essential component concerned with managing the replicated and conditioned physical information of the company. As the "heart" of the information infrastructure, it is under the control of the user via the Information Directory. The Information Database handles requests for information, the administration of its contents, and the physical management of the actual data.

Discussed in greater detail in the next chapter, the contents of the Information Database have been carefully selected and filtered. As much as possible, it contains information that is thorough, accurate, and unbiased, maintained at the lowest level of detail and at the highest level of quality, and kept for as long as needed. The Information Database contains the full range of needed information types.

It is important that information be physically organized and stored in *as neutral a form* as possible, to allow for the greatest flexibility for unanticipated uses and combinations. The ability to think about information in a "natural" form, such as tables, rows, and columns, is not only important for user effectiveness but for eliminating much of the implicit relationships present in information. When needed for analysis, those important relationships can be made explicit through the structures of the Business Information Model and by constructing user information views.

Information Database Administration

The Information Database is subject to critical administrative functions that are responsible for the maintenance, integrity, coordination, protection, and synchronization of its contents. These functions may be classed into several groups as follows:

- *Refreshing* of information, such as automatic calculations of totals and averages
- *Aging and archiving* of selected information segments from active to secondary storage
- *Backup and recovery* of information for smooth recovery in the event of failure
- *Administration of security* to prevent against unauthorized access
- *Management* of the movement of information throughout the company
- *Coordination and bulk loading* of newly extracted production information
- *Reorganizing* of information to reflect design changes and physical performance
- *Feedback* to source systems regarding information format and value changes
- *Synchronization* of updates to culled information copies

- *Reactivation* of information from archived or secondary storage
- *Retirement* of information by physically removing or destroying information

Information Database Engine

The Information Database is powered by industry-standard database management systems or *information database engines*. Such systems generally control one specific class of data (e.g., conventional or character-based information, text information, image information, etc.). The types of database technologies utilized in the EIT Design are discussed in Part IV. The ability to work with several information types at the same time is provided by the integrating functions contained in the Information Directory, and especially by the directory's use of information objects for representing and integrating all needed information types.

The information database engine is responsible for a range of basic functions such as receiving and handling requests, parsing them into suitable form, routing them to the appropriate components, reading and writing records, ensuring integrity and backup throughout the process, optimally retrieving requested data, and formulating a final response to the requester.

THE INFORMATION INTERFACES

In addition to the three EIT Information Infrastructure components discussed above, there is also a general class of capability that provides the necessary connections between them (hardware connectivity is a physical requirement and dealt with in Part IV). *Information interfaces* deal with the receipt, translation, and transmission of various forms and types of information, and the EIT Design calls for standard interfaces that link the three major components for commonly used transfer and conversion functions.

Having standard interfaces drastically simplifies the world of the information user. It results in more effective exploitation of the available information resources and provides a built-in and consistent "traffic cop" for managing the access, manipulation, and movement of information requests, information responses, and the information contents themselves. The major types are described briefly below.

The *information desktop interface* links the user to the other components of the EIT Design's infrastructure, either to "energize" functions at the Desktop, to get "information about information" from the Directory, or to access the physical contents of the Information Database. It translates high-level user requests for submission, and receives and prepares responses from those components for the user. This interface also enables connections with other users, with local databases (information physically resident on the same Information Desktop but outside the scope of the EIT Design), and with information from other databases (such as production data).

The *information desktop–directory interface* receives, translates, and coordinates requests from the Information Desktop. These requests are either for information or services from the Information Directory or the Information Database. Both types are intercepted and analyzed, and a suitable response is determined, and either sent back to the requester or routed to another function. The information desktop–directory interface helps integrate a diverse user community with disparate computers, software, and operating styles.

Ultimately, of course, the user wants access to the contents of the Information Database. The Information Directory helps the user understand what's available, what it means, and how best to access it. With that accomplished, the *information database–directory interface* prepares a request for the Information Database and sends it in a form most likely to be cost-effective and rapidly handled. Results of this request are received and forwarded to the user at the Information Desktop. In certain cases, interaction is between the Information Desktop and the Information Database.

Requests for information from the Information Directory or the Information Desktop are received and handled by the *information database interface.* Because requests may be coming in from hundreds of users at one time, this function manages both the translation and coordination of incoming messages. Requests have to be prepared and routed to the correct database request-handling functions, especially if a company has a number of different information types and storage locations. Results of the processing are received, packaged, translated, and transmitted to the requesting user. This may be a one-line display on a screen or 10,000 records.

9

EIT Information Transformation

This chapter looks at *Information Transformation,* the EIT Design's central set of information capabilities. It presents arguments for giving users the tools, information, and autonomy to operate effectively and creatively. The chapter presents ways to accomplish that goal—by providing functions for Information Design, Acquisition, Analysis, and Delivery. Each capability is accompanied by an example that illustrates the function and its part in the larger process.

AT THE TOP OF THE INFORMATION FOOD CHAIN

A major global airline carrier wanted to unleash the creativity and productivity of its employees by providing powerful capabilities that would help them to specify requirements using a comprehensive information directory. This, in turn, would help them access a central database that contained detailed information about passenger fares, flight segments by customer, flight number and time, competitive rates, frequent flyer mileage, routing, yield analysis factors, mileage program promotions, and a great deal more.

The system is in its early stages, with the implementation team making further refinements as more users come on board. One senior team member commented about the purpose of the new capability: "We want to give our knowledge workers the opportunity for directly defining their requirements, for getting results without having to seek out a hard-to-find programmer. We want them—there are close to a thousand—to work out their needs as they go along, to not be concerned that each request is a big deal and that once it's defined, they're not going to get another shot at it, much less at requesting another.

"This incremental, learn-as-you-go approach is the way people really work," he added. "And we want to capture that spirit in the new system. Our biggest problem will be success. We know what will happen if we fail. Things stay the way they are today, that is, barely adequate. But we're really in the dark if things come about as we plan. Can you imagine one thousand liberated users and what that could do for this company?"

Or what they could do for any company for that matter. This kind of thinking shows why the user is at the true center of the EIT Design. And nowhere is that more evident than in information transformation, where its capabilities position the user as the simultaneous designer, acquirer, analyzer, and deliverer of information, placed alone at the top of the information food chain.

To accomplish this means providing an information environment that frees users to meet their information needs without unnecessary delays, hassles, go-betweens, or restrictions. Whether to satisfy the need for reorganization of information to reflect a new hypothesis, to quickly add an information item, or to choose from a broad range of tools, features, and services, the user is given the full power to work with information to meet business needs.

It was shown earlier that classic automation limits the exploitation of information. Conventional techniques tend to reduce human thinking to stock mechanical patterns, to tightly constrained procedures, and to the often unproductive results of serial logic. To avoid this and to free up the creativity and resourcefulness of the enterprise's employees requires that people not only have access to excellent information when and how they need it, but that they are free to work in ways other than those prescribed by the narrow structures of automated thinking.

But what are the characteristics of excellent information? And what capabilities can liberate the user from the restrictive paradigms of conventional automation, encouraging them to be creative and effective in working with information? Each company will answer these questions in somewhat different ways. However, there are some benchmarks that may be used to help address these important issues. These are presented below and summarized in Table 9-1, Information Transformation Benchmarks.

Information Must Answer the Important Questions

One benchmark is providing information that helps answer the most important questions about the organization as a whole, its functions, its customers, and its central goals and problems. This was clearly seen in the Smarter Stores example. The most fruitful way to find out what these questions are is to ask the people best equipped to articulate them—the managers and executives of the company.

The most important questions are those which, if answered with accuracy and insight, have the potential for dramatically improving the company. A possible list might look like those in Table 9-2, Important Business Questions. These types of questions provide an excellent starting point to determine what information is needed to address the company's most important areas and issues.

TABLE 9-1   INFORMATION TRANSFORMATION BENCHMARKS

Information must answer the important questions

Information must be truly comprehensive

Information must encompass all available types

Information capabilities must provide drill down

Information capabilities must support automatic monitoring

Information capabilities must adapt to each user's style

Information capabilities must support creative work paradigms

Hidden in these seemingly simple questions are the clues and relationships that matter most. Out of the process of analyzing the many aspects of these questions come answers and yet other questions that begin to liberate the organization from the clutches of deadly fixed hypotheses. Take the question: "Who are our best customers?" Best in what sense? Revenue? Revenue growth? Margins? And over what time period? Three years? The past year? This month? What ranking should be given a customer who is number one in revenues yet is the number one customer of the company's biggest competitor as well? For managers to truly answer a question like this requires answering a host of other, related questions.

It is likely that the answer to this question will require accurate and detailed sales, pricing, and cost information by customer and product for the past several quarters, listed and ranked by revenue, revenue change, margin, and margin change. Assuming it exists, the data will then need to be extracted, scrubbed, organized, and placed in usable categories for the periods in question. The results must be joined with real-world knowledge and subjected to careful evaluation.

By the end of this process, it will be obvious that the seemingly simple question is, in fact, extremely complex. By taking a comprehensive approach to answering this question, and others like it, the company gains a greater understanding of the factors that are truly relevant. Striving to answer the most basic questions is an excellent way to understand the full extent of how and what information is needed.

Information Must Be Truly Comprehensive

The value of information is proportional to the comprehensiveness of the information. This is because large amounts of information can be used to produce finely carved insights that pay off in very big ways. For example, the grocery marketer who only has sales for the past month at the product and store levels must resort to general merchandising programs, can only mass market products based on factors such as average prices and inventories. The finely-tuned marketer, however, knows what has been purchased by customer, product, and store for the past year, and can tune his radar to pinpoint pricing strategies that encourage

TABLE 9-2   IMPORTANT BUSINESS QUESTIONS
_____

Who are our best customers?

Which are our best products?

Which are our most productive sales offices?

Which are our best channels and dealers?

Who are our most valued employees?

Who are our biggest competitors and how do our offerings and sales differ?

How are we perceived by our major customers, partners, and competitors?

How has market share shifted over the past 18 months?

What are our weak points in customer satisfaction?

What is the relationship between increasing customer satisfaction and additional revenues, and how does that relationship change as the numbers go up or down?

By how much can we increase prices for top-selling products before losing revenues?

What are the areas where we can squeeze more margin and profit without reducing customer satisfaction or employee morale?

How do our earnings per share, over the past five years, compare to those of our competitors, of the industry as a whole, and of other industries with similar characteristics?

What innovations can we apply to improve the company's overall health and prospects?

Where can we add actual or perceived value with existing resources?

Where do we fall short in terms of quality?

What are our most successful product niches, and should we expand them?

What makes people buy or not buy our products?

How can we least painfully reduce costs by 10 percent?

Can we promote our products more effectively?
_____

sales of the highest-priced products that will sell to a class of customers in specific stores and areas for the period in question.

The fortunate marketer, i.e., the one with the rich, detailed database, can also produce individual shopper profiles that, with a great degree of accuracy, can project what an individual consumer is likely to buy over the next few weeks, allowing targeted programs to encourage the customer in those desirable purchasing patterns. The enabling capability that makes possible such highly focused marketing efforts is a massive and detailed base of information.

To deliver that massive base of information requires extending the borders of information to where it is virtually unlimited in width, depth, and history. The *widest range or scope* includes information about all functions and areas of the business (sales, marketing, shipping, distribution, purchasing, etc.) as well as important competitor information. The *greatest depth or level of detail* includes the most granular of information instances, captured either at the basic transaction level (a customer order, an ATM transaction, a premium payment, a manufacturing run, a service call, etc.) or at a level one step above. The *historical or length extension* includes information that encompasses the greatest periods of time for an area (2 years of detailed daily sales transactions, 5 years of shipping information, 10 years of financial results, etc.).

The further these extensions are taken, the greater the opportunity for realizing the full benefits from information. Information that is broad in all its extensions provides users with the ability to analyze situations in new and insightful contexts, to monitor and compare performance across organizational and functional boundaries, and to discover the most important, and usually hidden, relationships and patterns—at the most general levels and at the most microscopic of dimensions—allowing new sources of leverage for creating competitive advantage.

Information Must Encompass All Available Types

As dependence on the company's information resource grows, users' information reach extends still further, to all areas of the company and to important external sources. The ability to combine several forms of information from different departments, time periods, and disparate production systems becomes critical for getting a grip on what is going on and for focusing closely on areas of particular interest. In addition, more qualitative information—about competitive moves, industry developments, government actions, economic changes, or technical discoveries—adds greatly to the value of information.

To realize its highest potential, information must include other types of data as well. Users may need, for example, text information to search databases for important records, for last year's progress report, for yesterday's newspaper article, or for that now-relevant position paper. Users also may require that this free-form information be combined with numerical or graphical information to create integrated documents for other executives and employees. For example, if the Eastern sales region is losing business to a competitor in one area, an executive can quickly plot the last two weeks of sales activity and combine it with text from a press release about the competitor's recently announced product strategy. This multimedia document would help raise awareness and spur action to reduce the impact of the bad news.

Capabilities Must Provide Drill Down

Conventional capabilities provide periodic, categorized, and summarized information in a fixed form specified in advance. They also offer detailed backup information, usually in the form of massive reports or on microfiche. Such capabilities are important but inadequate because they do not provide an easy and flexible way to *drill down* beneath the surface to see what's going on. For information to be of the greatest value, users must have the ability to uncover the pertinent details as conditions and instinct warrant, without formal specifications, and when under the pressure of a serious problem or crisis, i.e., on the fly. Here are some drill down examples:

- What is the significance of a decline in sales in a particular product for the month?
- Was customer demand off during that time period, and if so, why?
- Were there shifts in distribution channels, and if so, what were they?
- Did the planned promotional activities produce the anticipated results?
- Has a competitor suddenly taken over a sacrosanct niche?

To answer these types of questions, standard decision support and executive information systems pile up layers and layers of summaries. But clearing away those layers to get at what's underneath is seldom straightforward, especially if a question requires opening up a new path of investigation not already provided for.

Advances in information technologies can provide this vital capacity. With icons and a mouse at the ready, a user is presented with summary information about an area of interest. If an unexpected change is detected, the user clicks on the item and proceeds to systematically drill down through the layers until discovering the source and potential cause of the irregularity. This ability offers users, and especially managers, a new dimension for gaining valuable and untampered-with insight, providing them with first-hand and objective knowledge of their business operations.

Capabilities Must Support Automatic Monitoring

Users should also be provided with capabilities to automatically monitor information for changes and conditions of the greatest importance. Once deviations, thresholds, or trigger conditions are detected, flash information can be immediately provided. For example, daily changes greater (or less) than 5 percent in either sales or units for certain product, market, or customer categories can be automatically accumulated and matched against new sales activity. When activity levels exceed the boundaries, a note is sent to the user. If the user wants more information, additional details are presented. Further drill down can then follow, depending on the severity of the condition in question.

Capabilities Must Adapt to Each User's Style

Creative and insightful information use depends on the ability to easily adapt information transformation capabilities to the style of each individual user. Some like to see information in tabular form, others prefer graphics. Some want summaries first and details when needed, others want to work up through the details. And some respond best to pictures, colors, and symbols, while still others prefer their information in narrative form. Each user has a decided preference for working with information in certain ways.

The EIT Design acknowledges these differences, providing users with the means to request, either directly or through use, the modes best suited for particular information handling scenarios. Such customization is made to general-purpose capabilities to avoid limiting the general usefulness of those capabilities (as when, for example, there are changes in users or management styles). Tailoring information transformation capabilities to accommodate individual styles is accomplished by using general-purpose approaches modified according to the profile of each user.

Capabilities Must Support Creative Work Paradigms

Creative work is iterative in nature, halting in progress, tentatively concluding, and constantly inferring connections and hypotheses. For raw data to be changed into hard-hitting business knowledge, the user requires capabilities beyond those offered by standard automation. The discovery-bound user requires new paradigms for thinking about and working with information, and capabilities that support those paradigms.

With such capabilities, users are free to make and revise information connections and relationships, and are able to leap from one set of working assumptions to another without having to go back to ground zero. They are empowered to use automation to assist the search for conditions and patterns that shed light on underlying causes, and encouraged to explore hunches, test radically different hypotheses, and take possibly ground-breaking paths of investigation.

What are these creative ways of working with information? Some have to do with complex approaches to the organization and incorporation of segments of information into a companywide view, and with refining that view as needs change and knowledge grows. Others have to do with comprehensive methods for re-engineering and conditioning information for use in intensive analysis. Still others concentrate on techniques like intelligent query, machine learning, and pattern matching to analyze or unearth subtle but important information conditions.

Information processing paradigms are constantly changing, with new approaches, combinations, and variations surfacing all the time. The right information capability must embrace the full range of these evolving modes of working. In doing so, it helps users make the leap to higher information ground from where they may better survey the company's problems and performance. With this power, fixed points of view give way to deeper explanations, challenging concepts, and penetrating insights.

THE INFORMATION TRANSFORMATION CYCLE

EIT information transformation provides capabilities for creating excellent information and for creatively working with that resource. It makes it possible for users to survey, extract, mine, and refine the company's information, and become proficient in recovering 24-carat nuggets of business knowledge.

As stated in Chapter 1, information is data endowed with relevance and purpose. To transform data into information requires a rigorous yet flexible process for exploiting the quantity and diversity of information found in large companies. The EIT Design provides transformation capabilities that are comprehensive, standard, user-managed, user-modifiable, and part of an overall process. Throughout this process (see Figure 9-1, EIT Transformation Process), there are continuing opportunities to create valuable information from unconditioned data.

For example, a pressing business problem under analysis may open up new patterns and insights into information's subtle meanings and arrangements (and more comprehensive structures and relationships can be placed in the Business Information Model). Or, working through the information design process may reveal new shades of knowledge about the business and information's potential for new applications and use (and perhaps help a manager meet critical objectives by making smarter decisions and watching certain aspects of the business).

In its most fundamental form, information transformation is continuous, cyclical, and iterative. The *cycle* moves from design, to extraction and conditioning, to analysis, to interpretation and presentation, and then "back" again to enhancement, as new information is added or current information altered. Information transformation is also *iterative,* as when a user realizes in analyzing information that other information is needed, and must return to extraction, or even to information definition, before continuing. Finally, information transformation is *continuous,* as each cycle works to raise the quality and value of the information asset, endlessly transforming new data for inclusion in the Information Database. It is also a continuous process because nothing stands still, least of all information, which, if designed and used well, is constantly being altered to reflect the state of a dynamic business enterprise.

This process has the potential for enormous impact, especially with hundreds or thousands of users transforming data into useful business knowledge. Presented below are the major categories of EIT transformation: Information Design, Acquisition, Analysis, and Delivery.

INFORMATION DESIGN: MODELING THE FORM AND NATURE OF INFORMATION

Information design is the process by which users establish or change the specifications, structures, and relationships of the information with which they need to work. Designing (or modeling) information has the potential to engender discovery of new aspects in information and to remove much of the uncertainty and ambiguity that plagues most production data. It also creates the basis for common understanding throughout the company.

Information design changes the contents of the Business Information Model, and highlights the concepts, arrangements, rules, processing, and facts of greatest interest. Once the new information is incorporated in the Business Information Model, data from production systems can be extracted, conditioned, and stored for analysis. Information design includes information definition and re-engineering, organization and modeling, incorporation and implementation, and enhancement and redesign functions.

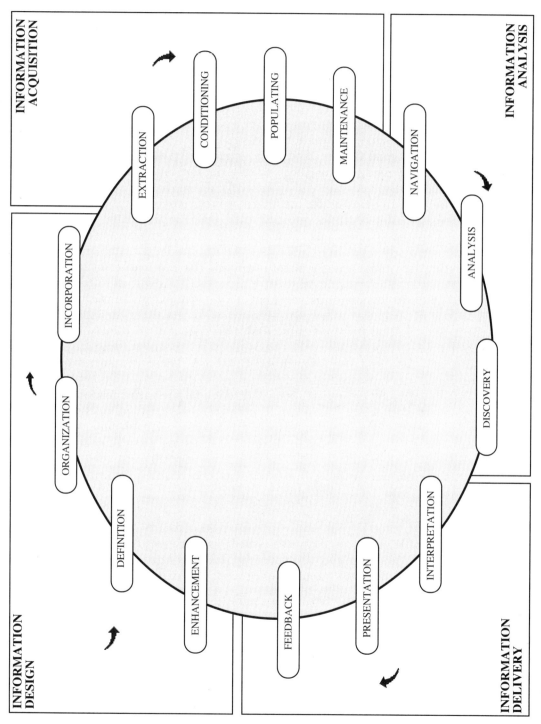

Figure 9-1. EIT Transformation Process

INFORMATION ACQUISITION

INFORMATION ANALYSIS

INFORMATION DESIGN

INFORMATION DELIVERY

EXTRACTION

CONDITIONING

POPULATING

MAINTENANCE

NAVIGATION

INCORPORATION

ANALYSIS

ORGANIZATION

DISCOVERY

DEFINITION

INTERPRETATION

ENHANCEMENT

FEEDBACK

PRESENTATION

Information Definition and Re-Engineering

In *information definition,* users first determine and describe the information they need. They specify the actual types of information and their definitions, formats, values, ranges, sizes, and other telling characteristics. The motives and means for doing this vary by business area and approach. One way, discussed above, is to articulate the most pressing business questions. Other requirements will emerge from understanding what it takes to satisfy a critical business strategy. Whatever the problem or opportunity at issue, defining information is essential to the information transformation process.

Information must be identified as to source, with the needed timing, transfer, extraction, and conditioning rules and criteria. For intense users of information, sources are many, and vary widely in terms of accuracy, relatability, timeliness, and reliability. In many cases, the true status of source data is not known. Accurate determination of this is a critical task. Once accomplished, it must be constantly updated as conditions in the business and source systems change.

Information re-engineering helps users determine the proper form and content of existing data and is a major factor in guiding the information design and acquisition process. This may be achieved by analyzing the formal definitions in the source production systems (usually kept in data dictionaries and adjusted by specifications in computer programs), or by viewing the contents of the databases themselves. Recent developments allow a good deal of this analysis to be done automatically. The results are the basis for the "information mappings" between the source data and the Information Database. These cross-over formats are stored, along with the information definitions, in the Business Information Model.

(Note: The following example is used throughout the entire description of information transformation. It is drawn from the real-world experiences of a company very similar in nature to the fictional Huck Fizz, although some aspects have been altered to make discussion clearer. All functions have been subject to real conditions and demands, and the information about their use and outcomes has been gathered from articles, first-hand experience, and a general knowledge of the industry and the technologies involved.)

Case Study Example

Huckleberry Fizz, Inc. is a grower-owned, package-goods cooperative with 500 members. It produces and distributes a designer-line of popular soft drinks, juices, and juice drinks. The eight-ounce Huck Fizz drink is its main product, selling through supermarkets and retail outlets, with sales volume approaching $350 million a year.

Until recently, the company tracked sales and market share using syndicated warehouse and retail store data from industry information providers, along with its own shipment data. The marketing department decided it needed greater insight to enhance its merchandising and distribution capabilities. With the widespread use of retail store scanner information and universal product codes (UPCs), users were quick to identify the information they needed to expand competitive capabilities. They contracted for consumer data from a major information provider.

The new information included unit volume, sales volume, market share percentage, and merchandising tracking measures (such as percent store distribution and average price). Each of these had to be available by UPC (versus currently available aggregate brand data), for individual store chains (versus no breakouts), 35 market territories (versus 5 geographical regions), captured on a weekly basis (instead of monthly), and eventually broken down by individual consumers and households.

The new capabilities required the acquisition of data from several source systems as well as from the information provider's marketing data. Automated re-engineering helped to determine the processing needed, for example, to convert Huck Fizz's internal product codes to the industry-standard UPCs. Also necessary was conversion of several years of sales history using older Huck Fizz's product brand codes into both current internal codes as well as industry brand groupings. Based on careful re-engineering analysis of both actual contents and formal definitions, users were able to create standard conversion formulas, along with master files for exception handling.

Information Organization and Modeling

The identified information is organized into structures and relationships that enhance its usability, meaning, and form. *Information organization* translates the user's business requirement into a focused information model that meets specific needs and is capable of fitting into the larger information view of the company (as contained in the Business Information Model). This model includes the rules, criteria, and procedures that are an integral part of the structure or are required for information transformation.

Case Study Example

Huck Fizz users organized the information they needed into the representation shown in Figure 9-2, A Business Information Model Example (the model presented is only a portion of their Business Information Model). There is a new information segment being created—Store Consumer Sales—and two others being modified, Product and Customer (these are highlighted).

The Store Consumer Sales segment contains information about each store's sales of products for both Huck Fizz and its major competitors. The UPC makes it possible to link information from the outside information provider (competitor product sales information, industry brand groupings, and industry merchandising measures) to their internal shipment, inventory, and sales information. Future expansion will include Household Purchases linked to Store Consumer Sales.

An example of information processing is shown in the "Line Item Business Rule." It governs the mechanics of customer orders, and resides, along with the structural information, in the Business Information Model. It is invoked anytime an update affects either of those information segments. Not shown in the example are the extraction and conditioning procedures associated with the various information items.

The *physical* impact of these dozen or so new or changed items is considerable. Because of weekly (instead of monthly) information capture, UPC (instead of

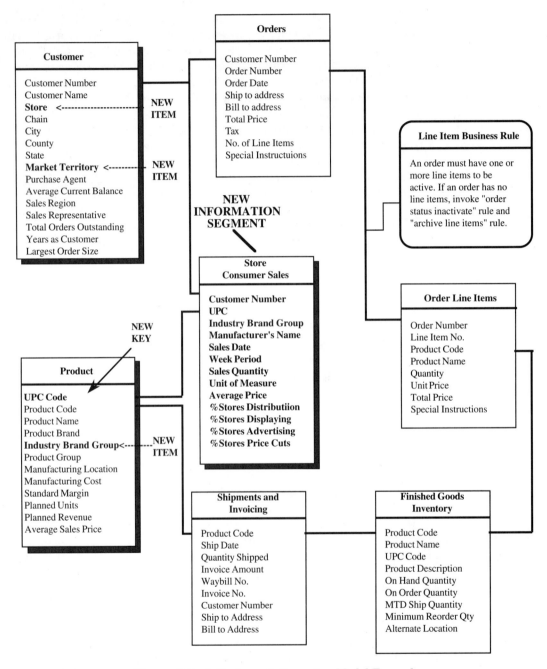

Figure 9-2. A Business Information Model Example

brand-level) detail, 35 market territories (instead of 5 regions), and competitor information not captured before, the increase in Huck Fizz's Information Database will be three to four times its current size.

Information Incorporation and Implementation

Once the information specification is defined and organized, it is incorporated into the Business Information Model. In *information incorporation,* a user determines how the new requirement compares to existing definitions and structures, resolves any conflicts, makes any necessary alterations, and implements it.

If the requirement represents a new information area, for example, it directly expands existing Business Information Model structures, both in terms of detail and scope. If, however, it overlaps portions of existing information territories, it will require changes to the requirement, to the Business Information Model, or to both. This may require negotiation between users if the overlap involves a conflict in design or in the meaning of similar information. The Information Directory prohibits changes that conflict with existing structures and relationships.

If the new requirement is wholly encompassed within the current Business Information Model, the user may simply use existing structures to access already available information. In this last case, the full utility power of the EIT Design comes into play as increasingly more information areas are added, for less new information additions are required to meet each new business need.

With the acceptance of the requirement into the Business Information Model, it is *implemented,* i.e., it physically alters the Information Directory and its linkages to the Information Desktop and Database. Information activities may now be invoked by any user who wishes to access that segment of information. For example, when the store consumer sales information is being conditioned, these specifications will be called upon to provide the definitions and rules to perform that task.

Case Study Example

Incorporating the new requirement into Huck Fizz's Business Information Model involved adding the new segment—Store Consumer Sales—and linking it to the Customer and Order segments via Customer number, and to the Product and Shipments segments via UPC number.

Information incorporation also required that new Store and Market Territory information items be added to the existing Customer segment, which expanded that segment from containing customers at the Chain-Region level (e.g., Von's Southwest) to individual Stores (e.g., Von's Santa Monica). The Product segment picked up the Industry Brand Group code and shifted over to UPC for its major identifier. Huck Fizz's internal product code was still being used to track orders, inventory and shipments.

Information Enhancement and Redesign

Information enhancement follows and improves the initial efforts at information definition, organization, and incorporation. It provides users with the means to take the sometimes painful experiences acquired in working with information and reflect that knowledge as refinements to the Business Information Model. In doing so, it requires that information be redesigned, i.e., redefined, reorganized, and reincorporated.

Hence, information enhancement precedes as well as follows information design. It recognizes the need for continuous information enrichment, an important consideration in advancing the company's ability to meet all of its Information Automation requirements from the common Information Database. Information enhancement provides capabilities to improve the form, meaning, and usability of information while users are under pressure to deliver results. These capabilities include altering, refining, or adding to the structures, specifications, and rules in the Business Information Model.

Case Study Example

Huck Fizz's users became adept at information enhancement, although the frequency of alteration dropped after most of the initial design errors were detected. Since then, changes have been mostly minor, concerned typically with "tweaking" the Business Information Model. However, there have been basic information structures redesigned from time to time, either to make them easier to understand or more efficient for access and manipulation.

INFORMATION ACQUISITION: CREATING QUALITY INFORMATION FROM PRODUCTION DATA

Information acquisition is the bridge between the company's production systems (and external systems) and the Information Database. Using the Business Information Model's rules and definitions, it provides standard but customizable functions for the extracting and conditioning of data from source systems, and for populating and maintaining conditioned information in the Information Database. In the short-term (see the discussion in Part V about the possible timing of implementing EIT Design functions), information acquisition seeks to create highly organized and quality information for the user. Longer-term, it is an active and dynamic connecting mechanism that keeps information synchronized with changes on either side of the "automation interface."

Information Extraction

Information extraction locates, selects, and extracts (or copies) required data from production systems. The rules and definitions for this vary by information element and as conditions change, and are maintained in the Business Information Model. Captured during information design, these parameters contain the logic, controls, and values needed to perform extraction of information from source systems.

Information extraction may be done by the periodic reading of production files that produces batches of *high-volume loads or updates* to the Information Database. These may be full or partial information replacements (or snapshots) or the most recent status updates and changes. There may be dozens and dozens of extract programs active at any one time, all tied to the Business Information Model. Information that is updated less frequently or that occurs in massive volumes is a good candidate for this form of extraction.

Extraction may also be done by *propagation,* an on-board facility that passes along individual transactions as they occur for "trickle-charging" the Information Database. Propagated information is usually held in a special staging area for later information conditioning. Highly perishable or frequently updated information is a good candidate for propagation.

A third form of extraction is by a connection that directly and immediately *hot-links* the production system with the Information Database. Hot-linking is an extreme form of propagation; instead of staging the propagated information for later conditioning (as in the two modes discussed above), it invokes procedures that provide for immediate inclusion in the Information Database. A candidate for this type of extraction is important correction data that is transmitted immediately.

Case Study Example

From Huck Fizz's production databases, information extraction pulls selected information about daily sales, inventory, and shipping databases, allowing access to the previous day's operational activities. In addition, on-line customer changes are trickle-charged from the customer production system as they occur. They are staged and fed into information conditioning every eight hours or on demand (as when, for example, there are important changes taking place in an entire chain).

There are also weekly extracts from customer order databases, which provide users with information on all current open orders, average current balance, and total orders outstanding. In addition, there are weekly processing extracts of almost all of the UPC marketing information (from the information provider), excluding, for the time being, less-important product groups and householder information (which will be fed in at a future point in time). Finally, there is a hot-link from the external provider for last-minute promotion or advertising program information, either for a major competitor or from one of its chains.

Information Conditioning

After extraction, information is subjected to an *information conditioning* process that corrects or flags errors, checks for unreasonable conditions and inconsistencies, provides structural, context, and synchronization checking and alterations, creates new information through derivation procedures, and performs quality-control monitoring. Once conditioned, information is in the proper form to populate the Information Database. Like in information extraction, the rules and definitions reside in the Business Information Model.

Case Study Example

The Huck Fizz conditioning process deals with most of the categories discussed above. For example, it checks that the "same" information from different sources is, indeed, the same (such as the customer status code from the order entry and accounts receivable systems). It scans incoming information to check that any one day's sales levels are not greatly in excess of the past few cycles: maybe someone doubled up the Dallas transmission again.

Huck Fizz's conditioning also performs needed reconstruction. It combines shipment and invoicing data into one information segment. It alters existing information structures, translating "industry brand" into a Huck Fizz "product group." It creates a numeric variable "age group = 25 to 50" instead of "age = 41." And conditioning checks for exceptional conditions as well, such as the customer who has made an unusually large purchase. Such rogue information throws off statistical analyses and must be flagged to exclude it from later analysis.

Huck Fizz's information conditioning also includes controls that check to see if record counts are reasonable or if there are holes (missing values) in important information items. If an entire section of data is erroneous, the information is worse than useless—it has the potential to eliminate the value of good data as well.

Information Populating

Information population is the entry point into the Information Database. The conditioned information, 1 record at a time or 50 million records over a week-end, populate the Information Database according to agreed-upon processing arrangements and the rules and procedures in the Business Information Model. Because of the size and complexity of this task, a great deal of planning and control is needed.

Provisions must be made to avoid possible processing errors, such as applying the same group of information twice. The use of flexible and comprehensive preparation, staging, backout, and coordinating procedures are essential to ensuring accurate and timely information populating. Information and systems administration capabilities need to be constantly refined as the use of the Information Database expands and intensifies.

Case Study Example

Huck Fizz's daily sales, inventory, and shipping data are posted to the Information Database each evening. Customer changes are updated in small batches every eight hours or, as mentioned above, on demand. Weekly updates apply information received from the customer order database. Over the weekend, populating occurs with the weekly store consumer sales information sent by the information provider. Finally, real-time population is run for information received by satellite transmission.

As Huck Fizz downsizes their mostly batch mainframe systems to local area networks, real-time updates to the Information Database will take the place of the daily and weekly updating cycles. This will become essential as Huck Fizz expands its system to include information on all its products, as well as the enormous volumes of household purchase data. The result will be a much larger and more dynamic environment in which users will be able to take the pulse of the business in ever smaller intervals, while increasing their ability to make improvements in its operations.

Information Maintenance

Once resident in the Information Database, that conditioned information must be maintained to keep its quality and relevance at peak levels. Some *information maintenance* functions are standard, such as aging, backup, and reorganization (see Chapter 8). Others are focused on correcting errors for, despite the extensive efforts to condition information, errors sneak by. Occasionally, they may be introduced during information transformation.

One important correction ability is prevention of erroneous data from entering the system. Once an erroneous condition is detected, the user alters the extraction and conditioning specifications in the Business Information Model. Information maintenance also handles correction of unacceptable information already in the Information Database. This may be done by altering the data in the source system (allowing the corrected information to pass into and adjust the Information Database), or by directly changing the contents of the Information Database (and creating an audit trail to correct the source system).

The audit procedures in information conditioning may not spot all anomalies in incoming information. What is needed are more powerful ways to analyze its status and contents. One approach is to set up intensive analysis capabilities that track changes in information content as compared to past patterns and norms, i.e., to define an information integrity model. Another approach is to use software to locate hard-to-find conditions that reflect atypical or subtle patterns, or that approximate user-supplied rules or constraints. These rules are refined as new patterns are recognized.

The other important maintenance capability is annotating the contents of the Information Database. Such annotations may warn about the potential problems in using a specific information item, or explain how the information was created. Users can comment about the uses made of information and on the results that followed.

Case Study Example

Huck Fizz uses all these types of information maintenance. They automatically age and archive fulfilled order line items and shipments after six months. They archive consumer product sales data for products no longer being sold. Older products that have taken on new names or packaging characteristics are kept in active storage with conversion procedures that are invoked when a user wants to merge the older information with the new product name. Backup and recovery procedures are rigorously followed and duplicate copies of key information are kept at a remote plant site.

Huck Fizz users discovered many problems with the data in their new system. One especially annoying problem was that the grouping of product codes into brands was not being done consistently. This was discovered when attempts were made to compare consumer sales using the industry-standard brand codes with Huck Fizz's shipments using their internal codes. Apparently, one of the production systems had never been changed to reflect the new categories. Users corrected the errors in the Information Database and altered the Business Information Model to trap erroneous codes with new conditioning procedures. (Note: This was done without adjusting the sensitive mission-critical production system, a difficult change that was instead added to the "fixes list" that gets periodically implemented during more quiet times of the year.)

Huck Fizz users also proved to be heavy annotators. Their comments ranged from short notes about the surprises they encountered in certain product and market categories to involved explanations of prevailing marketing measures. These comments saved a lot of unnecessary work as others began to use the same information. Users freely noted the information items that were suspect, as well as the information that had proved to be especially useful in making promotion, distribution, and pricing decisions.

INFORMATION ANALYSIS: TESTING AND CREATING OPINIONS

Information analysis is the general process that enables users to exploit and leverage conditioned information by turning it into useful business knowledge. Once available in the Information Database, information can be subjected to extensive analysis, manipulation, and investigation. This generally consists of placing selected portions of information in the context of a particular problem or analysis scenario.

Information analysis is concerned with both planned and unexpected needs for information. It helps users navigate the complex structures of information and map the most interesting sections, formulate focused inquiry and deductive analysis, and oversee discovery and inference analysis.

Information Navigation and Mapping: Getting the Right View of Things

The first step in working on an information-related problem involves knowing what's available. Will the needed information items have to be first designed and acquired? If they're already available, are they in a form that can be used, or do they require further manipulation? What are the major information groups and structures, what is each element's business definition, and what relationships exist with other information? And what are the demographics of an information segment?

Information navigation provides capabilities for users to answer these questions. And by providing access to the Business Information Model and Information Directory, users can see what previous analyses have been performed on similar information, what the results of those analyses were, and what rules and processing were used. Annotations and comments raise awareness and help reduce the need to reinvent the wheel.

Once a user has a fix on the information possibilities, the next step involves mapping the structures in the Business Information Model to those elements and relationships of interest. Creating profitable information clusters requires selection and rearranging of information into a user information view. As discussed earlier, this view can be a partial window of the Information Database or information kept in a separate physical collection.

With a large-scale information map to work with, a user can gain a better sense of the demographics of the information area and its value for addressing the problem at hand. This is done by comparing the information values believed possible to those that actually exist; by calculating the frequency and distribution of existing values; and by taking important averages, ranges, minimums, maximums, and standard deviations. These basic statistical techniques help a user understand information's shape, its discontinuities, and underlying characteristics. Revealing information profiles emerge, creating new areas of interest for potential exploration.

Case Study Example

Information navigation at Huck Fizz consists of a number of heavily used capabilities, used especially by management and those new either to the company or the system. These people roam through the Business Information Model seeking information of interest, notice an existing user information view, and run simple demographics. For weekly store consumer sales, for example, this might reveal that:

- Eight-ounce Huck Fizz drinks represent 94 percent of all Huck Fizz purchases
- Eight-ounce Huck Fizz has an average sales quantity of 1.2 and an average price of $2.25
- The minimum price for all eight-ounce soft drinks was $1.85 and the maximum $2.25
- A price increase of eight-ounce Huck Fizz in New York *increased* unit sales
- Koka Kolabear sales are 44 percent of the market, and Huck Fizz sales are 22 percent
- Overall percent store advertising went up 5 percent, with Chicago the greatest at 8.5 percent

Users at Huck Fizz also regularly create new information views, such as Weekly Sales By Area, illustrated in Figure 9-3, Constructing a User Information View (the segments on the right are in the Business Information Model, the segment on the left constitutes the view being created). In this slice of the Information Database, the user requests the information for a summary report on weekly shipments of eight-ounce juice drinks showing sales volumes, sales quantities, and changes from the preceding week.

This view automatically creates a procedure that compares the calculated Invoice Amount to the same calculation from the previous week to derive Net Sales Change. Invoice Amount is renamed Sales Volume, Quantity Shipped becomes Sales Quantity, and Ship Date is converted to Sales Week, there being no interest in daily sales activity.

Information Analysis and Inquiry: Testing Prevailing Opinions

With a carefully crafted view of information and knowledge of its demographics, the user can turn to powerful information analysis and inquiry capabilities to

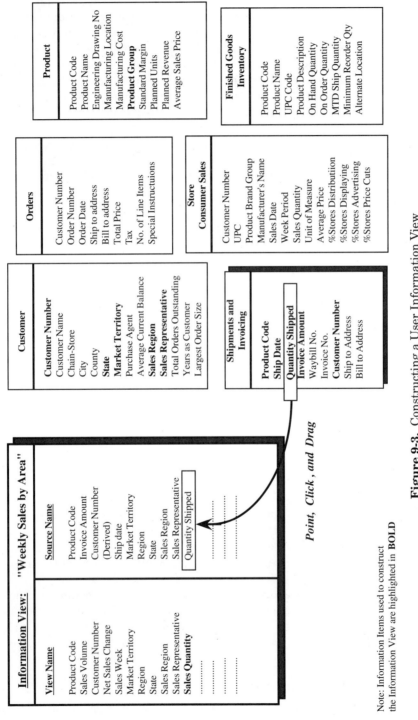

Figure 9-3. Constructing a User Information View

Note: Information Items used to construct
the Information View are highlighted in **BOLD**

provide further insight into the business problem under consideration. *Information analysis* subjects information to predescribed and deductive treatments, typically under the control of a guiding hypothesis or analysis scenario.

In *deductive analysis* (inductive analysis is discussed as part of information discovery below), the user, starting with an initial premise of how things are and how they work, wants to test that opinion by exploring its ramifications on specific real-world observations and conditions. The user may be motivated by a desire to predict future events, to estimate possible effects, or simply to corroborate a hypothesis with a different set of observations. Intensive analysis can lead to synthesizing new facts and hypotheses as it creates the basis for larger and more comprehensive explanations.

Information analysis and inquiry capabilities cover a wide range of power, purpose, and technique. They provide an analytical environment where users can employ packaged, off-the-shelf applications or their own custom-developed capabilities, always tied to the Information Directory and Information Database through standard interfaces. Basic capabilities include standard query languages, exception reporting, spreadsheets, graphic representations, query-by-example inquiry, simulation models, decision support systems (DSSs), executive information systems (EISs), non-procedural or fourth-generation languages (4GLs), and intelligent "front-ends" that use GUIs to simplify the generation of requests.

More advanced capabilities use expert systems for performing intelligent query, English-like (or natural) languages to simplify request preparation, fuzzy logic to handle vague or contradictory questions, and automatic request invocation for triggering analysis when conditions match criteria. Some capabilities accumulate knowledge and modify analysis on-the-fly.

Case Study Example

Huck Fizz continues to expand its analysis capabilities since the availability of store purchase data. Their system contains over 300 million records, utilizes 85 tracking measures, covers 50 geographic markets and 1500 retail stores, and has accumulated this information for 3 years. Every month the system grows by 40 million records.

Tracking the critical business measures and success factors and ferreting out the important news in all this information is made possible by a comprehensive set of analysis capabilities. Huck Fizz has developed a number of standard functions and user information views that regularly report on the state of the business. There are more than 50 statistical routines certified for common use within the company, along with hundreds of other standard functions. Customized versions are created by modifying these baseline views and functions.

An example of a standard function is one that generates line-of-business performance results displaying operating status and trends, changes in market share, sales dollars and units, and up-to-date key merchandising factors. These are available for every product, product brand, market territory, and region in the company. Changes are based on previous week, current month, past month, six months, and year ago numbers. Typically, they are automatically summarized and ranked based on these changes:

Region	Market Share	Change
Southwest	38.7%	6.2% increase
Northeast	35.5%	4.3% increase
Midwest	33.1%	3.9% decrease

But the heart of Huck Fizz's analytical capabilities is FizzFindings, a capability that tracks and interprets marketing success factors. Based on a combination of modeling, statistical, ESS, and DSS concepts, it analyzes weekly store consumer sales information and compares it to past information in an intelligent fashion.

FizzFindings highlights key events reflected (and often buried) in the Information Database. It provides users with top-line summaries and analyses covering a wide range of situations. Specific applications include monitoring the effects of competitive actions and price changes, discovering strengths and weaknesses in a market or region, assessing possible causes for purchase shifts and likely remedies, and tracking new product introductions and promotions.

This is done automatically as follows: FizzFindings summarizes information from the bottom-up, analyzes the top-most results, notes and ranks the major market share and volume changes, selects the products and markets furthest from the average, calculates and ranks the causal factor changes, and selects and reports which of the top causal factor changes are furthest from the average.

For example, if eight-ounce sales in the Southwest region showed the greatest change in market share, it would drill back down and determine what was happening in distribution, displays, price cuts, advertising, and average pricing. Based on predetermined weighting factors, it would report that performance for the Southwest—eight-ounce Huck Fizz sales were up 15 percent and eight-ounce Koka Kolabear sales were down 14 percent—was caused by some combination of the following:

- % store advertising increased 18 percent for eight-ounce Huck Fizz
- % store advertising decreased 12 percent for eight-ounce Koka Kolabear
- Average price was down 10 percent for eight-ounce Huck Fizz
- Average price was up 7 percent for eight-ounce Koka Kolabear

The brand manager can decide whether there might be other, more qualitative factors (e.g., Huck Fizz's extensive Super Bowl promotion or Koka Kolabear's image recently tarnished by injury claims) involved in the dramatic increase in sales and market share, and how to weight the impact of the various factors.

Information Discovery and Inference: Creating New Opinions Automatically

Buried in a company's information are important clues and indicators that help reveal the effectiveness of and problems with its business operations, provide insight into its most important products and customers, and confidently measure the prospects of its most strategic programs. But *finding* these clues and indicators is the trick.

One way to find them is to have a user take different samples of information, run analysis after analysis from contrasting perspectives, scrutinize and painstakingly match the results, add up the matches looking for logically and statistically significant levels of occurrences, weight and rank the several elements in the relationship, and repeat the process until finally spotting that one critical fact or one subtle connection that sheds light on a difficult problem. With a great deal of luck and effort, perhaps a previously unnoticed relationship or pattern is discovered that has the capacity to reveal something quite new.

Performing that process in a complex information environment is uneconomical and time-consuming. In addition, there are not only limits to the number of combinations the human brain can handle, there is always bias, whether in the process, the person at the controls, or in the form the results are made to take. *Information discovery,* using creative combinations of information automation to simulate human inference, is a better way to find those rich nuggets.

Information discovery uses automation for assisting the process described above, performing statistical sampling and value frequency ranking, logical (inferential) induction, numerical pattern recognition, statistical inference via graphical representation, threshold and significance testing, weighting and rank factoring, and machine learning. Some of this is done separately with much human intervention; in other cases, these capabilities are integrated into a single, larger process. However packaged and used, information discovery creates and tests new working hypotheses based on the specific and concrete conditions in information. It simulates human judgment by attempting to conclude (infer) something interesting from known facts using a combination of automated statistical, logical (i.e., expert systems), and numerical reasoning.

Assessing the true cause-and-effect relationships between information elements is a highly complex and subjective matter. Information discovery is an important aid in this difficult task, helping the user test enormous numbers of possibilities. Once set in motion, it can endlessly mine the astronomical possibilities in the Information Database. Information discovery also avoids the all-too-human weakness of being trapped within the narrow boundaries of stubborn opinion.

Case Study Example

Huck Fizz uses information discovery to expose the hard-to-detect patterns and conditions in their operations. These insights have shed light on low product yields, packaging trouble-spots, recurring distribution delays, unexpected clustering of marketing costs, excessive expenditure blips, potentially troublesome customer demands, and small but persistent factors contributing to lower profit margins.

Discovery has highlighted new areas of opportunity. One example was a newly discovered shift in buying patterns which resulted in the company quickly moving inventory to an area of expected greater demand. Another was gaining a competitive edge over Koka Kolabear by quickly isolating newly emerging factors affecting new customer purchase patterns in key market areas, i.e., an aging population and shifting population racial demographics.

They also use inferential techniques to determine if the key marketing measures in FizzFindings are correctly weighted, comparing them to changes in sales and market share. An inductive analysis of two years' information determined that increases in average price correlated 95 percent of the time with decreases in consumer purchase dollars of eight-ounce Huck Fizz—but only if there were corresponding decreases in Koka Kolabear's eight-ounce average price as well. Apparently, consumer purchases did not drop off if there was only an increase in average price of eight-ounce Huck Fizz. This led them to conclude that sales dropped off only when both conditions were present. This knowledge allowed them to increase prices incrementally as long as they believed Koka Kolabear would not match their moves. Needless to say, this automatically inferred finding did not square with the original marketing model dynamics.

Information discovery has helped Huck Fizz successfully challenge prevailing opinions in other "sacred cow" areas: in beliefs about the deeper connections at work in customer repeat business; in the rule-of-thumb that consumers act more-or-less the same throughout the country within particular age groups; and in the maxim there is a one-to-one relationship between percentage of stores advertising and the level of sales. Refuting or refining these hypotheses has resulted in revenue increases, better promotion programs, and more accurate merchandising measures.

INFORMATION DELIVERY: ALTERING OPINIONS FOR EFFECTIVE BUSINESS ACTION

With solid results from information analysis, information continues the transformation process from operational data to business action. *Information delivery* is the part of the cycle concerned with interpreting those results, crafting a presentation that can best alter prevailing opinion, and judging the effects of that information on the business for possible feedback for subsequent information use.

Information interpretation is the first step, where conclusions, results, and findings are matched by the user to the realities of the business to determine their potential usefulness. This process is greatly enhanced by users who have a good knowledge of the business and a deep sense of the meaning of the information. Once the user has verified that the findings are accurate and reasonable, and that they can be supported by clear and compelling facts or statistically significant occurrences, it is necessary to separate the interesting from the boring and the important from the irrelevant.

Do the findings, if accepted and acted upon, have the promise for translating into significant business impact? In other words, will anyone care? And what is the prevailing climate of opinion and reception? After all, Copernicus had great knowledge to impart, but to a world unwilling to receive it.

Information presentation introduces the results of information transformation—however numerically definite and however conceptually attractive—to the broader context of business and interpersonal reality. In doing this, a user is involved in the process of articulating a new idea or concept that has the potential for being accepted as truly useful knowledge. This will require an excellent sense of judgment and timing, and the necessary skills for presentation.

For a concept to become knowledge and a precursor to action, it must be capable of going beyond the originating user and present itself in the most critical light for verification. It must pass the barriers of self-interest and frozen thought, and gather a broad consensus. Finally, it must gain the blessing of authority, logic, and experience. That new and hopeful concept must have the potential for intersecting and improving the quality of prevailing opinions.

For that to happen, the user must determine how the information is best presented, what issues and factors affect the way management will regard the results, i.e., how the information will be viewed, and how well the organization receives surprises and responds. Is it possible management doesn't want to know about any of this, because if they do, they will be forced to act on a situation whose consequences may be unpleasant? If so, will the messenger be shot?

The user must assess the different types of reactions that are likely to occur. Reaction to new knowledge may be immediate or deferred, positive or negative. Other responses have to do with whether the information was: already known and has confirming value, already known and has no value, already known and has negative value (as when information only serves to make things worse), and not already known but of no possible interest.

Judging the degree of usefulness precedes the act of presentation, a skill that involves understanding the best timing, form, setting, and audience for presenting the idea for consideration. Often presenting the problem by itself is insufficient, as most executives expect to hear the response or solution paired with the finding. Doing this well greatly improves the chances of insightful discussion, and for receiving strong responses in a constructive and thoughtful fashion.

If the finding is accepted and acted upon, the user is in the unique position to see first-hand the effects of that action on the business situation. *Information feedback* takes those outcomes and looks for ways to further raise the value of information for future business use. This is the point where the knowledge gained and the information accumulated are ready to enter another round of transformation, their being applied to still another, possibly more important business problem. The company benefits greatly when users reflect the results as an enhancement or redesign of the Business Information Model and the contents of the Information Database.

Case Study Example

Huck Fizz has a management team basically receptive to *news,* however unpleasant. They were far-sighted enough to understand the importance of information for their business, and serious enough to provide the support needed to bring it about. In fact, it is difficult to separate the information user from the managers at Huck Fizz. A new finding may just as often come from the CEO as from a market research analyst or brand manager.

Hence, there is an open and free exchange of opinion with regard to all potentially important facts and hypotheses about the business operations and markets.

The only requirement is that any conclusion or finding be first subjected to standard validation using the tools and techniques discussed above. Hunches, anecdotal-driven findings, and personal agendas are still alive and well at Huck Fizz. But they must be backed by solid information before top management will give them the kind of attention the promulgator wishes. Hick Fizz has become an information-driven company, a result of determined pursuit of the benefits of information transformation.

part IV

INTEGRATING THE INFORMATION TECHNOLOGIES

10

An EIT Integration Model

The present chapter begins the third component of the EIT Enabling Framework and is concerned with how a company can best implement the EIT Design's infrastructure and transformation capabilities. It provides integration strategies that an organization can use to adapt to its unique business, technological, and information environments.

This chapter offers an EIT Integration Model for evaluating and configuring information technologies. Chapter 11 discusses more than twenty general technologies that are key to providing infrastructure and transformation functions. Chapter 12 reviews "packaged" information visions offered by leading information technology vendors and contrasts them to the EIT Design and Integration Model.

REALIZING THE BENEFITS OF THE EIT VISION

Preceding chapters have provided a vision and design for transforming a company's information asset into ongoing competitive advantage. But to receive the actual benefits from information requires not only grasping information's full potential and articulating an approach for seizing it, but also understanding how to implement working capabilities. More than a few companies have come this far, only to fall short in making it a business reality.

Many of the failures to go the distance can be traced to the obstacles discussed earlier: to the subtle but pervasive problems involved in taming information; to an inability to separate the two types of automation (and their very different needs and solutions); and to a timidness in applying technologies to the handling of massive collections of information.

To be complete, any approach to harnessing the power of information must provide concrete and practical ways for implementing capabilities, especially by identifying the critical enablers and how they may be used. The single most important enabler is the integration of proven, available, attractive, and compatible information technologies. Doing that technology integration task well ensures a cost-effective, coherent information solution that can be rapidly deployed over the widest possible range of uses and users.

ENABLING EIT CAPABILITIES

There are many ways to turn the EIT vision into a business reality and establish the features and capabilities called for by the EIT Design. It can be built from scratch, custom-tailored to the specifics of the individual organization. However, despite the tremendous power of new tools and techniques for building information systems, this seems unwise from a number of standpoints, not the least being the large development cost and time. Besides, the EIT Design relies heavily on general-purpose capabilities that generally require development skills most technology-using companies do not have in abundance.

Or, a company can cobble together the technologies already present in the organization to fashion EIT capabilities from what has worked in the past. This may meet some immediate needs but risks creating serious complexities and an overall environment that grows progressively more unwieldy and less responsive. The hope of creating a common information utility is very unlikely with this strategy.

Alternatively, a company can elect to follow the global architectures and flagship technologies of the leading vendors in this area, relying on a single source to package and deliver a total information solution. This has its obvious dangers and attractions, and for those so inclined, that possibility is explored in a later chapter.

Finally, a company can choose to bring EIT capabilities to life by uniting the "best of breed" technologies under one structure. This model takes advantage of "ideal" technologies in a way that greatly reduces new development, gains the benefits of industry-standard approaches and architectures, and ensures a flexible and changeable technology environment. Of course, there are several integration models to consider when taking this approach.

OBJECTIVES (AND LIMITS) OF THE EIT INTEGRATION MODEL

What are the ideal technologies for enabling the capabilities called for in the EIT Design? How are they best integrated to reduce implementation and support costs, enhance flexibility and functionality, meet needs for reliability and performance, and resist obsolescence? What are the criteria for judging information technologies in the face of a bewildering array of approaches, architectures, standards, consortia, and committees (not to mention conflicting vendor claims and hyperbole)?

The Integration Model presented below helps make sense of much of that confusion, and of the technologies that affect the implementation of an EIT capability. It is grounded in the notion that most, if not all, of the technologies needed to establish this broad capability can be acquired, adapted, and employed with little net new invention. The model helps companies configure a coherent information environment, providing a flexible structure for technologies to be integrated. Such a model assures that this structure remains effective over the life of the information capability and is flexible for modifications to accommodate changes in the business and in technology.

Some caveats: The use of a general model to erect the technology base for EIT functions is going to be affected by factors constantly in a state of flux. Obviously, the technologies themselves are highly dynamic in nature, with developments constantly occurring—today's new paradigms of automation are tomorrow's disdainful calls for radical replacement. Also, the melding of many complex technologies into an integrated, cost-effective, and coherent system is still mostly an art form, perhaps analogous to large-scale musical composition. Therefore, the EIT Integration Model is intended to be reworked by the implementing organization, giving greater or lesser weight to different features, functions, and technologies as conditions and priorities change.

EIT ENABLING CRITERIA

The EIT Integration Model includes a set of enabling criteria that helps a company evaluate and select the technologies, methodologies, tools, techniques, approaches, and arrangements best suited to the components and functions of the EIT Design. In general, a company should select solutions that resist obsolescence, are designed to be extendable and modifiable, that do not lock it into a single vendor or approach, have widespread market acceptance, and provide built-in avenues of escape.

Having satisfied these more general demands, the most attractive solutions must respond favorably to a set of criteria that takes into account a range of important information, technology, cost, and other issues. These are summarized in Table 10-1, EIT Enabling Criteria, and discussed individually below.

Storage Capacity

This criterion deals with the technologies needed for handling massive-sized databases. The greater the storage capacity, the greater the ability to maintain information at the lowest levels of detail and for the longest periods of time. As discussed earlier, this allows for an increase in the value of information by providing greater flexibility, more powerful exception spotting and tracking, more precise projection and modeling capabilities, wider and more subtle relationships among the various parts of the business, and richer capabilities for information selection, segmentation, and consolidation.

Massive storage capacity means that a replicated central information resource can be realistically maintained, resulting in a number of critically important benefits (see Chapters 2 and 3). The most important of these benefits is reduction of

TABLE 10-1   EIT ENABLING CRITERIA

Storage capacity
Processing performance
Price-performance
Functionality
Connectivity
Sharability
Availability
Reliability
Security
Modularity
Productivity
Standardization

the large number of copies of information to (essentially) one copy. By accomplishing that, a single massive Information Database is capable of reducing the total information storage capacity throughout the company. For large companies, without factoring in non-traditional information such as image or text, important categories of information can easily exceed several hundred gigabytes—and quite a few, a terabyte or more.

Processing Performance

This criterion calls for very high levels of processing capabilities for superior response and throughput. An EIT capability must support the most complex analyses and queries imaginable, and the technologies used must provide adequate power for handling those requests quickly and efficiently. This capability directly bears on enhancing user and operational productivity.

The other dimension of performance is information throughput, which deals with the ability to process enormous quantities of data (e.g., for functions such as information extraction and populating). A simple example is the daily loading of 25 million records into the Information Database, a process that using older technologies takes more than 24 hours to complete. Obviously, the technologies used must have the horsepower to solve this "impossible" problem.

Price-Performance

This calls for the use of technologies that meet the very highest levels of price-performance. These important measures include average cost per MIP (millions of instructions per second) for processing and average cost per megabyte for storage. This criterion balances power against price, and provides a critical measure of technological cost-benefit for the adopting organization. As will be seen in the next chapter, microprocessor-based computing platforms and smaller format disk drives offer extremely attractive price-performance ratios, with little improvement let-up in sight.

Functionality

This criterion calls for infrastructure and transformation software technologies that provide powerful and rich functionality. This functionality should be built over a general-purpose design that permits a great deal of expandability, scalability, customization, and modularity. The user-based ability to plug-in additional capabilities as needed, and provide the means for rapid and cost-effective development of new capabilities, is very important. Examples are information processing capabilities that allow users to easily create complex information queries or establish sophisticated information relationships without having a high level of technical knowledge or skill.

Connectivity

This criterion calls for technologies capable of linking every user and organization in the company into an effective network of information handling platforms. Enterprisewide, industry-standard and open (more on "open" below) connectivity eliminates restrictive computing arrangements, allows multi-vendor and multi-product environments, and permits the cost-effective sharing of information.

Sharability

Widespread and easy sharability of information goes well beyond the transferring of information from one workstation or platform to another. It calls for the complete sharing of a single-copy of information by anyone anywhere in the company. Preferred technologies must provide for widespread and common access to shared central information, with all or most of the processing done at the user's Information Desktop. This arrangement increases the opportunities for achieving important business benefits and for taking maximum advantage of the economies of scale of a single information resource.

Availability

This criterion calls for users to have assured information availability whenever they need it. Information availability is more than systems or hardware availability (i.e., lack of down-time). It requires technologies that not only provide high levels of simplicity, reliability, fault tolerance, and recovery, but also enable high-speed, effective delivery of information to the user wherever he or she is physically located.

Reliability

Related to information availability, this area is concerned with basic hardware and software robustness, durability, resilience, and recoverability, especially when information technologies are subjected to massive work loads or equipment and software changes. This criterion demands, for example, that the technologies support the highest levels of error-free operation and, in the event of a failure, provide immediate and uninterrupted recovery of all information affected during the failure. Facilities for providing extremely high levels of reliability include total component redundancy, automatic diagnosis and servicing, information mirroring, fallback processing, and unsupervised operations.

Security

Information security is the ability to actively limit access to or manipulation of information that is either sensitive, potentially damaging, compromising, or embarrassing, without restricting or discouraging legitimate use. Legitimate use may include uses not specifically authorized or in pursuit of a recognized business objective. Once portions of information are designated as secure, the technology must support protection requirements in the most efficient and unobtrusive fashion. Of great importance is the protection of information from accidental destruction or dissemination.

Modularity

This criterion calls for highly compact and modular technologies that can notch up or down in small but useful increments as needs and conditions change. Paying for unused capacity, extra features, or capabilities that aren't needed should be kept to a minimum, with incremental upgrading as a means for deferring new expenditures as long as possible.

Inherently modular systems approach linearity (i.e., a unit increase in capacity and performance matches a unit increase in cost), and offer attractive economies of scale as capacity reaches upper limits. They contain capabilities for onboard reconfiguration and expansion, on-site replaceable units, reduced technical support, uninterrupted operations, and automatic administrative functions (such as redistribution of data when capacities are altered).

Productivity

The preferred technologies must also provide for greatly simplified functions for cost-effective operations and support. They should require fewer people to manage and operate than conventional systems of automation and reduce the difficulties of data and systems administration. In other words, the technologies should have fewer knobs to turn, with most of their complexity hidden, and the full power and range of use revealed and available.

Standardization

This criterion calls for employing technologies that are industry-standard and non-proprietary, i.e., they are "open" in design, allowing multiple vendors the opportunity to offer alternative value-added solutions. The technologies should also enjoy widespread marketplace acceptance. Examples of standard technologies and architectures include:

- SQL as a data manipulation language
- POSIX for software portability
- OSI for wide area network communications
- The Intel 80X86 chip (i.e., the 80386, 80486, 80586, etc.)
- Relational database management systems
- Unix and OS/2 as the LAN Server operating system
- Novell's NetWare for local area network management
- DOS Windows as the desktop GUI

A company should choose standard technologies for clearly beneficial reasons: for preserving the company's technology investment, for assuring continuing support and cost-effectiveness, and for retaining the maximum number of options for change and expansion.

EIT PROCESSING ARCHITECTURE

Evaluating specific information technologies and approaches cannot be done in a vacuum. They must be looked at in the context of a processing framework or architecture in order to position and link them together. Chapter 2 described the prevailing visions of information in most companies today. The most common and successful visions are those supported primarily by centralized or distributed processing arrangements. While those arrangements may be appropriate for a company's production systems, a different architecture is required to satisfy the EIT Design.

A distributed database arrangement can only achieve the goal of a single image of information and the benefits of local processing through extensive and expensive information synchronization. A centralized arrangement is an easier information environment to manage but requires that all processing be centrally managed and controlled, a less than ideal arrangement. *Another alternative is to have the information centralized and the processing distributed.* This reduces the amount of synchronization needed, while taking full advantage of the benefits of local processing. The processing architecture best suited for doing that is *client/server.*

Client/Server Architecture

While not the only approach, *client/server* provides an excellent basis for selecting and integrating products and solutions most suited to the EIT Design. It is an architecture that separates the tasks of managing information from those that handle its use. Client/server is an inherently open, industry-standard solution that facilitates a heterogeneous computing environment in which products from multiple vendors can interact. It provides a great deal of flexibility in handling information interfaces.

Client/server architecture takes advantage of technologies that satisfy most of the criteria presented above. It provides a high degree of information sharability and connectivity. It lends itself nicely to attractive technology modularity and standardization. In addition, client/server fits well with the highest price-performing technologies. Finally, it is compatible with solutions that are rich in information functionality and designed to be easy to use and operate.

With client/server, each platform performs special-purpose, dedicated tasks while remaining connected to other platforms. Its architecture calls for a program resident on the client platform to obtain services from another program operating on the server platform. A server may satisfy multiple clients, and a client may access multiple servers. This arrangement places the right amount of processing power where it's needed to achieve the most cost-effective solution. Dedicated platforms perform a specific function (or a limited number of closely related functions) as efficiently and as powerfully as possible.

Servers dedicated to handling information are called *database servers.* They may be further specialized by type—text, image, voice, or conventional data, and by level or function—central, department, or local. Servers may handle requirements other than information (such as running a laser printer, executing "compute" cycles, managing optical drives, or handling complex network management functions).

The EIT Design is best furthered by a processing architecture that naturally divides work into its corresponding functions. For example, the client platform may be dedicated to supporting a powerful, intelligent, and easy-to-operate GUI (the Information Desktop). This permits greater user capabilities for manipulating information provided by the server. When the server supports the Information Database, it has the sole responsibility to store, manage, and deliver information to requesting clients, either the Information Directory or Information Desktop.

Configuring the EIT Design as a client/server architecture permits an arrangement similar to the one illustrated in Figure 10-1, EIT Integration Model, Client/Server Architecture. This architecture positions the components of the Information Desktop as a client platform; those of the Information Database as a server platform; and the Information Directory as both—it is both a server to the user at the Information Desktop (a client) and a requester of services (a client) from the Information Database (i.e., a server). These platforms are connected logically by information interfaces and physically by communications and network connections.

Large-Scale Client/Server Architecture

Client/server processing is typically employed in local area network (LAN) environments that satisfy the needs of a relatively small and homogeneous group of

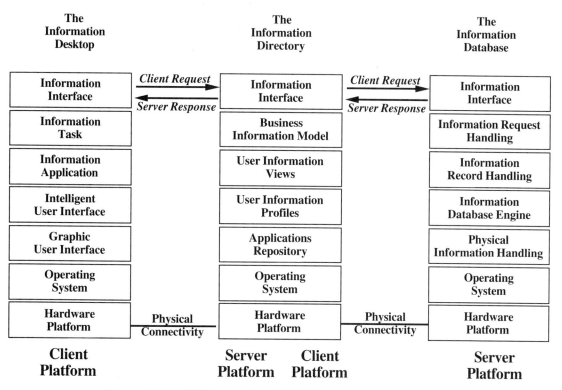

Figure 10-1. EIT Integration Model Client/Server Architecture

users. With advances in new software and hardware technologies, the client/ server paradigm has been extended well beyond the single user group or department. Standard information structures and request languages, faster and wider connectivity, and more powerful database computing platforms have made *large-scale client/server architectures* both possible and attractive for large company information environments.

Large-scale client/server architecture offers the ability to access terabytes of information from client platforms anywhere in the company. This is a basically simple, powerful, and infinitely configurable processing arrangement that allows a great deal of flexibility to expand and adjust. With large-scale client/server computing, there is a further improvement in information sharing and connectivity over the local client/server form (i.e., LAN-based).

The focus of this "peer" processing arrangement (see Figure 10-2, EIT Integration Model, Large-Scale Client/Server Architecture) is the central database server. Based on very powerful and dedicated technologies, it makes possible the handling of truly massive quantities of information in a single physical location. Tied to a companywide or backbone network that links information to every user at a workstation, it permits extensive freedom of processing while retaining the benefits of central information. Local database servers are used to download culled information segments for processing that is best handled locally or separated from the central database server.

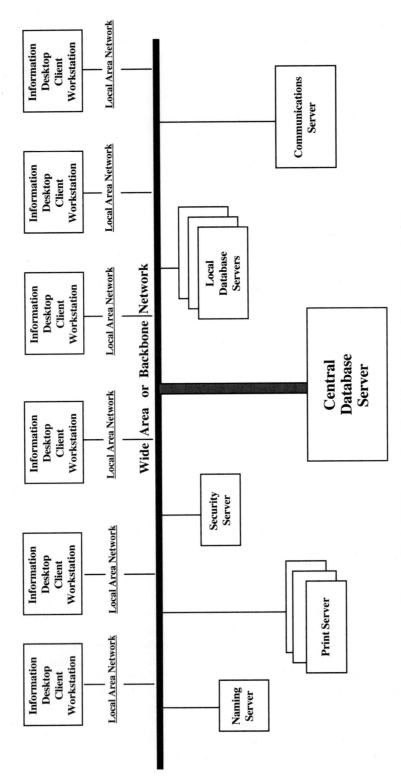

Figure 10-2. EIT Integration Model Large-Scale Client/Server Architecture

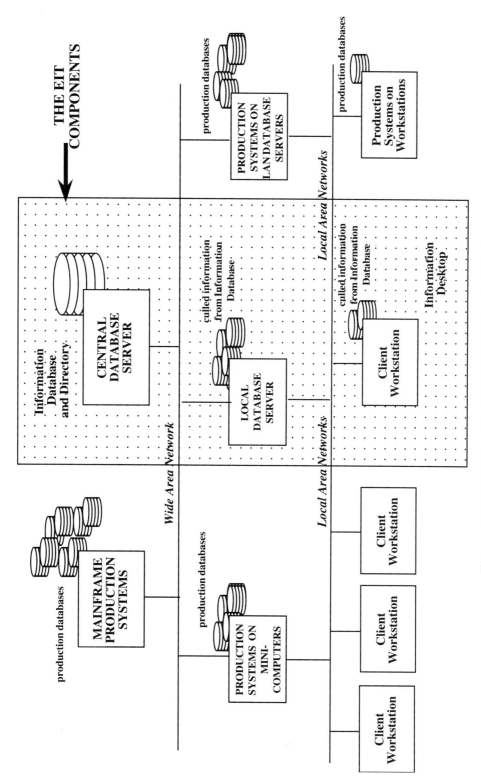

Figure 10-3. EIT Integration Model Fully Integrated Environment

143

INTEGRATING THE EIT ARCHITECTURE INTO THE EXISTING SYSTEMS ENVIRONMENT

How do the component technologies of the EIT Design, when based on the large-scale client/server architecture, integrate with a company's existing computing and communications environment? Assuming that its production systems are based on a mix of central mainframes, departmental minicomputers, LANs, and individual workstations, the EIT components could take on the arrangement depicted in Figure 10-3, EIT Integration Model, Fully Integrated Environment.

In this arrangement, all components connect over a peer network and common interfaces. Production data is extracted, conditioned, and transferred from source systems residing on any of a number of platforms to the Information Database. That information can be accessed by any client workstation or computing platform. The Information Directory, while shown in the illustration as residing in common with the Information Database on the central database server, may be located on another computing platform—a mainframe, minicomputer, or dedicated directory server.

11

Enterprise Information Technologies

This chapter discusses the several classes or categories of enterprise information technologies that provide capabilities and functions called for in the EIT Design, and that are compatible with the EIT Integration Model. It also offers important examples of these classes of technologies (examples are illustrated in Figure 11-1, Enterprise Information Technologies).

Two types of examples are offered: archetypes and alternatives. *Archetypes* are specific products, artifacts, or other tangible manifestations that are either an original prototype of that class of technology, or that have become, through use or through the influence of the vendor, the de facto standard. *Alternatives* are products or artifacts that provide equivalent and typically more advanced capabilities (coming as they usually do after the archetypal product). Together, they help clarify the nature of the class of technology under discussion and establish clear boundaries for their place in the overall EIT Design and Integration Model. In some cases, neither archetypes nor alternatives are presented because currently available technologies do not adequately meet EIT needs or the area is simply too new.

The technology categories and examples are presented in a sequence that moves from the general to the specific and correspond to the groups of capabilities described in the EIT Design in Part III. Generic technologies are presented first (i.e., those needed throughout and that underlay many of the other technologies), followed by technologies that deal with infrastructure capabilities: the Information Database, Directory, Desktop, and Interfaces. EIT transformation technologies are presented as part of the needed information design, acquisition, analysis,

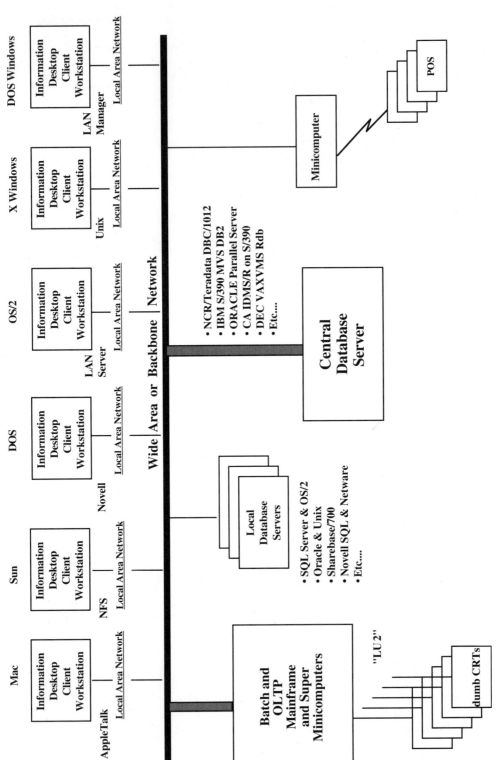

Figure 11-1. The Enterprise Information Technologies

TABLE 11-1   THE ENTERPRISE INFORMATION TECHNOLOGIES

Generic Technologies
Microprocessor technologies Object technologies Expert systems technologies
Database Technologies
Central database server technologies Local database server technologies Relational database technologies
Directory Technologies
Business Information Model technologies Complex information representation technologies
Desktop Technologies
Client workstation technologies Intelligent user interface technologies
Interface Technologies
Interconnected LAN technologies Information interface technologies
Design Technologies
Information re-engineering technologies
Acquisition Technologies
Analysis Technologies
Information analysis technologies Information discovery technologies
Delivery Technologies

and delivery capabilities. These areas are summarized in Table 11-1, The Enterprise Information Technologies.

Some caveats: While there is a great deal of ground covered in this chapter, the technologies presented are not the only ones that may be used by a company to enable the functions of the EIT Design. Different technologies, and different arrangements of the same technologies, are not only possible, they may be preferable, depending on conditions in the implementing company.

An EIT-bound organization should carefully consider what is presented as a point of departure rather than as a recommendation for selection. This is because continued and rapid changes in technology, and especially in the quickly moving tradeoffs of costs and benefits, may make this set of technologies less than ideal (or even available) in a short time. Nonetheless, the technologies offer compelling advantages that should be considered by any organization serious about implementing EIT capabilities.

It is not possible for a company to select each of the archetypal products and integrate them, as they may be based on different underlying structures, architectures, philosophies, or standards. A simple example would be trying to use IBM's DB2, the archetypal relational database system, on NCR/Teradata's Data Base Computer, the archetypal central database server. It just can't be done. Fully integrated packages of all the enterprise information technologies are not yet available, although some vendors are moving in that direction (see Chapter 12).

GENERIC TECHNOLOGIES

Generic technologies are those that cross specific functional boundaries of the EIT Design or do not neatly fit into one category or group. The microprocessor is a generic technology available for use in all EIT hardware platforms. Object technologies and expert systems are used heavily in Information Directory and Desktop components and in transformation functions such as information design and analysis.

Microprocessor Technologies: Providing Finely Calibrated Scalability

At the center of enterprise information technologies is the humble *microprocessor,* that basic CPU-on-a-chip that grows ever faster, ever cheaper, and ever more powerful. Despite enormous progress, there appears no sign that the improvement curve will lessen. This movement can be seen in the march of Intel chips from the 8088 to the 80486 (with the 80586 on the horizon) in less than a decade—four generations of staggeringly impressive price-performance improvement (see Table 11-2, Mainframe and Microprocessor MIP Comparison). Assuming such development continues, what will not be possible with a 80986 chip in the next decade?

As much as possible of an EIT's hardware should be based on the microprocessor—desktop computers, communication links, processing platforms, and database servers. While the advantages of the microprocessor have been vividly demonstrated on the desktop, with a few exceptions, its use in other areas has not reached nearly the same high levels of exploitation. The most dramatic applications of microprocessor technologies are likely to occur in those areas over the next few years.

TABLE 11-2   MAINFRAME AND MICROPROCESSOR MIP COMPARISON

IBM mainframe	Intel chip	MIP* Ratio
Model 3080	8086	30 to 1
Model 3090	286	15 to 1
Model 3090F	386	7 to 1
Model 390 Summit	486	4 to 1

*MIP—millions of instructions per second

Incrementally scalable machine hierarchies based on the microprocessor are starting to appear, allowing an organization the ability to apply the exact amount of processing power to a specific task. Such finely-tuned calibration might employ single microprocessors for Information Desktop needs, two-way or three-way loosely linked microprocessors as LAN Servers, dozens of tightly-coupled symmetric processors functioning as general-purpose mainframes or large departmental Servers, and hundreds or even thousands of processors linked in massively parallel configurations to meet supercomputer and extremely large database server needs.

This expanded use of microprocessor technologies is making it possible for companies to replace their conventionally designed mainframes with networks of smaller platforms running downsized Business Automation applications. It is also enabling clusters of tightly linked microprocessors to provide mainframe power for large, centralized applications. The EIT Integration Model fits well in this milieu, drawing information from either mainframe systems or downsized networks, and relying on large numbers of compute clusters to power its massive information processing needs.

- The archetypal microprocessor chip is the Intel 80X86. Common alternatives include Motorola's 680X0 chip, Sun's Sparc chip, IBM's RISC chip, and a few others.

Object Technologies: Enabling High-Level Information Structures

Information objects were introduced in Chapters 8 and 9, those high-level, high-density information units that satisfied a number of purposes: for grouping complex sets of choices and processing under an icon at the Information Desktop; to add organizing and semantic capabilities and for storing rules and procedures in the Business Information Model; to represent complex information constructs such as knowledge, text, and image in the Information Directory; and for enabling functions such as information design, modeling, navigation, and mapping, among others.

These and other uses of information objects are essential to EIT capabilities. While there are other ways to provide these important capabilities, *object technologies* are the most attractive of those currently available. Object technologies (or object-oriented technologies) have advanced the computer user's ability from working with simple information structures (a standard list of year-to-date payroll quantities and matching employee numbers, for example) to multifaceted and dynamic representations that closely mirror the real world (such as interactive three-dimensional color graphs, photographs, narratives, and sound).

Object technologies are used for creating apparent simplicity by hiding the complexity that gets in a user's way, for encapsulation of standard information transformation functions, for creating powerful information query and processing expressions, and for automatically invoking procedures based on the status of events. How are object technologies of value to the information user? What can they do to help improve the performance of information tasks? They can trigger an update in the user's copy of information when the central information copy has changed. They can automatically integrate a newly created information design requirement into the Business Information Model. They can perform automatic aging and archiving functions of designated portions of information. And so on.

There is great power in information objects. Typically, they are used to support relatively simple functions, such as opening a document at the Information Desktop. As information users grow in skill and knowledge, however, entire applications can be built in this fashion, with objects calling other objects ad infinitum. With this unlimited scripting power, users become the authors of their own Information Automation procedures—the developer-users of the future.

Object technologies have other benefits. They produce capabilities that are readily reusable and sharable. They can be requested as needed or invoked automatically. They are easily modified and expanded. For example, a user can call up a statistical procedure developed by someone else, modify it to reflect a change in the parameters, and apply it to a different collection of information. The results can be hot-linked to another object, in this case, a spreadsheet, where the insertion of numbers from the first object triggers the recalculation of new spreadsheet totals.

Object technologies are most critical to the EIT Design in their ability to represent and manage information, and specifically in the modeling of the structures that organize and control the Information Database, i.e., in the Business Information Model. As discussed later in this chapter, standard business data is stored as a collection of tables—rows and columns organized into segments based on certain rules. Tables (supported by relational database management systems) are an intuitive way to use information. They allow for the most effective separation of the user from the underlying mechanisms while providing a neutral view of information. They also provide easy-to-use and flexible analysis capabilities. However, tables lack powerful organization and semantic abilities, especially those needed to create a comprehensive information picture of the business. The EIT Design erects its Business Information Model on top of these neutral tables, building layers of higher-level structures with object technologies.

- The archetypal object-oriented language is Smalltalk-80 by ParcPlace (called ObjectWorks). Usage has, however, made C++ the de facto standard. Alternatives include Digitalk's SmalltalkV and Prolog++, and several others.
- The archetypal object-oriented tool is Asymetrix's Toolbook. Alternatives include Knowledge Garden's KnowledgePro, Whitewater Group's Actor, Interactive Images' Easel, MDBS' Object/1, Borland's Object Vision, Microsoft's Visual Basic, and others.

Expert Systems Technologies: Augmenting Information's Intelligence

Expert systems (or expert reasoning systems) technologies are an important part of the EIT Design. Derived from developments in artificial intelligence, these technologies perform difficult tasks using a logical inference process that makes deductions based on a knowledge base of expert rules, procedures, strategies, and "rules of thumb." Expert systems technologies create new facts and conclusions by comparing information to existing facts, premises, rules, and conclusions.

An EIT knowledge base may contain, for example, the exact relationships that exist between two information items, perhaps sales volume and price changes, and deductions of how those variables interact under conditions of uncertainty (i.e., less than 100 percent). This knowledge will be changed by a "reasoning engine" to reflect new dynamics in the environment (customer purchase behavior) and can be viewed, changed, and applied as needed. A user may ask, for example, to be notified when that rule no longer holds based on new information.

Expert systems technologies can assist in the transformation tasks of modeling, re-engineering, and incorporation, especially where a knowledge base helps the user choose between complex design strategies by taking advantage of knowledge about existing relationships in the Business Information Model. They can help find out what a user is *really* interested in, perhaps by working with a requirement that is close to, but not exactly, what is needed.

Expert systems technologies can also provide support during information acquisition, such as by applying complex rules to verify incoming information, in restructuring information, and in deriving information from data in source systems. In maintenance of the Information Database, they are used in generating self-modifying database actions for automated aging or archiving of records as time or information conditions change.

Expert systems technologies are heavily employed in information analysis, where they are used to support a wide range of requirements. They provide intelligent query formulation, using knowledge about the user and the target information. They automatically analyze observed changes in information content and availability, so that if some information item drops below a threshold, a series of special analyses are automatically invoked. They perform query optimization, where an expert systems-based process automatically chooses the processing paths most likely to get the needed results in the shortest time (i.e., least cost).

Expert systems technologies help provide an easy way to express complex requests that involve powerful declarative features (what-if rules, predicate calculus, and complex logic) by embedding those smarts in GUI-based information query and analysis tools. These technologies are also a critical part of information discovery, especially in those capabilities that use machine learning techniques to create new understandings about information based on detailed instances.

Expert systems technologies are also used to assist or instruct the user in performing complex or new functions by employing dynamic user information profiles based on expressed preferences or patterns of use. They automate or "default" much of the busy work involved in information handling.

- The archetypal expert systems language is LISP. Alternatives include Prolog, Poplog, Pascal, Interlisp, and a few others.
- The archetypal expert systems development environment is OPS. Alternatives include Teknowledge's S.1 and M.1, IntelliCorp's KEE and Kappa, Inference's ART, Aion's ADS, AICorp's KBMS, Software A&E's KES, and others.

- The archetypal expert systems shell is Mdbs' Guru. Alternatives include IBI's Level5, Neuron Data's Nexpert Object, KDS's KDS, Gold Hill's Goldworks, AICorp's 1st-Class, Inference's ART-IM, Paperback Software's VP-Expert, and many others.
- The archetypal database with expert systems capabilities is Ask's Ingres Intelligent Database. Other database vendors are providing additional intelligence to their core products.

DATABASE TECHNOLOGIES

Historically, database technologies supported business needs that called for high levels of performance, were limited to small or modest volumes of data, operated in an environment where there was little structural change to the information, and supported mostly predetermined access and reporting requirements. Information Automation needs, however, are far more dynamic and volatile, and require unplanned access to massive quantities of detailed historical information.

To meet these very different needs, the Information Database is supported by two closely matched technologies: high-performance database servers and relational databases. These core technologies are further augmented by modeling and enhancement facilities in the Information Directory, by an enterprisewide network that connects them to the users' Information Desktops, and by interfaces that link them to other functions and applications.

While the importance of non-traditional information (image, text, sound, etc.) has been recognized and provided for, the emphasis in the EIT Design is on traditional information, where there are large and immediate business benefits to be seized. In addition, the current stage of technological development does not make it feasible to intermingle large quantities of different types of information physically in one database system. However, the EIT Design provides for managing and integrating information from these different media and forms by the use of information objects in the Information Directory and Desktop.

Central Database Server Technologies: Industrial-Strength Processing

The EIT Design calls for an Information Database to be supported by a dedicated, massively powerful, fully accessible *central database server,* with tight links to local database servers, local area and wide area networks, and desktop computers. The central database server is an industrial-strength, information processing platform with extremely high levels of reliability, availability, serviceability, and recoverability. It handles very complex analyses that manipulate large quantities of data while providing high levels of security and integrity control and important systems administrative functions.

The central database server takes a request from any client platform, parses, and dispatches it to available processing units, executes the request, sorts and merges the results, and returns the final "net answer set" to the requester. If a user wants to see a subset of records from a 500-million-record database, only the results, maybe a few hundred records, travel back over the network. The millions upon millions of records are completely processed at the central database server, freeing the network and the client workstations for other uses.

Information is stored on one of several storage media, placing, for example, high-demand information on faster and more expensive magnetic disks (and in semiconductor memory), and either less-frequently accessed or very large collections of information on write-once, read-many (WORM) optical media. Archived information is usually stored on optical or magnetic tape storage media, with the ability to retrieve some or all of that information upon request.

The central database server must be capable of handling massive quantities of information. Most large enterprises have from 100 gigabytes to a couple of terabytes of information to manage. If non-traditional information is included, especially text and image, it can quickly climb into the petabyte (or quadrillion byte) range. The central database server needs to deliver incredibly high levels of performance, providing great information-crunching power for handling requests quickly, such as a response of 20 seconds to analyze information from 10,000 records.

The central database server must also have very high levels of throughput, as is required, for example, in the weekly updating of 3 million records in 16 hours. The central database server may also be asked to handle one set of processing requirements at 10 A.M. on a typical Monday, another set immediately before a major new product promotion is launched, and yet an entirely different set of information at quarter-end on a Sunday at midnight. Similarly, it may be necessary to update information from several source systems while responding to hundreds of queries.

There are two basic classes of technology for satisfying these world-class information requirements. The first repositions the mainframe or large minicomputer as the central database server, either as a single and massive central processor or as a tightly linked cluster of several machines. This approach trades off robustness and high rates of internal speeds against a more costly and rigid environment that must handle other functions (i.e., applications, multitasking, communications, and printing).

While not as compatible with the large-scale client/server model nor as attractive as the microprocessor's inherently excellent price-performance, the mainframe is nonetheless a serious alternative for many large companies. This alternative is even more attractive for an organization with excess capacity and smaller databases, or that has other, more specific processing needs that lend themselves well to this approach.

The other general class of central database server technology leverages large numbers of microprocessors and smaller disk formats. This technology provides high levels of performance and throughput at much lower costs. Massive parallel processing takes requests that run in hours on mainframes and runs them in minutes (see Table 11-3, Mainframe and Microprocessor Database Comparisons). Just as important, conventional database systems running on serially oriented

TABLE 11-3   MAINFRAME AND MICROPROCESSOR DATABASE COMPARISONS

Elapsed time comparison of parallel linearity

# Processors	Power	Effective processing rate
1 CPU =	3 MIPS =	2,400 Records per second
effect: 5 million records would take 2,000 seconds or 35 minutes		
10 CPUs =	30 MIPS =	24,000 Records per second
effect: 5 million records would take 208 seconds or less than 4 minutes		
50 CPUs =	150 MIPS =	120,000 Records per second
effect: 5 million records would take 42 seconds		

MIP and data capacity cost comparison

Microprocessors	30MIPS, 20 Gigabytes	$1.5M
Mainframe	28MIPS, 20 Gigabytes	$5.2M
Microprocessors	50MIPS, 40 Gigabytes	$2.7M
Mainframe	49MIPS, 40 Gigabytes	$9.7M

Scalability

Linear (parallel systems) versus exponential (uniprocessor systems) cost rise when based on straight-line power increase

Cost per MIP comparison

Mainframes	$75,000–$125,000 per MIP
Microprocessors	$ 5,000–$ 25,000 per MIP

The bottom-line

A query on a mainframe costs approximately $15.00. That same query on a workstation using a microprocessor-based database server would cost approximately $.01

(i.e., conventional or Von Neumann) mainframes "hit the wall" at certain volumes, resulting in absolute processing limits. Parallel systems expand beyond the wall by simply adding more processors.

To get an idea of its full power, imagine a massively parallel system in which each microprocessor is a 3-MIP 80386 controlling four disk drives of a gigabyte each. Putting together 1,000 processors brings more than 3,000 MIPS to the task of managing an Information Database, along with 4 terabytes of information. No mainframe can match the "speeds and feeds" of a system such as that at comparable costs.

In addition to the sheer brute power and outstanding price-performance, parallel systems offer excellent modularity, sharability, connectivity, and productivity. They tend to suffer, when compared to the mainframe, from lower availability and functionality, and often considerably lower reliability and security.

- The archetypal microprocessor-based massively parallel central database server is Teradata's (now NCR's) Data Base Computer/1012. Alternatives systems include Oracle Server on nCube, scalable Sybase or Oracle Server on the

NCR 3600 and 3700, the ShareBase Server/8000, and systems from Intel, Kendall Square, and Thinking Machines. Other parallel server technologies, such as the transputer, are being employed in machines offered by companies such as White Cross, Meiko, and Parsys.

- The archetypal mainframe-based central database server is IBM's symmetric multiprocessor cluster of S/390s running DB2 under MVS. Alternatives include Software AG's ADABASE on IBM S/390 MVS, and CA's IDMS/R on IBM S/390 MVS.
- The archetypal minicomputer-based central database server is DEC's VAX multiprocessor clusters running VMS with either Rdb or Oracle. Alternatives include HP's larger 3000 models running Allbase, Tandem's NonStop SQL, and a few others.

Local Database Server Technologies: Synchronized Information Downloading

Local database servers handle information processing when it is best done separate from the central database server. An example might be a user who is testing a new set of information definitions and relationships and wishes to experiment on selected information independent of the central copy. Another example is snapshotting, in which a copy of information is frozen at a point in time and maintained intact on a separate database platform. Yet another example is off-loading processing that overburdens the central database server at a time when it is being heavily used.

These and other reasons call for the central database server to download culled datasets of information to local database servers while keeping that information current with changes to the central copy. The functional characteristics of a local database server are essentially the same as those of the central database server, except that less power is required and fewer connections need to be maintained.

Local database servers tend to be based around standard microprocessor hardware and operating systems, and are widely used to meet the demands of desktop users on LANs. They are also used as gateways to central production systems and their databases.

- The archetypal local database server is Microsoft's SQL Server on OS/2 running on Intel 80486 platforms. Alternatives include Oracle and Ingres on Unix or OS/2, the Sharebase Server/700, Gupta's SQLBase Server on OS/2, CA's IDMS Server, IBM's OS/2 Database Manager, Novell's SQL under Netware, and XDB under DOS.
- Many of these systems also run on higher-performance platforms, such as Compaq's SystemPro, Sun's Sparc Server, IBM's RS/6000, NCR's 3550, the Relational Accelerator from Charles River, and NetFrame.
- Minicomputers repositioned as local database servers include IBM's AS/400, HP's 3000, and DEC's smaller VAXs.

Relational Database Technologies: Managing the Information Database

While the Information Database may be based on information structures other than tables, columns, and rows (using *relational database technologies*), the EIT vision's most fundamental benefits will be seriously diminished or even lost without those critically important abilities. For relational database technology is at the very core of the Information Database, the EIT Design, and its client/server-based Integration Model. Relational database systems (RDBMSs) handle a number of important functions, almost all of them standard, such as:

- Request handling, parsing and optimization
- Backup and recovery
- Creation and maintenance of logical user information views
- Basic conflict management for accessing information
- Physical management of the database
- Basic populating functions
- Basic maintenance functions

RDBMSs use structured query language (or SQL), an industry-standard language, for handling the definition, modification, query, and control of relational information. SQL manipulates information relations based on well-defined paradigms such as relational algebra and set theory. SQL can be used in its native form or generated by intelligent user tools and programs.

Relational database technologies are ideal for supporting EIT capabilities because they help establish an open information environment and are supported by an impressive array of user tools. They are attractive for performing transformation functions because they treat information in ways that users normally think about information (in tabular representations using declarative requests), are inherently extendable so that new meanings, relationships, classifications, and organizations may be added to the basic information structures, and because they handle information in sets rather than as individual records, thereby allowing dedicated hardware solutions to achieve very high levels of performance.

There has been a proliferation of relational database technologies over the past 10 years, with some vendors offering versions that run on almost every operating system and computing platform. A few are designed to operate only on high-performance platforms such as database machines or fast database servers. Others are finely tuned, robust, and mature products that have been used for years in demanding and general-purpose information environments.

- The archetypal relational database technology is IBM's DB2 for S/390 MVS. Common alternatives that operate in large information environments include Oracle, NCR/Teradata, Ingres, NonStop SQL, Sybase, Informix, IBM's SQL/DS, DEC's Rdb, ShareBase, and a few others.
- Non-relational database technologies include IBM's IMS, DEC's VAX RMS, Software AG's ADABASE, and CA's Datacom/DB, and IDMS.

DIRECTORY TECHNOLOGIES

As mentioned above, relational database technologies provide core information capabilities, but there is still a need to extend those abilities to provide additional "informing" power. *Directory technologies* contain the complex, high-level information structures that extend those simple tables, columns, and rows while retaining their advantages. These structures (using object technologies) make up the Business Information Model, the user's lens to the company's Information Database.

In addition, directory technologies satisfy the need for the representation and management of other forms of information: stored processing procedures, business rules and policies, the knowledge information used by expert systems technologies, and unstructured information types such as text, hypertext, and image. *This provides a means for representing under one capability many disparate forms of information.* With it, users can seamlessly combine the following as requirements demand:

Information Objects Handle:	That Enable or Support:
Information entities, relationships	Information design, acquisition, analysis, etc.
Program code, rules	Information Automation applications
Frames, slots, values	Knowledge Base for expert systems
Objects, classes, attributes	Object-oriented tools and languages
Documents, concepts, nodes	Text and hypertext functions
Diagrams, graphs, vectors	CAD and drafting functions
Audio and visual images	Multimedia functions
Photographs, drawings	Paint or drawing functions

Except for a few ground-breaking efforts that have so far failed to produce a viable commercial prototype, there is no true archetype of directory technologies. However, there are many technologies that provide some capabilities needed for this most central portion of the EIT Design and Integration Model.

- Foremost of the self-contained directories (i.e., those structurally independent and that readily interface to a variety of DBMSs and tools) is IBM's Repository Manager, the de facto industry standard. Alternatives include Tangent's Navigator, Brownstone's Data Dictionary, RelTech's DB Excel, and InfoSpan's IRMS*/RM.
- Directory technologies offered as part of CASE or relational capabilities include CGI's Pacbase, Appleton's Leverage, Knowledgeware's Encyclopedia, Texas Instrument's Repository, Intersolv's LAN Repository, Oracle's CASE* Dictionary, Manager Software Product's DataManager, DEC's CDD/Repository, CA's Data Dictionary, and Andersen Consulting's Foundation.
- The directory standard is ANSI's Information Resource Dictionary Systems (IRDS).

Business Information Model Technologies: Extending Information's Meaning

At the heart of the Information Database lies a large collection of business information. At its most atomic level, this information is made up of letters and numbers organized into higher-level structures according to the rules and specifications of relational database technologies. The most basic structures are columns, rows (or records), and tables (or files). The Business Information Model builds on top of these neutral information structures by allowing more complex information structures and relationships. Some of these relationships were presented in Chapter 9, where it was seen that the Business Information Model and user information views helped users perform information modeling, navigation, and mapping functions.

With the use of the Business Information Model, tables that directly relate to each other can be further grouped into larger information structures called subject areas. These are information groups basic to the enterprise's structures and operations. Subject areas are organized according to primary classifications having to do with products, customers, and equipment, or according to basic business functions, such as cost accounting, product distribution, and inventory control. When integrated, all of a company's subject areas make up the contents of the Business Information Model. The Business Information Model also uses information objects for managing the rules and criteria for handling information tasks.

- Archetypal and alternative technologies for enabling the Business Information Model were presented under directory technologies.

Complex Information Technologies: Providing the Conceptual Hooks

In addition to standard information types and the important need for high-level information structures, there is another large world of information that consists of non-traditional or more complex information types. While the value of these forms of information vary by company and by application, the EIT Design provides for these as well, integrating their unique characteristics and supporting technologies with core relational database information through directory technologies. As mentioned above, the use of information objects makes it possible to provide a common place for all information representation in the company, while information management facilities are generally handled separately. As far as the information user is concerned, there is only one place to go to understand what kinds of information are available and how they are constructed.

The major types of complex information were described in Chapter 8 and include: expert knowledge (for artificial intelligence and expert systems), text information (to handle narrative, concepts, topics, documents, and keywords), hypertext (for browsing through unstructured information), graphic coordinates (for handling precision geometric objects), and image information (for managing photographs, drawings, voice, audio, video, and animation).

Directory technologies permit the bounding and identifying of these complex information types within an information object in order that it may be represented in a consistent and accessible form. It provides users with the ability to identify and qualify complex, unstructured information entities, access them by tags or complex pattern recognition, dynamically adjust these objects for better representation, and combine several types of information at the Information Desktop. Using information objects with the proper interfaces, the EIT Directory can work with the technologies and examples presented below.

- The archetype text technology is IBM's Stairs. Alternatives include Information Dimensions' BasisPlus, Fulcrum's Ful/Text, BRS Software's BRS/Search, GE's GEScan, Infodata's Inquire/Text, CP International's Status/IQ, CCA's Text/204, and NDX's Creatabase.
- The archetype concept-based text technology is Verity's Topic.
- The archetype hypertext (and to a limited extent) hypermedia technology is Apple's HyperCard. Alternatives include Software Artistry's Knowledge Engine, Spinnaker Plus, Silicon Beach's SuperCard, and Asymetrix's Toolbook.
- Computer-aided design (or CAD) examples are AutoCad and VersaCad, along with others.
- Expert systems technologies (and their knowledge base capabilities) were described earlier. Multimedia technologies (that manage image information mixed with standard information) are still relatively new and evolving, making it difficult to identify archetypes or examples.

DESKTOP TECHNOLOGIES

Users at the Desktop are supported by two major technologies: the mostly standard hardware and software that provides *client workstation* functions; and the *interface mechanisms* that buffer them from lower-level operations—both capabilities making the Desktop more amenable to their needs and styles of working.

In the EIT Design, the Desktop supports the exchange of complex requests. A standard Information Automation process is that of a user sending a request for creating a new information segment. This high-level representation is submitted to the Information Directory which checks the request and returns it for correction. The user manipulates the Business Information Model until it reflects the desired representations. The user then prepares a request for extracting source data and conditioning it; this might involve several sessions. With that accomplished, the user then prepares a request to access and manipulate portions of that information, beginning yet another complex and interrelated series of exchanges.

Not only are these requests (and responses) complex from a processing standpoint; they are complex in terms of the information structures and processing paradigms that a user is constructing and attempting to carry out. Desktop technologies must provide effective support for this kind of creative information work.

Client Workstation Technologies: Putting Mainframes on the Desktop

With the power and price-performance of the microprocessor, client workstations are bringing the capabilities of million-dollar mainframes to all company information users, with functionality previously available only to highly trained people working under tightly controlled circumstances. As a result, there are probably more MIPS humming away on the desktops in the world than on mainframes, even though, as seems the case in so many companies, workstations are used only a small portion of the time (while mainframes are almost totally utilized).

Client workstation technologies employ powerful, industry-standard CPUs, a mouse, high-resolution color screen, large disk drive, accelerator board for numerical processing, LAN interface card, and remote communications interface. These are controlled by an operating system that manages all the underlying hardware functions, the execution and coordination of multiple tasks and applications, and interfaces to the user via a GUI. The client workstation also contains the interfaces that link the user to local and central database servers.

The client workstation needed for the EIT Information Desktop is far more than a PC. With powerful information transformation capabilities, it is a responsive and fully integrated information environment capable of satisfying a user's full set of business information needs.

- The archetypal client workstation technology is the Intel-based IBM PC and its many clones, especially those based on the 80386 and 80486 chip. Alternatives include Motorola's 680X0 systems such as the Apple Macintosh, and RISC-based systems such as Sun and IBM's RS/6000.
- The archetypal client workstation operating system is Microsoft's DOS. Alternatives include IBM's OS/2, Macintosh OS, Next, and many Unix operating systems. Microsoft's NT operating system is expected to be a strong alternative if not a new archetype.

Intelligent User Interface Technologies: GUIs and More

The EIT client workstation is both intuitive and nontechnical in nature. This requires, at a minimum, GUI capabilities that are both powerful and simple to use. It must lend its look-and-feel to all applications and functions, ensuring quick and easy learning and use of all capabilities. To better visualize this, Table 11-4, GUI-Enabled "Simultaneous" User Tasks, describes a range of functions that an industrious user might perform more-or-less at the same time.

Additional intelligence may be added to this environment by the use of intelligent features and expert systems technologies, either as part of a specific application or as a more general capability. An example is the use of user information profiles, where expert reasoning is used to improve the effectiveness of functions such as information navigating and analysis.

- The archetypal client workstation GUI comes with the Macintosh (or more accurately, Xerox PARC's prototype GUI that led to the Macintosh). Despite the Mac's power, the much greater use of Microsoft Windows has made the latter the reigning de facto standard. Other alternatives include IBM's OS/2 Presentation Manager, and the many Unix "flavors" of X-Windows, Motif, and OpenLook.
- The archetypal intelligent GUI is HP's New Wave, a capability that runs with Microsoft Windows. Alternatives include the NCR Desktop, DEC's DECstations with Compound Document Architecture, CA's CA90s User Interaction Manager for multi-GUI consistency, and Oracle's OracleCard.

TABLE 11-4   GUI-ENABLED "SIMULTANEOUS" USER TASKS

Making notes for a report using an outliner system

Drawing a chart for that same report

Running a request for information using a query program

Writing specifications for matching the query results against a set of criteria

Preparing to run the results of that request through a statistical analysis program

Using a spreadsheet program

Browsing through the Information Directory looking for an information category

Using a word processor to write a narrative to accompany the final report

Checking incoming electronic mail

Keeping track of appointments and "things to do" in a calendar system

Preparing an electronic message to be faxed to a supplier

Preparing an overhead presentation

Accessing an electronic research database of market data

Proofing an internal newsletter using a desktop publishing system

INTERFACE TECHNOLOGIES

With the capabilities of the Database, Directory, and Desktop technologies discussed above, the EIT Design and Integration Model require additional "glue" technologies that connect these infrastructure components. This consists of both physical and information connectivity, and is accomplished by linking LANs into a common enterprisewide network, and establishing standard information interfaces that permit different client applications to communicate with the database technologies on local and central database servers without special effort by the user.

Interconnected Local Area Network Technologies: Linking The Enterprise

EIT capabilities are facilitated by widespread, redundant, reliable, and rapid connectivity. These technologies connect the far-flung parts of the company, linking it both internally and externally with agencies, customers, suppliers, and partners. Such communications connectivity is becoming increasingly standard, as better capabilities emerge in terms of speed, quality, flexibility, and price/performance. People work where they're most effective and are always in touch with the rest of the company. Everything worthwhile is done on-line and in real-time.

The EIT Integration Model achieves enterprisewide connectivity based on interconnected LANs that are expanded or contracted as conditions require, are industry-standard in design, and incrementally scalable. Literally built from the ground up, they extend information capabilities to every user and computer platform. With industry-standard connectivity, a company can capitalize on its current hardware, software, skills, and information, preserving its investment by taking advantage of the flexibility and extensibility of interconnected LANs. Hence, connectivity is critically important, whether looking at what exists today or what's to come in the future.

EIT connectivity technologies link heterogeneous client and other processing hardware, central and local database servers, diverse operating systems, various communication and network software and protocols, and other computing resources. The basic technology is the LAN—the low-cost combination of transmission media, hardware, and software configured under a basic processing arrangement or topology, and operated according to certain communication protocols.

Bridges and routers provide connections between LANs, and between LANs and the company's backbone network—generally a high-speed medium such as fiber optic. Special gateways link workstations on LANs to mainframe proprietary architectures. Remote LANs link via high-speed modems.

- The archetypal LAN media is twisted pair cable. Alternatives are coaxial cable, fiber optic, and wireless (radio, microwave, etc.).
- The archetypal LAN topology is Ethernet. Alternatives are Token-Ring, Token Bus, and Star topologies such as Ethernet 10Base-T and Starlan.
- The archetypal LAN operating system is Novell's Netware. Common alternatives include Microsoft's LAN Manager, Banyan's Vines, and IBM's LAN Server.
- The archetypal basic operating system supporting the network operating system (and other processing software) is Unix. Alternatives include IBM's OS/2 and DOS.
- The archetypal wide area (or backbone) network protocol is TCP/IP, originated at the Department of Defense. Common alternatives include IBM's Systems Network Architecture (SNA) and DEC's DECnet, both of which, short-term, coexist under TCP/IP, and long-term, support OSI's ISO Reference Model (such as X.25 packet switches as a backbone network).
- The archetypal inter-enterprise communications protocol is Electronic Data Interchange or EDI.

Information Interface Technologies: Common Information Exchange Mechanisms

The EIT Integration Model also requires standard *information interfaces* that, riding on the physical connectivity described above, link the requesting user or platform to the information in the Information Directory and Database. These functions, described in Chapter 8, require several different types of software, ranging from packing and unpacking low-level information messages (for transmission over physical media) to handling the more sophisticated forms of information translation and validation.

One kind of information interface involves the passing and handling of SQL, the industry-standard language that is so integral to relational database technologies. SQL interfaces fully support the separation of functions between client and server platforms, a separation critical for implementing the large-scale client/server architecture that underpins the EIT Technology Model. They not only link the tables in the Information Database with a wide variety of user applications and tools on the Desktop, but also with requests from the Information Directory.

Another type of information interface handles complex information objects that are part of the Information Desktop and Directory. These rich, multi-level structures move from the highest levels of the user interface at the Desktop through layers of applications and operating system software, and back up to equivalent levels in the Directory. This type of interface tends to be unique to the tool or software in use, to the platform on which it resides, and to the specific object technologies implemented.

- There is no archetypal SQL interface technology at this time. Alternatives include Information Builders' Enterprise Data Access/SQL (EDA/SQL), Apple's Data Access Language (DAL), Gupta's SQLRouter, and Micro Decisionware's Database Gateway.
- DEC, NCR, and a number of vendors support open interfaces based on the SQL Access Group standard. IBM has its own interface standard called Distributed Relational Data Access (DRDA), which is less open.
- Industry-standard object-oriented interface technologies do not exist at this time.

DESIGN TECHNOLOGIES

Information design in an EIT environment represents a very different design paradigm from that found in standard Business Automation applications. It is grounded in the notion of continuous information refinement, enhancement, and expansion by many users simultaneously designing information to solve business problems. More formal and static information design activities performed by professional systems people are replaced by the on-line user.

Computer-aided systems engineering (or CASE) technologies are a major source of tools and methods for designing information. While the EIT Design environment shares similarities with most CASE approaches, it also differs in several ways. For example, information is modeled during the development of a business response, not before, as in the standard CASE scenario. Also, creating a Business Information Model does not, as in conventional automation, drive the sequence of automation development; on the contrary, business needs determine the sequence of applications, which, in turn, create and expand the Business Information Model.

Further, in conventional CASE approaches, the information aspect is secondary to the process being automated. Even in development programs based on *information engineering* (where the information side is considered fundamental), it is still, once again, the business process that determines the general success of the effort. Only in Information Automation per se is the design of information the primary and only focus. Hence, EIT Information Design finds the most suitable technologies where the emphasis is exclusively on the engineering of information.

Finally, even with a strong information orientation, most CASE technologies fall short of satisfying information design needs, targeted as they are for use by technology professionals. The EIT Design requires technologies that eliminate the need for these specialized technicians, offering capabilities that are as smart as the folks who today are called in to handle issues of optimum design, resolve conflicting requirements, and generate efficient physical database schemas.

Information design technologies are numerous, change rapidly, and cross a broad spectrum of orientation and purpose. Commercial technologies for a true user-driven, information-oriented process have yet to appear. Like Directory technologies, there is no archetype for EIT information design technologies.

- Technologies that provide some of the information design capabilities are Bachman's Data Analyst and Database Administrator, Appleton's IDEF/Leverage, Chen's E-R Designer, TI's Information Engineering Facility, IBM's DevelopMate, Manager Software Product's DesignManager, CA's DB:Architect, Knowledgeware's Information Engineering and Applications Development Workbench (ADW), Intersolv's Excelerator, Oracle's Case*Designer, and LBMS's Systems Engineer.
- The archetype information design modeling paradigm is Entity-Relationship Diagraming (ERD). Alternatives include Chen's Entity-Relationship (E-R) Model, IDEF1x (a government and aerospace standard), Ross, and LBMS.

Information Re-Engineering Technologies

Here, too, the EIT environment presents a somewhat different set of requirements from the more traditional forms of *information re-engineering*. The latter is primarily concerned with migrating a collection of information from one form to another in order to support the same business process in a new way. It is a one-time process in which the old system is turned off. EIT information re-engineering, however, creates information that is continually re-engineered and placed in the Information Database in a different, yet equally valid structure. In this case, there are two sets of definitions that co-exist side-by-side. The old system is not shut off, and a new one arises alongside.

Information re-engineering technologies range from analysis of database specifications in source systems to analysis of the actual values and relationships in source databases. In the former or deductive case, the "truth" is determined by what a system says it is doing. By looking at the actual data itself, the inductive alternative, information re-engineering is based on what is actually happening, searching for patterns that determine information dependencies and relationships. In either case, the results are used for refining the Business Information Model, and in establishing the links between the "from-side" and the "to-side" for the extraction and conditioning process.

- The archetypal *deductive* information re-engineering technology is Bachman's Data Analyst and Database Administrator tools. Alternatives include Chen's SchemaGen, XA Systems' DataTEC, On-Line Software's (now CA's) ADvance, Intersolv's Gateway, and VIasoft's Via/Insight.
- The archetypal *inductive* Information re-engineering technology is DBSoftware's RE/generator. An alternative is IntelligenceWare's Database Supervisor.

ACQUISITION TECHNOLOGIES

The EIT Design calls for general-purpose, user-operated, and customizable extraction and conditioning capabilities that are tightly linked to the rules in the Information Directory. Once considered utility or secondary in nature, *information extraction* technologies are beginning to be available as dedicated capabilities or as part of capabilities such as information re-engineering or analysis. Many enterprises, however, still write ad hoc extract programs in standard programming or fourth generation languages.

Like information extraction, function-rich, general purpose *information conditioning* capabilities are not abundant. Many enterprises have expanded or adapted 4GLs and data transfer utilities to provide this capability. Still others have built elaborate capabilities from scratch, using conventional third-generation languages. A few vendors are integrating conditioning capabilities into their extraction software.

(Note: Information population and maintenance, the other information acquisition capabilities, are always provided by relational database technologies, augmented by the procedures and rules in the Information Directory.)

- There is no extraction technology archetype. Examples include IBM's DXT, MCC's (now Evolutionary Technologies') Extract, Carelton's CQS Convert2/DB2, NCR/Teradata's Multiload, IBM's Data Propagator, Information Builders' EDA/SQL, Sterling's Presentation/Answer, XA Systems' (now CompuWare's) Data-Xpert, and others.
- There is no conditioning technology archetype. Examples include Evolutionary Technologies' Extract, Carelton's CQS Convert2/DB2, Tools and Techniques' Data Junction, and XA Systems' Data-Xpert.

ANALYSIS TECHNOLOGIES

Information navigation, analysis, and discovery technologies are a critically important part of EIT capabilities. While analysis and discovery tend to be offered as separate capabilities (see Table 11-5, Information Analysis Technologies), *information navigation* technologies are closely related to or are an integral part of directory and relational database technologies (they handle user information views, for example).

Many analysis technologies with a statistical lineage tend to have capabilities that allow a user to map and restructure information segments from common

TABLE 11-5   INFORMATION ANALYSIS TECHNOLOGIES

Basic Analysis Technologies

Basic query languages
Graphical analysis
Intelligent front-ends
Query-by-example systems
Spreadsheets
Statistical analysis systems
User declarative (or non-procedural 4GL) systems

Advanced Analysis Technologies

Automated machine learning
Automated pattern recognition
Decision support systems
English (or Natural) languages
Executive information systems
Fuzzy logic systems
Intelligent query systems
Simulation modeling

Discovery Technologies

Case-based reasoning
Logical pattern inference
Numerical pattern inference
Statistical and graphical inference

database formats. While these are not as integral as the EIT Design's navigational abilities, they provide alternatives to more formal navigational and directory technologies.

Information Analysis Technologies

EIT information analysis technologies are always available as stand-alone applications, although they are increasingly designed to work with industry-standard GUIs and SQL/relational database technologies. Some are specifically positioned for certain vendor software or information architectures. Others are part of product families that rely on a common technology base or end purpose. Still other analysis technologies do not fit neatly into a single category and may satisfy analysis needs in more than one area.

Immediately below are the more common information analysis technologies, with archetypes and examples wherever possible. (A caveat: this area is *extremely* dynamic, with products, architectures, and vendors appearing, changing, and disappearing rapidly and often.)

- The archetypal 3GL for writing analysis programs is Cobol. Alternatives include C, Basic, and Assembler. (This technology is obviously not intended for most information users.)

- The archetypal applications generator and/or 4GL is Information Builders's Focus. Alternatives include Must's Nomad, On-Line Software's (now CA's) Ramis, native SQL (offered by every relational database vendor), Blyth's OMNIS 5, JYACC's JAM, CA's Ideal, Oracle's SQL*Forms, Unify's Accell/SQL, Gupta's SQL Windows, Uniface's 4GL, and others.
- The archetypal spreadsheet is Lotus 1-2-3. Alternatives include Microsoft Excel, Borland's Quattro, Sinper's TM/1, ManageWare's Complete Modeler, Paperback's VP Planner, and others.
- The archetypal front-end query tool is IBM's Query-by-Example. Alternatives include IBM/Metaphor's DIS, IBI's Focus, Micro Decisionware's PC/SQL Link, Andyne's GQL, Claris' EQT, CA-Dataquery, Borland's Paradox, Acius' 4th Dimension, Datura's SQL Commander, Brio's DataPivot and DataPrism, SPC's InfoAlliance, and many others.
- The archetypal natural language query tool is AICorp's Intellect. Alternatives include Programmed Intelligence's Intelligent Query and Natural Language's Natural Language.
- The archetypal general analysis tool (with SQL/relational links) is Lotus 1-2-3. Alternatives include SAS Institute's SAS, Microsoft's Excel, SPC's Harvard Graphics, and others.
- The archetypal statistical technology is SAS. There are many, many alternatives.
- The archetypal graphics capability is Harvard Graphics. Alternatives include Microsoft Excel, Lotus 1-2-3, Odesta's DataDesk, IntelligenceWare's Data Visualization Tool, and many others.
- The archetypal simulation technology is SPSS Inc.'s SPSS. Alternatives include IBI's Focus, SAS, Comshare's System W, and others.
- The archetypal decision support technology is SAS. Alternatives include Execucom's IFPS, Forest and Trees, IBM's Metaphor, Decisus' Business Wits, and others.
- The archetypal executive information system is Comshare's Commander EIS. Alternatives include Information Resources' Express/EIS, Pilot's Executive Software's Command Center and Lightship, Software Publishing's EIS, Channel Computing's Forest and Trees, IBI's Focus/EIS, IBM's Executive Decisions, D&B Software's Smartview, Metaphor's DIS, Execucom's Executive Edge, and many more.

Information Discovery Technologies

Discovery technologies provide a company with one of the critical edges for gaining insight into its business and its major problems. It does this by utilizing automated inference to uncover and extract potential facts and relationships that might not otherwise be apparent. The basic technology is induction (as opposed to the deductive process of standard information analysis technologies), and is accomplished by creatively combining technologies that perform logical inference (or reasoning engines), numerical and statistical analysis, automated machine learning, and numerical pattern recognition.

EIT discovery technologies are among the most rapidly developing of the areas discussed. They are only available as stand-alone packages, with many still in the early development stages. As these technologies mature, they will almost certainly be offered in more powerful, integrated, and comprehensive forms, with, for example, embedded interfaces to industry-standard GUIs and relational database technologies. Examples are given below by category; archetypes are not presented due to the newness of the technologies.

Statistical inference is a process that interacts dynamically with a user who does not know much about the information's demographics. It allows for the formal creation of meaning by using statistical inference techniques presented in dramatic and contrasting visual form, typically two- and three-dimensional graphs and scatterplots. Being able to visualize and manipulate that representation, statistical inference allows a user to understand the demographics of information without his being a statistical expert.

Logical inference seeks out patterns in information by combining logical induction, statistical analysis, sampling, iterative query submission, and machine learning. It ferrets out these relationships by determining the frequency of discovered patterns and groupings and presents them to the user when they cross a threshold. The process may be guided by setting controls.

Numerical inference is based on the use of mathematical techniques that recognize and learn from patterns of information occurrences. The software is trained using mathematical formulas and user input. Numerical inference (also referred to as *neural networks*) provides a continuously growing intelligence as conditions and structures in the information change and evolve.

Case-based reasoning is a class of inference that uses examples or cases as a basis for comparing new conditions. As cases are received and added to the history of examples, the range of possibilities increases, and with it, the hit rate for comparing new examples. In effect, the system learns, much as most human experts learn, as the library of cases increases in size.

- Examples of statistical inference technologies include Odesta's DataDesk, IntelligenceWare's Data Visualization Tool, SAS, and a few others.
- Examples of logical inference technologies include IntelligenceWare's IXL, HNC's Database Mining System, and TRW's Discovery System.
- Examples of numerical inference technologies include Inductive Inference's ADAM, IBM's Neural Network Utility, PLOGIC Knowledge Systems' pLOGIC, and Cognition Technology's neuroSMARTS.
- An example of case-based reasoning technology is Inference's ART-IM.

DELIVERY TECHNOLOGIES

There is a great need to use *information delivery technologies* to help users collect, interpret, and present findings. There are numerous such technologies available, many of them designed to interface with industry-standard GUIs and relational database technologies. These include spreadsheets, chart-makers, drawing tools, slide and projection organizers, paint and photographic image managers, numerical and statistical graph makers, topic and concept organizers, hypercard and hypertext-like information managers, and multimedia presentations combining data, sounds, text, images and motion. Examples of these technologies are not given, primarily because they are so plentiful, so well-known, and so constantly changing.

12

Vendor Information Visions

This chapter looks at those vendor strategies that come closest to addressing the EIT vision, deliver the capabilities in the EIT Design, and provide the technologies that correspond to the EIT Integration Model. These *vendor information visions* represent the information architectures and frameworks of today's leading technology vendors. Companies wishing to attain the benefits of EIT capabilities must look at viable alternatives. The previous chapter provided one—that each company select and integrate the best of the enterprise information technologies. This chapter offers another approach.

VISIONS FOR SALE

The packaging of information technology strategies and architectures is big business, fueled by the number of companies using (or wanting to use) information technologies to power their competitive strategies, and by the maturing nature of the computing industry. For a technology vendor, enticing a customer into adopting its information architecture promises not only a common language; it also creates a solid base from which future purchasing decisions can follow.

The EIT Design and Integration Model offer the technology-using company *an objective and vendor-independent strategy* that can help level the playing field. It gives the company a clear "best-of-breed" alternative for seizing competitive advantages from its information asset. As important, it can be used to assess the value of a vendor's information strategy. This chapter provides a basis for making that assessment and for understanding the core philosophies and nature of a vendor's information strategy.

It has been necessary to restrict the discussion to those vendors that come the closest to capturing the "EIT spirit," that offer solutions—individually and collectively—that compare well with its Design and Integration Model. As will be seen below, none map 100 percent, while a handful present intriguing similarities. Of the ones selected, hardware vendors are presented first, followed by software manufacturers. Other than that, they are not presented in any particular order. The six information strategies discussed are:

- IBM's Information Warehouse
- NCR's Open Cooperative Computing
- Teradata's Industrial-Strength Database Computing
- DEC's Information Network
- Computer Associates' CA90s
- Oracle's Parallel Server

Each description starts with an overview of the information strategy as promulgated by the vendor. That is followed by a discussion of that strategy framed against the EIT Design and Integration Model. The review concludes with general observations that seek to gauge the vendor's overall strategy, its applicability, and value for establishing EIT capabilities.

Aside from the opinions expressed, the information for these descriptions comes from documents (such as company literature, marketing collaterals, annual reports, industry newsletters and periodicals), and on-the-record interviews. The vendors have not reviewed these descriptions, and are not responsible for the contents or errors that may be found in them. Future capabilities, whether unannounced products or hoped-for directions, are avoided to keep the discussion anchored in the concrete and real.

The area that appears most subject to change, according to what is presented below, is NCR and Teradata. Since NCR's acquisition of Teradata, there has been no safe way to predict how its technology and vision of information will be assimilated within NCR's product strategies. NCR and Teradata are, therefore, presented as separate visions, i.e., according to the situation that existed prior to and during the acquisition, and at the time of the writing of this book. The evaluating company should keep this and the need for tracking NCR's evolving concepts in mind. In fact, this is good advice for all the vendor visions.

IBM—THE INFORMATION WAREHOUSE

Any strategy that comes from IBM must be included in an analysis of this kind, if for no other reason than to understand what the de facto standard is likely to be for many companies. However, IBM has presented a large and sweeping information blueprint for addressing many of the opportunities targeted by the EIT vision, a capability that, by itself, merits careful attention. *The Information Warehouse* is IBM's approach to meeting the Information Automation needs of large companies. It is consistent with IBM's more general computing, software, and communications strategies, and represents a major step forward by recognizing the need for enterprisewide solutions of this type.

IBM Vision Overview

With the Information Warehouse, IBM is providing an evolutionary framework for a set of tools and standards that provide information users with transparent access to databases anywhere in the enterprise. This initiative is a key element in making the mainframe the central database server, while linking data from multi-vendor mainframes, minicomputers, and desktop systems.

While heavily based on IBM's proprietary products, it is a more open strategy than many previous IBM frameworks, primarily because it uses industry-standard SQL and targets data on both IBM and non-IBM hardware and database management systems (DBMSs). The Information Warehouse integrates third-party software partner offerings with IBM's DB2 and OS/2 Database Manager using IBM's Distributed Relational Data Access (DRDA) and Information Builder's EDA/SQL.

IBM's Information Warehouse is positioned as the strategic direction for *informational systems* and represents an emphasis on non-operational computing requirements. Informational systems are concerned with providing a user with access to company information on a large scale for reporting and data analysis. Automation of this area is driven by business needs and the availability of improved tools for accessing data.

The Information Warehouse draws together the various strands of informational systems activity within a company, and creates an integrated *warehouse of company data* based on the relational database model. End-user access to this warehouse is simplified by a consistent set of tools provided by a common end-user interface and supported by a data directory (not announced but widely expected) that describes information in user terms.

IBM's Information Warehouse is a comprehensive architecture aimed at providing a cross-functional business information system that is easy to use and flexible to change as the business changes. The Information Warehouse absorbs developments in relational technology, including support for the information desktop, multiple file servers, and multiple database machines. It is designed to protect a company's computing assets while providing better capabilities to utilize information.

IBM Generic and Infrastructure Technologies

Although IBM's Information Warehouse employs microprocessors in its PS/2 systems and peripherals, its central platform is the S/390 mainframe. The Information Warehouse positions it as the central database server. Such an arrangement benefits from the strengths of the mainframe (greater performance, reliability, security, and to a lesser extent, functionality and capacity), but it fails to take advantage of the advantages of the microprocessor (greater connectivity, sharability, price-performance, modularity, availability, productivity, and standardization).

IBM's Information Warehouse positions its AS/400 and PS/2 machines as midrange and local database servers. Connected by IBM's proprietary network and data access architectures, SNA and DRDA, these systems are used to process downloaded information from the mainframe. IBM supports local area networking with its network operating system, LAN Server under OS/2, running Token Ring.

IBM's client workstation is either the PS/2 running OS/2 or the RS/6000 under Unix, with both supporting IBM's Common User Access (or GUI) standard. They are adaptable platforms that provide fast access to data for experienced users and maximum guidance for novices. They promise a common look to applications by supporting a consistent window for stored data. GUIs offered are Presentation Manager on OS/2 and Motif on the Unix RS/6000.

Although users access and manage information via industry-standard languages, interfaces, and communication protocols, the Information Warehouse is firmly grounded in IBM's proprietary DRDA access standard. This calls for keeping operational data on the mainframe, where most Business Automation currently resides, and extracting and placing it in an Information Warehouse based on IBM's flagship relational database system—DB2.

DB2, the archetype relational database system and the most functional relational system available, is also expensive, difficult to use, hard to operate and support, requires an expensive mainframe, and cannot readily handle the volumes of information needed by an EIT environment (capacities over 250 gigabytes, for example). To counter the last problem, IBM suggests heavy use of segmentation and aggregation of information, an approach whose disadvantages were vividly demonstrated in earlier chapters.

The Information Warehouse is grounded in relational and SQL technologies, and relies on advanced access technologies to supply DB2 with extracted, snapshotted, or propagated information from operational systems. As IBM repositions DB2 to serve a greater role as an EIT Information Database (instead of primarily production systems), it is hoped that IBM will expand its processing and capacity limits to handle the truly enormous sizes anticipated and to address some of the other concerns mentioned above.

IBM's Repository Manager/MVS is bidding to be the de facto directory standard. It contains specifications about the data in the Information Warehouse, as well as other computing and operational information. It uses objects to support information design, modeling, and semantic extensions, with access from a variety of platforms and tools. It is expected that IBM will continue to enrich Repository Manager, evolving it to the point where it provides the capabilities needed to support a Business Information Model (although it does not specifically address unstructured information or provide for expert systems technologies). IBM is also expected to port Repository Manager/MVS to microprocessor-based computing platforms for use in LAN environments.

IBM's probable long-term information strategy will be that a company shall manage all information in the enterprise as a single logical image (i.e., a central

information directory) with physical data distributed over a variety of local platforms and geographical locations. Over time, such a capability could evolve to the
point where Repository Manager knows where everything is located, what form it
is in, how to convert it, what network configurations to traverse, and how to
transport it quickly and safely.

IBM Information Transformation Technologies

Most of the transformation capabilities for IBM's Information Warehouse come
from third-party vendors. IBM's partnering strategy delivers information design
capabilities via CASE products such as KnowledgeWare's IEW and ADW, Bachman's products, and Intersolv's Excelerator. IBM also offers its own modeling
software, DevelopMate. These products work directly with IBM's RM/MVS and
DB2 technologies, and function within the general Information Warehouse
framework.

The Bachman products are especially strong on information re-engineering, and
their modeling tools are capable of capturing data designs from existing systems,
providing model-driven data delivery to the knowledge worker. With an expanded
Repository Manager, the Information Warehouse is expected to support the cross-
mapping requirements needed for information extraction and conditioning.

Information extraction functions are handled by IBM's Data Propagator and
DXT technologies, and by third-party products working directly with the Information Warehouse. There appear to be no IBM products to handle information
conditioning, except by using such third-party tools as Carleton's (see previous
chapter). It is expected that IBM will incorporate capabilities that address more
powerful data consolidation and enrichment functions. Information populating
and maintenance are an inherent part of DB2, although it does not yet have fully
automatic and precision archiving and restoration capabilities.

As mentioned above, IBM's Information Warehouse is expected to have the
equivalent of an EIT Information Directory and Business Information Model that
would provide powerful information navigating capabilities. Limited access to the
Repository Manager's metadata is currently available.

Analysis tools are abundant, provided by IBM and a large third-party community. Almost every popular analysis and query tool accesses data in IBM's DB2
system. This also holds true for information delivery technologies. Current IBM
technologies that will be integrated into the Information Warehouse include Data
Interpretation System (DIS), Personal Application System (PAS/2), Executive
Decisions (ED), Application System (AS), Query Management Facility (QMF) and
SAA LanguageAccess.

IBM Compliance with the EIT Integration Model

The Information Warehouse is based on IBM's other architectures (SAA, SNA,
DRDA, SystemView, and AD/Cycle), an environment that resembles the EIT Integration Model and large-scale client/server architecture in many respects, but
that remains clearly IBM-specific in its most fundamental orientation.

IBM's Information Warehouse is not totally compliant with industry-standard client/server and SQL architectures. It differs in its ability to support true heterogeneous hardware and software. There are notable differences in how responsibilities and tasks are divided, particularly between client and server platforms. True heterogeneous connectivity is possible only if non-IBM technologies use IBM's standards. DRDA's more elegant and powerful technology comes at the expense of simplicity, cost, openness, flexibility, and connectivity.

While promulgating its own standard with DRDA, IBM is also providing connectivity with relational databases from Borland, Gupta, Informix, Locus, MDI, Novell, Oracle, and Sybase. In addition, IBM is offering, through one of its partners, a more industry-standard technology that can access information using SQL in databases on both IBM and non-IBM computing platforms. Called EDA/SQL from Information Builders, it allows users of SQL-based products to access relational or non-relational databases via standard interfaces, translators, and drivers. EDA/SQL allows a variety of user tools to cross distributed and multivendor systems, and is compatible with industry-standard protocols and architectures.

IBM, then, is presenting two somewhat complementary strategies: a more open, less integrated but industry-standard alternative—IBI's EDA/SQL, and a more powerful and integrated, less open alternative—DRDA. Neither is fully complaint with a third alternative—the computer industry's SQL Access Group's common interface that enables clients and servers from multiple vendors to work together.

IBM General Observations

In addition to the concerns mentioned above, the Information Warehouse appears to be expensive. While there are no implementation costs available, the use of the MVS operating system and DB2 software alone are about $500,000 a year, with the MVS/Repository Manager pegged somewhere between $100,000 and $250,000 annually. The Information Warehouse is obviously a big-ticket item, and considerations such as the cost of the mainframe, operating system, training, and support must be factored into the justification analysis.

While it offers some real hope, the Information Warehouse has not solved the fundamental bad data problem present in so many production systems. Its distributed access strategy fails to address the need for transforming information before it can be used for Information Automation, and for modeling and storing the conditioned information in a single database. Nor has it offered the level of autonomy required by users to make them full partners in the "information harnessing" process. Many of the approaches advocated in the Information Warehouse are no different than some of the ineffective top-down, central information engineering efforts of the past.

Finally, despite its sweeping vision of going beyond distributed databases, the Information Warehouse doesn't offer a viable long-term vision for information— how to arrive ultimately at a single data store or single information image. In fact, the Information Warehouse would seem, by its very success, to perpetuate indefinitely the separation of information for operational and informational needs. Unless that end-state goal is provided for, this is a fatal flaw in IBM's otherwise promising vision.

On the positive side, IBM's Information Warehouse is a major step forward by the world's biggest computer vendor in addressing the information opportunities of business enterprises. It is IBM's response to the failure of most conventional mainframe-based solutions to satisfy the critical information needs of businesses. Despite its many faults, the Information Warehouse offers important capabilities and strategies that must be carefully considered by any organization seriously interested in exploiting the potential of its information asset.

IBM's ability to focus third-party software companies on important components is a major factor in making the Information Warehouse an exciting vision. Even if IBM provides little of the enabling technologies themselves, the mere presence of this framework allows others to produce needed capabilities while working within a de facto standard. Should IBM move to make this framework more open and cost-effective, it would be an attractive vision that any company would seriously consider.

The Bottom Line

The Information Warehouse will likely become, because of who's behind it and because of its singular range and depth, the standard for enterprisewide information architectures. If it never spawns the power and functionality called for by the EIT Design and Integration Model and that is needed to achieve truly sustainable competitive advantage, it will certainly create the momentum for approaches and technologies that will.

NCR—OPEN COOPERATIVE COMPUTING

NCR has shaken off its stodgy cash register image, and with a firm foothold in retail and banking data collection systems, is espousing some of the latest, industry-standard, open computing products in the marketplace. It has articulated an approach truly sweeping in nature and one based on a different and often compelling view of computing in general.

With its recent acquisition of Teradata (whose main offering is discussed separately), it has the ability to deliver immediately essential large-scale information technologies. And with its own acquisition by deep-pockets, technology-rich AT&T, NCR is well positioned to sustain a long-term initiative that some believe could remake the face of computing. That face is known as *Open Cooperative Computing.*

NCR Vision Overview

NCR's strategic information theme is based on an architecture called *Open Cooperative Computing* (or OCCA). This initiative combines the concepts of open systems and cooperative computing to permit enterprisewide interoperability so that processing can be physically located anywhere in the enterprise and in response to changing conditions. This strategy recognizes the needs of companies to manage all of their information in detail and on an enterprisewide basis.

OCCA is an overarching computing environment made up of three programs. The first is a family of *scalable, general-purpose computers* ranging from notepads to massively parallel computing machines. The second is *Cooperation,* an integrating environment for achieving enterprisewide cooperative computing. The third is *Open Networking Environment,* a set of networking products to enable enterprisewide connectivity.

NCR bases its strategy on the dominance of four technologies: the microprocessor, open system standards, parallel processing architectures, and user productivity tools (the last area is where NCR places relational database, object, and client/server technologies). The ultimate aim of this computing environment is cooperative computing. Companies may want to adopt OCCA because it provides significant economic and strategic advantages as applications are implemented under its architecture.

OCCA assumes the use of a transitional approach, carried out under a master plan by building more cost-effective computing gradually—by constructing new applications, by rearchitecting existing applications, and by extending the current computing infrastructure. NCR offers OCCA as the basis for transitioning to that future infrastructure.

NCR Generic and Infrastructure Technologies

NCR's OCCA, covering capabilities that range well outside the boundaries of the EIT Design, provides a rich set of computing and information technologies for the large enterprise. OCCA is built upon a hierarchy of computing platforms based around the Intel 80X86 chip family. Anchored in this archetypal microprocessor, the NCR System 3000 product line offers the price and performance advantages of that critical technology. Platforms range from small systems to massively parallel processors of more than 100,000 MIPS.

NCR System 3000 platforms are based on an implementation of client/server architecture, promising high levels of connectivity, performance, capacity, modularity and price-performance. Because the hardware is capable of providing for all aspects of client/server, it promises high levels of functionality, reliability and security as well.

The central database server is based on the System 3600 and 3700 models (plus the newly acquired Teradata DBC/1012). These are Unix-based, loosely-coupled parallel processing systems that handle thousands of microprocessors and terabytes of information, use small form-factor disk drives, and offer linear increments of power and performance. The NCR 3600, for example, offers four times the power of the largest conventional mainframes at one-tenth the price. Smaller models are positioned as local database servers operating under either Unix or OS/2.

While OCCA supports LAN protocols such as Ethernet, Token-ring, and NFS, and WAN architectures such as TCP/IP and SNA, its more general strategy is based on the OSI networking model. Its aim is to create efficient, reliable, and cost-effective communication networks with the flexibility provided by open standards, yet still connecting to proprietary networks. OCCA uses OSI-based networks to link clients and servers across the enterprise, and to provide network and systems management applications such as software distribution and security.

Client workstation platforms are based on the smaller System 3000 models, running either SCO Unix, Unix V, DOS, or OS/2. OCCA provides its own Information Desktop environment called NCR Desktop (based on HP's New Wave technology), an object technology that offers a comprehensive and intelligent GUI. NCR Desktop integrates advanced GUI functions with user script languages, standard PC and workstation applications, an executive tracking facility called Business Information Monitor (discussed below), and a file tracking and archival facility. NCR Desktop also handles automatic document conversion, office productivity functions, and resource scheduling management. Information users have access to all applications, databases, and other users in the enterprise through facilities that provide general-purpose information retrieval, analysis, manipulation, and reporting, along with decision support tools that incorporate personal and work group productivity functions.

One of OCCA's key technologies is relational database, with engines capable of running on platforms ranging from small servers on up to the largest machines. This interoperability allows information to be placed where it is most needed and effective. In addition to NCR's large-scale relational database engine on the System 3600 and 3700 (based on Teradata's technology), it offers the Oracle Parallel Server, an RDBMS that can run on any of the smaller NCR 3000 models, providing easy portability and upgradability. Access can also be to information in Oracle relational databases on minicomputers and mainframes via Oracle's SQL*Net. Also available on local database servers is Gupta's SQLBase, with its DB2 gateway and 4GL tools. OCCA provides facilities for user access to IBM DB2 databases on mainframes from any client workstation. A scalable version of Sybase is planned for the NCR 3600 and 3700.

While object technology is used extensively on its client workstation platforms, OCCA does not use it to provide semantics to the relational model or to satisfy complex information modeling capabilities. Hence, it lacks the advantages of an Information Directory, although its general architecture provides for the support of the IRDS standard. Nor does NCR's OCCA make use of advanced, embedded expert systems technologies for information requirements.

Unstructured information is addressed by OCCA's Text Retrieval and Compound Document Editor, both resident on the NCR Desktop. The latter produces compound documents of text, graphs, spreadsheets, and images; the former allows for retrieval of documents and text fragments using standard text search and matching algorithms.

NCR Information Transformation Technologies

At this stage, OCCA provides no real assistance for information design. This appears to be true for information re-engineering, extraction, and conditioning. Information populating and maintenance is provided by the System 3000 relational engines. OCCA also lacks information navigating facilities, since that is an inherent extension of an (also absent) Information Directory. However, OCCA offers a number of information analysis tools.

The NCR Desktop provides access to local databases under SQLBase, remote DB2 databases, and local and remote Oracle databases (tools for the SQLBase environment include SQL/Windows, JAM/DBi, Nomad, ZIM and SQL Commander). Its Business Information Monitor can query those databases as well as others (including older files and spreadsheet data) to provide management with a critical success factor tracking system. There is also a drill-down feature, allowing users to view the underlying relationships that exist between the key summary factors.

OCCA's object technologies allow some functions to be automatic, such as the ability to archive and track historical data, to provide needed security of information, to assist the user in preparing queries, and to issue alarms and alerts when the information changes from normal to urgent status. NCR's Information Storage Manager helps users access information from databases anywhere in the enterprise without their having to know specifically where that information resides.

OCCA's Application Development Environment (ADE) offers 3GL, 4GL, and object technologies for applications development that, while not specifically intended for the user, can build applications that benefit from a professional programmer. The object technology utilized at the NCR Desktop facilitates rapid applications development, and may serve as a base for new EIT capabilities. This would include true user-driven tools and capabilities, along with libraries of reusable procedures and requests. OCCA's SQL/Windows may be the first of such a series, with capabilities for users to build Information Automation applications directly.

OCCA lacks specific information discovery capabilities. It permits, however, the use of most of the popular information delivery tools, and goes a step further by providing the ability to easily communicate the results of information analysis to all users of the company.

NCR Compliance with the EIT Integration Model

OCCA strongly adheres to the basics of client/server architecture—it is a truly open and cooperative approach to information architectures, combining the most compelling and effective technologies into a broad scheme for enterprise computing. It doesn't designate how an enterprise should organize and locate its information, a philosophy similar to the Scatterplot Vision described in Chapter 2.

However, the EIT Integration Model is based on the *large-scale* client/server computing model, a processing environment that, with its critical central database server technologies, brings its own set of requirements with it. While OCCA doesn't *prevent* an organization from using its technology to enable the EIT Design, at the same time, it doesn't specifically satisfy the requirements and problems inherent in such an approach.

For example, OCCA provides capabilities to track automatically the location of information anywhere in the enterprise (an important requirement in a distributed or scatterplot environment), but lacks capabilities to download information from the central database server to a local database server and keep it tightly synchronized. The significance of this is that OCCA's underlying philosophy is more attuned to the needs of Business Automation than to Information Automation. This distinction aside, OCCA closely matches the characteristics of the EIT Integration Model.

NCR General Observations

NCR's Open Cooperative Computing architecture has taken some of the more promising information technologies and integrated them under a general architecture, adding value by providing small but critical linking components. This can be used to save work in developing or customizing these types of capabilities. The benefits of such an integration strategy are high levels of connectivity, sharability, modularity, price-performance, productivity and standardization; less certain are the benefits of capacity, performance, functionality, reliability, security and availability.

Because it is still relatively new, the true cost of implementing an EIT Design under OCCA is not clear. Certainly, the use of microprocessor technology will tend to keep it at high levels of price-performance. But hardware costs are only part of the story. Development costs, people and training costs, implementation costs, support costs—these and others need to be factored into the analysis. They are mostly unknown in the world of cooperative open computing.

Being a general-purpose solution, OCCA has the disadvantage of not specifically addressing the objectives and requirements of the EIT Design. Is a fully integrated but less focused solution a fundamentally better approach than picking the "best of breed" technologies and integrating them into a less-than-perfect overall solution? Which adapts better to major change? Which holds up better over the long-term, especially as new technology threatens to replace the underlying components? What happens when the demands of the EIT user exceed the capabilities of an integrated and open solution?

OCCA, like IBM's Information Warehouse, has not specifically addressed the bad data problem in current systems. OCCA has provided a way for redesigning a company's production systems while taking advantage of client/server and microprocessor technologies. This could serve as the basis for changing OCCA's scatterplot orientation to one more closely resembling the long-term vision of a single information image. If NCR's large parallel machines can handle the massive information processing requirements of such an environment, OCCA becomes a viable alternative for organizations implementing the EIT vision of information.

The Bottom Line

OCCA offers an exciting and reasonable approach to enabling the EIT Design. Given some success stories (here, Teradata can help a great deal), OCCA has the potential to usher in a new wave of technology-based computing that can unleash the power of information to create and sustain significant competitive advantage.

TERADATA—INDUSTRIAL-STRENGTH DATABASE COMPUTING

(Note: At the time of the writing of this book, NCR had consummated a friendly takeover of Teradata. The two companies had previously collaborated on major research and development projects, suggesting there is a good fit of Teradata's technology with NCR's overall OCCA vision. Such an acquisition could help ensure the long-term viability of Teradata's underlying technology. As mentioned above, their two information architectures are presented separately.)

Teradata offers a large database computer that handles massive volumes of information in a shared and open environment. It produces this power by employing parallel processing of large numbers of cost-effective microprocessors and disks. Unlike hardware vendors that have several, often overlapping proprietary architectures, Teradata relies primarily on industry-standard connections and interfaces to provide access to and manipulation of the information stored in its *Data Base Computer / 1012 (DBC / 1012)*.

Teradata has been successful in enabling some striking "information success" stories. While small as a company, Teradata's technology is by no means small, and it offers very large-scale relational database handling capabilities that have been unsurpassed by any other technology (it is the archetypal central database server; see previous chapter). Teradata's information strategy can be described as enabling a shared information environment using industrial-strength database computing.

Teradata Vision Overview

The heart of Teradata's guiding vision is a central and single image of information accessed by users throughout the enterprise. With a technology that can conceivably support that goal, it has led the way with customers whose competitive needs require the transformation of massive collections of information. Most of Teradata's customers have used the DBC/1012 technology to meet the kinds of business needs discussed in this book. Long-term, the Teradata parallel processing technology is intended to handle all of a company's information, for both Business and Information Automation needs.

Teradata Generic and Infrastructure Technologies

Teradata's technology is based on Intel's microprocessor. Its four generations of database machines have matched the evolutionary stages of the Intel 80X86 chip family, each progression bringing with it large advances in power and price-performance. Teradata's current offering, the DBC/1012 Model 4, is therefore based on the 80486 chip. Arrayed to its theoretical limit of 1,012 processors (the basis for its name), the system can deliver over 9,000 MIPS. Each processor has 8 megabytes of memory, along with 2 megabytes of non-volatile disk cache (temporary data storage) at an average cost per MIP of $25,000 (one fourth to one-third the cost of mainframe MIPS).

The Teradata DBC/1012 uses standard small form-factor disk devices that can store over two gigabytes per drive. With a theoretical maximum of 4,096 drives in a system, the DBC/1012 can hold over 10 terabytes of information (or over 10,000 billion bytes). The drives and processors are connected in a unique parallel fashion (the Ynet) that permits a linear increase in power as units are added, i.e., there is no loss of power due to increasingly complex overhead or systems administrative functions.

The DBC/1012, positioned as the central database server, can be connected to a variety of heterogeneous computing platforms (mainframes, desktop systems, and minicomputers), all acting as clients in a true client/server architecture. The overall effect is to deliver precise modularity along with sharability, connectivity, productivity, and price-performance without loss in performance, capacity, or availability. Compared to the mainframe, the DBC/1012 delivers less functionality, reliability, and security.

Teradata also offers local database servers via its Sharebase product. The DBC/1012 connects to popular networks (Ethernet and Token Ring), PCs and workstations (IBM PCs, Macintosh, and Sun), operating systems (DOS, Windows, OS/2, Macintosh OS, and Unix), minicomputers (DEC VAX) and mainframes (IBM, Unisys, Bull, Siemens, and AT&T), either through LAN gateways or direct attach. This allows a company to place and access information on the DBC/1012 without changing its current equipment, software, or operating systems.

The DBC/1012 uses industry-standard relational database technologies. It makes no use of object or expert systems technologies, although it provides interfaces to products that do. It does not have an Information Directory, although once again, through interfaces, it can link with certain third-party Directory technologies. There is no provision in the DBC/1012 for the management of unstructured information, although there is an interface to optical disk storage systems.

Teradata Information Transformation Technologies

Teradata relies on third-parties for its transformation technologies. It provides transparency software (referred to as TS/API) that permits systems that access IBM's DB2 to access the DBC/1012. This permits DB2-based tools and technologies to gain access to the parallel processing benefits of the Teradata platform.

Teradata does not offer information design capabilities, and there is no support for industry-standard CASE products. It currently offers Multiload, a product that handles a wide range of information "acquisition and apply" functions using data from extracted databases. In many cases, this powerful utility eliminates the need for some extraction and populating functions. Standard information populating and maintenance are provided by the core DBC/1012 relational database engine.

Teradata's DBC/1012 does not provide information navigating capabilities. It offers, however, both its own SQL query tools (BTEQ, ITEQ) and a number of third-party information analysis tools. These are enabled either by direct interfaces or by industry-standard gateways such as IBI's EDA/SQL, Gupta's Router, Micro Decisionware's SQLServer, and Apple's DAL.

The information analysis products include Metaphor's DIS, Microsoft's Excel, and Asymetrix's Toolbook under DOS Windows, Micro Decisionware's PC/SQL Link, Andyne's GQL, Cognos' PowerplayEIS, Gupta's SQLWindows and Quest, NeXT, Must's Nomad, IBI's Focus, Unisys' Mapper, AICorp's Intellect and KBMS, CA's Ramis, IBM's QMF, Apple's Hypercard, Ingres' front-end, and Aion's ADS. IntelligenceWare provides capabilities that address information discovery with IXL, Database/Supervisor, and Data Visualization. Products such as Microsoft Excel support information delivery functions.

Teradata Compliance with the EIT Integration Model

Although the DBC/1012 began life as a "back-end" to IBM mainframes, Teradata's shared information philosophy and its other capabilities are fully compliant with current notions of large-scale client/server architecture. The DBC/1012 relies on the separation of application and database processing, is an inherently open architecture, and uses industry-standard interfaces, languages, and protocols. Client platforms may be of almost all popular hardware and software combinations.

Teradata's technology is firmly rooted in microprocessor technology, gaining its power by interconnecting them together via parallel connections and dedicating them to a single database task. It uses industry-standard relational database and SQL technologies, builds on LAN technologies, and provides high-speed links to IBM (and other) mainframes where the truly large collections of information are located (typically through very-high-speed magnetic tape channels).

Teradata falls short of full compliance with the Integration Model by relying on a proprietary operating system (although they are working on a Unix-based system), and in lacking capabilities to automatically synchronize information changes with local database servers.

Teradata General Observations

In many ways, Teradata's technology comes closest to meeting the EIT Design and Integration Model. While other technologies are beginning to match the DBC/1012 for sheer horsepower, it is still at the center of a broad wave that is sweeping older approaches before it—client/server architecture, the microprocessor, massive parallelism, enterprise connectivity, relational, and SQL. The advantages of Teradata's technology are capacity, availability, sharability, modularity, overall performance, price-performance, standardization, and productivity.

But there are problems. The technology is not well-known or widely accepted, despite successes at some large companies. Another concern is that, despite an approach that points it directly at EIT objectives, Teradata has seen itself as a player in all automation, supporting OLTP, batch production, and decision support applications alike. As was argued earlier, it is unlikely that any business organization could take full advantage of such capabilities, even if they existed.

Further, with a few exceptions, the DBC/1012 lacks important directory and transformation technologies, especially those that take full advantage of its massive parallel technology. A final concern is scalability at the low end. The initial buy-in for the smallest DBC/1012 is likely to cost a minimum of a half million dollars, leaving a lot of room between it and local database servers. While a small DBC/1012 buys a lot of processing power, it also limits sales to those customers who can afford the initial price tag.

The Bottom Line

Teradata technology offers massive power at attractive prices. It enables central information with distributed (or local) processing. It is compatible with IBM and industry standards. For companies with truly massive databases, it may be the only alternative. It is, therefore, an important vision to explore for those seeking the biggest payoffs from information.

DEC—THE INFORMATION NETWORK

Digital Equipment Corporation, the largest minicomputer vendor in the world, has positioned itself as the leader in multivendor computing and connectivity solutions. Historically a niche company that sold department-level proprietary minicomputers for functions such as manufacturing, distribution, and factory automation, DEC has moved into the 1990s as an important player in large and medium-sized computers, in information architectures, and in fostering some very leading-edge and industry-standard technologies.

Over the past few years, DEC has unveiled several tightly interconnected strategies and architectures designed to meet the business demands of the 90s. More recently, it has turned its attention to the issue of enterprise information by articulating *The Information Network*. As would be expected, the core technology of this vision is centered around DEC's mainstream products, extended by a host of advanced and integrating technologies.

DEC Vision Overview

DEC's strategic database direction for the 1990s is the Information Network. It is a software framework that extends DEC's Network Application Support (NAS) to encompass technologies that allow users to transparently integrate and manage data dispersed across a distributed computing environment. Hence, the Information Network is oriented towards coexistence with multivendor technologies in a true industry-standard open environment. To make this a reality, DEC has invested aggressively in database technologies and is leading the push towards standards-based capabilities.

The Information Network is a vision of distributed and tightly linked databases connected to source or legacy systems (typically on IBM mainframes) and to desktop workstations on LANs. It aims also at integrating diverse information structures such as conventional data, text, graphics, and multimedia. The Information Network's primary technologies are open systems, distributed relational databases, a system-wide repository, and industry-standard products.

DEC positions the VAX line as central and local database servers, while NAS provides the connectivity to link DEC's client and server platforms, as well as with other vendor databases and platforms. With this broad connectivity, information can be shared from numerous heterogeneous environments while providing users with a single, consistent interface. They have robust and open access to other computers and databases for information extraction, access, and distribution.

All the definitions for these distributed collections of information are described and enforced by a central and active metadata directory called the CDD/Repository. Using object technology, the CDD/Repository provides a single, logical information model for an enterprise's information, regardless of its physical location and format. Finally, DEC's Information Network allows organizations to take advantage of a large suite of tools and products, from those provided directly by DEC to many third-party products.

DEC Generic and Infrastructure Technologies

Except for the Desktop incarnations of the VAX, the venerable DEC line does not avail itself of the full advantages of the microprocessor. VAX price-performance is somewhere between that of the Intel chip and an IBM mainframe. DEC has provided, however, a wide range of scalability to its VAX models, ranging from the small 3100 to the new mainframe 9000 series. Hence, the VAX user benefits from a high degree of modularity and scalability.

The Information Network employs a mainframe-sized VAX (6000 or 9000 series), clustered or multihost, as the central database server. Such an approach suffers from the same tradeoffs of using any mainframe as a central database server. However, because of DEC's efforts to open its proprietary systems and to utilize industry-standard connectivity and technologies, this positioning retains more of the benefits of the mainframe-as-server approach without giving up the advantages of a truly open, microprocessor-based server.

The Information Network deploys smaller VAXes (3000 or 4000 series) as local database servers tightly connected with the central server—a feature missing in most of the other vendor's architectures. These systems store the off-loaded information for local PC/LAN processing. Users access the local and central information via DEC's SQL/Services (comparable to the SQL Access Group's standard).

Enterprisewide connectivity is provided by DECnet (a quasi-proprietary protocol which includes components of the OSI standard) or by TCP/IP linked to LAN Manager or NetWare. Information is moved from the central to local database servers using DEC's Data Distributor. Access to information on IBM platforms is via a DECnet/SNA gateway utilizing the access and extract capabilities of Rdb-Access or VAXlink, which, in turn, populate the VAX/Rdb central "data warehouse."

The client workstation can be any industry-standard platform such as the Intel PC (running DOS or OS/2), the Macintosh, Sun workstations, other Unix workstations, and of course, DEC's own DECstations and VAXstations under VMS. Information Network includes Compound Document Architecture, a specialized Desktop software facility that provides simultaneous presentation of text, graphics, and tables.

The Information Network positions DEC's flagship relational database technology, Rdb, at the center of its architecture. Rdb is a widely installed technology that exceeds industry-standard SQL specifications. It can be linked tightly with other copies running on other servers, and is probably the most functional distributed relational database system available. It is engineered to take advantage of VMS and DEC's VAX clustering technology, which provides more power for higher throughput and faster response times. Much of this improvement is designed for production processing.

DEC's Information Network utilizes object technologies to enable its CDD/Repository. This technology integrates tightly with Rdb to allow an interaction that meets some of the more advanced requirements of the EIT Design (for example, an active directory that immediately reflects changes in the Information Directory or Information Database). This active mechanism helps ensure that users access information according to the definitions, rules, and views resident in the Repository, and that any desired changes are carefully and fully serviced and implemented.

The CDD/Repository is the central intelligence for all enterprise information, whether in its own systems or others. It stores user queries for modification or reuse, and is "open" for integration with DEC's CASE and information access tools, as well as products from third parties. DEC's Rdb utilizes expert systems technologies to automate the information design process, especially in translating a conceptual design into physical specifications for implementation. Rdb also supports unstructured information types such as text and image, and employs its Desktop Compound Document Architecture to provide access, integration, and presentation of multimedia information.

DEC Information Transformation Technologies

The Information Network's information design capabilities are offered by DEC's CASE technologies and third-party CASE tools. It does not, however, address the functions of information re-engineering, extraction, and conditioning, although it does provide general utility products that handle rudimentary extraction capabilities from different databases. VAXlink extracts information from MVS databases such as IBM's IMS, SQL/DS, DB2, and VSAM; Software AG's ADABAS; and CA's IDMS. VAX Data Distributor provides for information replication, extraction, and roll-ups from DB2, Oracle, RMS, VSAM, and Rdb to populate a Rdb data warehouse. Information populating and maintenance is provided by Rdb, including advanced trigger capabilities for automatically enforcing database integrity constraints.

The Information Network provides industry-standard access gateways to the information stored in databases under Rdb, regardless of user or information location. Tools and applications using SQL and one of these standard interfaces are provided by both DEC and various third parties. They include IBI's Focus, Borland's Paradox, Cognos' Powerhouse, Lotus 1-2-3, Must's Nomad, Apple's Hypercard, Acius' 4th Dimension, Digitalk's Smalltalk V, SAS, Microsoft's Excel, Andyne's GQL, Brio's DataPrism, and Neuron's Nexpert Object.

DEC offers VAX Rally, a 4GL development system, DECquery, a broad suite of tools for the user to build, store, revise, and share queries, and analysis capabilities such as Teamdata, DECdecision, and Datatrieve. Information navigation capabilities are enabled by access to metadata in DEC's CDD/Repository. No specific DEC supplied information discovery tools are provided, although IntelligenceWare offers IXL for the VAX.

DEC Compliance with the EIT Integration Model

The Information Network, buttressed by DEC's NAS, conforms to some of the tenets of the EIT Integration Model and its large-scale client/server architecture. As discussed above, it offers an industry-standard interface between all clients and servers, utilizes SQL and relational technologies, operates in an open, heterogeneous connectivity environment, and espouses wide access to information anywhere in the enterprise.

The Information Network falls short of full compliance with the EIT Integration Model in that it positions a general-purpose computing platform as the central database server, relies on less attractive minicomputer technology, and links its servers according to the distributed database model (instead of the distributed copy and synchronization model).

DEC General Observations

DEC's Information Network presents a promising approach to seizing the advantages of information. It exploits attractive new technologies such as object, client/server, and enterprisewide connectivity. Opening its VMS operating system presents an alternative to intrinsically open (i.e., vendor neutral) Unix. Striving for open access to all platforms and products improves DEC's chances of being the vendor of choice. Making Rdb faster and better increases its attractiveness.

All this serves to improve DEC's products, making them more extendable and modifiable, more open, and more likely to avoid obsolescence. DEC has been previously thought of as an expensive but high-quality computing vendor, recognized for its engineering prowess, honesty, and support. DEC will probably have to make its pricing more attractive to effectively compete with microprocessor-based systems.

The Bottom Line

There are at least two dimensions to be considered in utilizing DEC's strategies for the EIT Design. First, the Information Network is based on the distributed database vision—it is primarily oriented to Business Automation application requirements. As with the other distributed database visions, it carries most of the same problems when adapting to the needs and circumstances of Information Automation. Reconciling the differences, exploiting the major advantages, and judging the net value that remains requires careful analysis.

Second, if an organization highly values the benefits of open systems, it needs good reasons to choose DEC's Information Network over other, more truly open alternatives, because DEC, despite its efforts, is still proprietary at its core. If that same organization, however, values results, robustness, and functionality at the expense of an open computing solution, it must justify a strategy that takes its operational data off IBM mainframes (where it probably resides today) in order to get the extra advantage that DEC brings to the table.

Perhaps what DEC is really offering is a compromise between these two choices, in allowing an organization to reap immediately the advantages of better information for running its business while moving gradually to a fully open information environment.

COMPUTER ASSOCIATES—CA90s

Computer Associates is the largest independent software vendor in the world, having built its position primarily from acquisition of other software companies with large customer bases and well-established technologies. CA has worked hard at melding these sometimes disparate, sometime overlapping, sometimes duplicate technologies into a cohesive program to address market needs.

With two flagship database products anchoring the company, CA has eschewed the relational model for database management and has, instead, leveraged older DBMS technologies as a base from which to offer some leading-edge solutions. This unusual approach creates a different set of problems and opportunities from those presented by some of the other vendor visions. The company's general strategy for promulgating this vision is called *CA90s*.

CA Vision Overview

CA90s (CA's formal and central architecture) is an amalgam of dozens of products and systems crafted into a general software architecture whose objective is to offer business enterprises a viable cross-platform database strategy. Whereas most of the other information visions focus primarily on information, CA focuses on information as part of an overall situation. CA is a major presence in the computing industry (there are few large business enterprises that do not have their products), and their DBMSs account for a good deal of the legacy data in production systems.

CA90s has no inherent hardware bias, although it is obviously IBM mainframe-oriented. It provides a framework for introducing new technology in a nondisruptive fashion while protecting current investments. CA90s allows CA to systematically bring its broad range of solutions to all computing platforms in a way that achieves unprecedented levels of automation, integration, and portability. The strategy employs a layered design that insulates software solutions from hardware and software. The layers are referred to as User Interface and Visualization, Integration, and Distributed Processing.

CA90s is based on the concept of a single database supporting the operational and Information Automation needs of the enterprise. Its objective is to standardize on database and software technology to satisfy an enterprise's entire computing needs. Hence, CA's database products are designed to meet production and Information Automation needs, as well as to offer transparency to programs and interfaces that use other DBMSs.

CA DBMSs are not inherently relational, although they use SQL as a data access language to retrieve and manipulate information. CA90s allows for the layering of new technologies such as information modeling and semantic extensions by placing them on top of the basic database structures. This has resulted in powerful active and integrated data dictionaries that are the foundation of CA's information repository.

While CA90s offers a single database for all processing needs, it positions that database to operate identically on a variety of microcomputer, minicomputer, and mainframe platforms. The databases on the several computing platforms may be tightly linked into a distributed database environment that provides support for multi-site retrieval and update. Through this distributed approach, CA90s attempts to address client/server and downsized computing solutions without having to replace the bulk of existing mainframe operational systems.

CA Generic and Infrastructure Technologies

CA90s is a mainframe architecture with provision for using microprocessor technologies as adjunct. To support the EIT Design, this strategy requires the use of an IBM mainframe running one of its two database systems. An organization could also elect to run CA's databases on PCs using their distributed software linkages. The central database server, then, is a CA database system on an IBM MVS mainframe.

This approach, like the other mainframe-based solutions, offers excellent performance, reliability, security, and to a smaller extent, good functionality and capacity, at the expense of price-performance, modularity, sharability, availability, connectivity, productivity, and standardization. Given the non-relational database strategy of CA90s, the "delta" between the benefits and losses of this scenario is less attractive than with a true relational database on IBM mainframes.

Local database servers, running different versions of the mainframe database system, operate on PC-connected LANs, which, in turn, are connected to the central database server via industry-standard and proprietary protocols. These include Ethernet, Token Ring, SNA, DECnet, TCP/IP, and OSI. Using a software layer to insulate applications from these protocols (Common Communication Interface), CA90s offers several connectivity options, ranging from true centralized processing to peer processing to client/server processing to distributed processing.

The client workstation is supported by another software layer that allows a variety of different user processing environments to all look approximately the same. CA90s links all GUI and non-GUI (character-based) screens with its own common look-and-feel. This not only makes primitive screens look and act more like powerful desktop systems, it also provides the basis for providing powerful capabilities such as information navigation and browsing, data formatting and validation, sophisticated Help and reporting functions, and graphics integration.

As mentioned, CA90s is an information strategy that does not rely on relational database technologies, although it utilizes SQL for access and inquiry. This is a major shortcoming, for it is in the inherent flexibility and ease-of-use of tables and set processing that the EIT Information Database is securely anchored (while CA has true relational solutions, they are not positioned in CA90s as the central components for managing information).

CA looks at SQL, information objects, and information designs as access methods or languages, instead of as extensions of the information structures themselves. This is a fundamental difference between the applications orientation of Business Automation and the information and business functions orientation of Information Automation. Because of this difference, CA90s fosters the notion of applications integration—an inappropriate basis for satisfying the objective of integrating information. While the former is valid, especially for Business Automation, it has much less value for the EIT Design.

CA90s uses object technologies based on the industry-standard IRDS specification to support its data dictionary and repository. These provide a single logical view of information, though the data is typically located in several places and probably in duplicate formats as well. Despite the general weaknesses of this approach, CA90s offers one of the best implementations of object technology for information design. Further, it is an *active* dictionary, something essential to a user-based capability and not generally available from the other vendors.

CA90s also incorporates expert systems technologies in its framework. It uses inference engines for user assistance and training, for intelligent query formulation, for diagnosis of the operation of the operating software, and for building customized "expert applications." CA90s does not support management of unstructured information such as text, although it does provide limited multimedia capabilities for tutorials and training.

CA Information Transformation Technologies

As already mentioned, CA90s offers an object-based dictionary and repository for design of information models and business semantics. Since it is targeted to the single database environment, CA90s does not directly support re-engineering, extraction, and conditioning capabilities, although there are third-party tools that meet those needs (including CASE tools). Information populating is not as much of an issue for CA90s (for the same reason), although it and maintenance are supported by the core DBMS engines.

CA90s provides information navigation capabilities with its User Interface layer. It also offers its own suite of information analysis and delivery tools such as spreadsheet analysis, 4GL development and prototyping, and user query. CA90s does not offer information discovery tools.

CA Compliance with the EIT Integration Model

CA90s is compliant with some of the aspects of client/server architecture, such as the separation of functions between client and server platforms. It also supports a heterogeneous or multivendor product environment and takes advantage of microprocessor machines and LANs. It spans proprietary networks like IBM's and DEC's.

Where it falls short in meeting the EIT Integration Model is in its absence of SQL and relational, in its failure to rely on microprocessor technology for enabling the central database server, and in its focus on distributed and independent database servers versus true synchronized local database servers.

CA General Observations

CA's unifying vision, CA90s, is based on a single database supporting both Business and Information Automation needs. This represents a fundamental difference in philosophy from that of the EIT vision, although the EIT long-term objective is to arrive at a single database. CA apparently agrees with the belief that the investment in existing systems and databases must be protected; they just go about it in a different way than that proposed by the EIT approach.

CA would keep those old and cranky DBMSs running and would layer new software on top of them. The marketplace, however, has placed its bets on relational database technologies. Hence, all the new and exciting tools, and even some of the new hardware, are based on relational and SQL technologies. CA90s technologies, while layered with some very advanced technology, are, fundamentally, based on technologies that are not going anywhere. Further, these core technologies do not promise the liberating and openness virtues of the newer technologies—they lock a company into proprietary software.

Beyond these concerns, CA90s is not user-oriented or even information-oriented. For example, CA90s is integrated at the applications level, not the information level. While its repository is excellent, it cannot be used in the ways an "EIT information user" would wish to use it—to bring about enterprise information access, to respond to expected and unexpected needs with equal efficiency, to allow changes made by simultaneous users, and to allow for design and analysis without the intervention of computer professionals.

From a cost perspective, while CA takes advantage of microprocessor technology, the basic components are still mired in the expensive, complex, and hard-to-support world of mainframes and their related technologies. Perhaps most damaging is the CA90s failure to address the problem of bad data in production systems. Given the problems of poor quality, incorrect formats, data not available, and so on, CA90s does not offer a viable alternative for transforming data into information for sustainable competitive advantage.

The Bottom Line

For the enterprise that wishes to conform to the model of a single database management system, to the concept of distributed databases, and to heavy use of the mainframe, CA90s offers an alternative information vision. For those who adopt the basic tenets of the EIT vision, Design, and Integration Model, CA90s has some serious problems.

ORACLE—THE PARALLEL SERVER

Oracle delivered the first commercial relational database system, and since then has aggressively sought to dominate the database industry. Its basic strategy is to offer ever greater functionality and performance while adapting its database engine to operate on dozens of hardware platforms and operating systems. To do that, it has developed a wide range of connectivity capabilities, user and developer tools, and business applications. As a result, Oracle is the leading supplier of database management software and services, and the third largest software company in the world.

Oracle has expanded the reach of its core relational database system by adapting it to operate on microprocessor-based, massively parallel computing environments. While targeted primarily at Business Automation needs that require very high levels of on-line transaction processing performance and reliability, the *Oracle Parallel Server* is nonetheless capable of supporting the massive information processing needs of the EIT Design.

Oracle Vision Overview

Oracle believes that to meet the business challenges of the 1990s, organizations must have a comprehensive information strategy that addresses all data processing requirements of the enterprise. Oracle addresses that situation by developing portable software products for database management, applications development, decision support, and office automation.

With the Oracle relational database system, organizations can integrate different computers, operating systems, networks, and database management systems into a seamless, enterprisewide computing and information resource. Oracle products provide organizations with complete information management solutions for cooperative computing. All of its products are open, portable, distributed, and integrated.

Open refers to Oracle's adherence to every major standard for databases, operating systems, networking protocols, and user interfaces, and to its provision of gateways to third-party products such as IBM's DB2. *Portable* refers to the ability of its database to operate on more than 80 hardware platforms. *Distributed* provides transparent access to Oracle databases anywhere in the corporate network with a single logical view. And *Integrated* refers to the interoperability of all Oracle's products, working together as a unified whole.

Oracle Generic and Infrastructure Technologies

Oracle's relational database system runs on microcomputers, minicomputers, and mainframes, either stand-alone or connected via industry-standard LANs and WANs. It has been most successful in enabling applications for the DEC VAX environment. The database has rapidly evolved from the somewhat limited world of minicomputers to where it can meet the requirements of enterprisewide database computing.

The Oracle Parallel Server is a version of Oracle's relational database system designed to take advantage of more complex computing arrangements. This allows Oracle to improve greatly its feeds and speeds, using technologies that break work into smaller increments for simultaneous processing. This, in turn, allows the handling of much larger databases (hundreds of gigabytes) and for serving larger and larger numbers of users (hundreds or thousands of users). The Parallel Server is being implemented on loosely coupled systems such as DEC's VAXcluster, Sequent, Pyramid, and IBM's S/390 Sysplex, and on massively parallel systems from NCR, nCUBE, Meiko, and Parsys.

The Oracle Parallel Server is a potentially excellent fit as the EIT's central database server. Because of its underlying technology, it promises excellent performance, capacity, and availability, with the additional benefits of modularity, sharability, connectivity, productivity, and price-performance. Because of its dedicated role as a database server (as compared to the mainframe), the Oracle Parallel Server is likely to deliver somewhat less functionality, reliability, and security.

Local database servers consist of the Oracle relational database system running on microprocessor systems using OS/2 or Unix, and tied to any of a number of popular LAN systems such as Novell or LAN Manager. The platforms could be any standard Intel system, such as IBM PS/2s or the smaller System 3000 models from NCR (or dozens of others). Client workstations are connected with the local and central database servers via Oracle's SQL*Net, a facility that communicates over all standard network configurations and protocols such as DECnet, TCP/IP, IBM's SNA, and ISO.

SQL*Connect provides user gateways to IBM's DB2 and DEC VAX files, allowing users concurrent access to information in Oracle and other databases. Further, with compliance to IBM's DRDA strategy, Oracle is positioned to provide direct links between its database engine and all IBM relational database systems (and those from similarly compliant vendors) under IBM's proprietary but important SNA environment.

This broad connectivity includes support of client workstations such as dumb DEC and IBM terminals, as well as PC DOS, OS/2, Macintosh, and Unix Desktop platforms. Oracle tools run under a variety of environments, such as character mode terminals, and GUI-based client workstations such as DOS Windows, OS/2 Presentation Manager, Macintosh OS, and Motif and DECWindows. Capabilities built using Oracle's toolkit can be moved among all of these environments. The Oracle RDBMS can also be operated on client DOS, OS/2, Macintosh, and Unix workstations.

Oracle has the ability to manage information designs that provide a repository, the CASE*Dictionary, for portable, multiuser access. Part of its CASE toolset, the repository generates applications by linking with Oracle's application generators. Oracle's technology is targeted at Business Automation development, and as such, is inadequate for meeting the more user-oriented, interactive nature of the EIT's Information Directory.

Oracle does not make use of expert systems technologies. It does, however, offer text management and retrieval capabilities by storing unstructured data types in the same Relational tables as traditional information. SQL*Retrieval extends SQL, providing a common language for text and standard business information. OracleCard allows DOS Windows and Macintosh users to integrate image, text, and other unstructured information with structured information at the desktop. It also supplies a powerful scripting language with hypertext capabilities.

Oracle Information Transformation Technologies

Oracle offers EIT information design capabilities only indirectly and as part of its CASE solution. These professional developer tools are tightly linked with the Oracle CASE*Dictionary and oriented primarily toward meeting Business Automation needs. As a result, Oracle provides only a minimum level of support for Information Design.

Oracle provides utilities for performing limited information re-engineering, for producing default physical database designs, for moving information definitions from one dictionary to another, and for comparing current information definitions to what actually exists in the database. Further, with SQL*Connect, information from DB2 source systems and others may be extracted for population to an Oracle database.

There is no provision for general information extraction and conditioning. Information populating and maintenance functions are performed by the basic engine. Advanced database intelligence functions, such as automatically invoked triggers and executing stored procedures in the database, are beginning to appear in the basic product.

Information navigation capabilities are modest due to the limited nature of the repository, with basic abilities such as reporting on the stored information definitions. Oracle offers its own set of information analysis capabilities, primarily for data access, report writing, and chart-making. These include SQL*Plus, SQL*ReportWriter, Oracle Graphics, OracleCard, SQL*QMX, Easy*SQL, SQL*Graph, SQL*Calc, Hyper*SQL, and SQL*Forms.

Text retrieval and hypertext capabilities already mentioned add a powerful dimension to this area. Oracle offers no capabilities for information discovery. Third-party tools that interface to Oracle include Borland's Paradox, Microsoft's Excel, Apple's Hypercard, Acius' 4th Dimension, Lotus 1-2-3, Blyth's Omnis 5, Silicon Beach's SuperCard, and many others.

Oracle Compliance with the EIT Integration Model

Given the Parallel Server, Oracle provides a very high level of compliance with the EIT Integration Model and its large-scale client/server architecture. It is based on industry-standard SQL and relational; it allows for the optimum balance of functional separation between client and server platforms; it separates tasks in a way that permits industry-standard connections and facilitates maximum choice; it operates in a basically heterogeneous and interactive environment. And while it doesn't directly control the platform it is used on (being portable in nature), it provides software that takes advantage of these microprocessor and network-based technologies.

Oracle supports the locating of its database engines in compliance with the distributed database model. Its technology is "neutral" enough to be deployed as a more-or-less true client/server architecture. Information copy and synchronization management between central and local database servers is not offered, but the use of common software, tools, and languages makes the creation of such capabilities feasible.

The Oracle Parallel Server places Oracle dead-center in the use of microprocessor technology to enable large-scale database computing and to meet enterprisewide needs for information with a single and replicated database solution. It is reasonable to assume that with initial success in the world of world-class Information Automation, Oracle will meet the needs for greater EIT-style capabilities.

Oracle General Observations

With the Parallel Server, Oracle becomes a viable alternative for enabling the EIT vision and Design. It offers attractive price-performance, extensibility, scalability, and openness. Given the current level of market acceptance of its relational database systems, Oracle is likely to find many takers for its approach. With it, Oracle can "ride the waves" of the new microprocessor parallel technologies, allowing Oracle the time and the experience to develop capabilities that round out a broader and more cohesive information vision.

Many, if not most, of the components for such a vision are already in Oracle's inventory in some form. If, however, Oracle chooses to concentrate its new technology exclusively on Business Automation (a large and profitable market), then Oracle will not be as successful in developing the solutions needed for serious Information Automation, and for achieving the high yields in exploiting a company's information asset.

The Bottom Line

If Oracle shakes off its minicomputer image and "one-size-fits-all" philosophy and concentrates on products that meet EIT requirements, its expertise in relational database management, in tools and applications, and in implementing business solutions, can be extremely important in providing workable and industry-standard solutions. If Oracle sees the possibilities as part of an EIT vision, it stands an excellent chance of articulating an exciting alternative to the hardware vendors.

BEHIND THE GLOWING VISIONS

Two important conclusions emerge when one looks at the vendor visions above. The first is that no vendor has articulated a vision as general or as comprehensive as the EIT vision put forth in this book. The second is that most of what they have in common is in what *they don't offer.* None offers on-line, real-time, user-based access to complex information objects for information design. No vendor is delivering comprehensive technologies that address general-purpose, user-augmentable information extraction and conditioning. Even the central role of an Information Directory is only partly acknowledged.

The fundamental EIT premise, the separation of automation for information versus production needs, is either ignored or minimized. True open connectivity and interoperability is given a great deal of lip service, with real support in only a few cases. And when it comes to embracing the enormous potential of the ubiquitous microprocessor, those vendors whose pasts are wedded to older technologies clearly shy away from the prospect.

What is it that these vendors are really offering? All of them, in one form or another (and with the possible exception of Teradata), are offering a vision of *distributed database computing.* Each is seeking to capture the high ground of microprocessor-based Business Automation, for owning the downsizing of business applications, either with proprietary or industry-standard technologies. As was seen early in this book, the distributed database model is only one vision. Even if it were the only vision, it is still a long way from being feasible for most companies. And when a vision of this type is asked to satisfy the needs of the EIT Design, there are some very big obstacles and problems to overcome.

Admittedly, much of the technology offered in these visions is relevant to the EIT vision. Rather, it is in the way their many components are "lashed" together that makes their applicability questionable. How useful these visions ultimately are in enabling the capabilities of the EIT Design will depend a great deal on which of two factors comes to dominate the motives of the technology-making and technology-using companies—the more objective cost-savings opportunities available from downsizing business applications; or the more subjective and competitive business-producing opportunities involved in Information Automation.

part V

IMPLEMENTING THE GENERAL INFORMATION SOLUTION

13

Establish the Implementation Environment

This chapter begins Part V, Implementing the General Information Solution, the fourth and last component of the EIT Enabling Framework. It provides a roadmap to establish EIT capabilities, and one that calls for a staged, pay-as-you-go implementation strategy, guided by a dynamic planning process that has business needs determining priorities and resource commitments.

The chapter offers ways to get EIT implementation moving. Chapter 14 discusses the steps for selecting and prototyping the most important information opportunity areas, and for justifying the EIT investment. Chapter 15 presents an approach for implementing the components of the EIT Design in a staged and incremental fashion.

IMPORTANT IMPLEMENTATION DIFFERENCES

Information technology practitioners have developed and in some cases perfected a pantheon of approaches, methods, and practices for implementing conventional systems. Many of these are useful, and some mandatory, for establishing EIT capabilities. However, organizations must not automatically adopt such approaches—at least not without understanding the inherent value and dangers.

Implementing Business Automation involves a series of the mostly linear tasks of planning, design, and installation. Once up and running, the formal implementation mode shifts to one of maintenance, as the system settles into ongoing operation. The scope of the system remains fixed in terms of its original requirements, functions, and users. Once in maintenance, mostly minor changes and fine-tunings are made. If radical and fundamental changes are needed, chances are excellent that the system will be replaced in its entirety.

In the realm of Information Automation, on the other hand, the scope of the EIT vision has no effective limits to its users' needs. Companywide in range and multipurpose in scope, it embraces requirements that emerge from anywhere and anyone, subject only to a general set of components and capabilities, and governed only by the relevant needs and policies of the business.

In this environment, users are constantly defining requirements, refining and extending information structures and definitions, testing working assumptions, prototyping different approaches, creating and altering complex requests and procedures—and not necessarily in any order. Some tasks are repetitive, others one-time in nature, still others performed only as needed. The redesign and enhancement of information, in particular, is ongoing.

There is a very strong sense of iteration and recycling in the EIT environment, a process that repeats and accumulates as new demands arrive, requirements change, and results are refined. Nor is there a clear demarcation between user and developer—today's information user is likely to be tomorrow's developer. Information solutions are as dynamic as the needs that caused them to come into existence. Planning becomes a matter of selecting from a set of intelligent reactions, instead of rigid, abstract, and discrete sequences.

Yet this is not chaos. There are a few critical anchor bolts that hold this constant swirl of activity fast and that give it a base for ongoing use and expansion. In addition to the EIT Design and Integration Model, there is the EIT *implementation roadmap.* This is a shared and common implementation process made up of the best of conventional practices and some new approaches, designed to sustain an organization seeking competitive advantage from its information asset.

PREPARING THE EIT GROUND

An organization must have the right environment for EIT implementation to take root and grow. These environmental underpinnings level-set the knowledge and opinions of members of the company and establish a common base of coordination. These initial actions (see Table 13-1, Creating a Favorable Implementation Environment) create the necessary momentum, aim efforts in the right direction, and keep the effort correctly oriented as conditions and players change. While there is never a guarantee of success, these actions help to minimize confusion, focus concentration, and assure conformity to the most critical EIT objectives and strategies.

FIND A POWERFUL CHAMPION

The EIT implementation program needs a champion, and it must be a senior executive, preferably the CEO. The closer the individual is to the operational seat of power, the greater the chances of success. Championed by a powerful CEO, and supported by programs that seek to improve quality, enhance customer-orientation,

TABLE 13-1   CREATING A FAVORABLE IMPLEMENTATION ENVIRONMENT

Find a powerful champion

Enlist the true information users

Create a tailored information vision

Establish a general information strategy

Put an effective information policy in place

Remake the information planning process

Provide the necessary incentives

Set tough but realistic expectations

Use appropriate controls

Assign implementation responsibilities

Head off the expected blockers

Guard against loss of momentum and complacency

and upgrade accountability, the plan for implementing EIT capabilities can turn slow, unimaginative, and ineffective organizations into business powerhouses.

ENLIST THE TRUE INFORMATION USERS

The best place to begin is with the primary users of information, those people responsible for realizing the goals of the business. The company must turn to these people to make progress in harnessing the power of its information asset.

But who are these people? They are certainly not the information technologists, the people who design and write programs, or who sell and supply technology. These professionals will have plenty to say on the subject but they're not the ones to start with. They're the *information suppliers.* Nor are the right people those folks in staff jobs, or that group of planning analysts down the hall, although they, too, use information a great deal and will almost surely have something to say. These people make their living from information, from gathering, manipulating, and presenting it to others. They're the *information manipulators.*

No, the information users who really count are those literally on the line—the only ones who understand the true value of information, who can correctly estimate the benefits, and who can commit to delivering those benefits. These users see information as clues, hints, and pointers to the problems and opportunities of the business. They're the *true information users,* the people who know where to begin, what information to collect, and how to proceed once the information is available. They at the ones who desperately need information to run their operations, make decisions, and sell and satisfy customers.

How does a company find them? They're the people who have been complaining about inadequate information the loudest and the longest. They are the people who have the most to gain from good information and are willing to pay for it. And they can commit to bottom-line business improvements from having that information.

CREATE A TAILORED INFORMATION VISION

Once those information users are identified, they must be encouraged to express their opinions, for there may be uncertainty, skepticism, or even resentment from past disappointments in this area. A working framework should be used to help them deal with the different information needs and approaches that will quickly emerge and vie for attention.

With the EIT Enabling Framework as that starting point, a company can validate and alter its baseline parameters to the known and expected information needs of the organization. That adaptation gives the company a solid base for creating a tailored information vision, one made up of high-priority information candidates, bold and relevant objectives, precise information requirements, a comprehensive design, and an attractive set of enabling technologies.

ESTABLISH A GENERAL INFORMATION STRATEGY

Critically important is the need to establish a general information strategy that articulates the company's Information Automation goals, values, and directions. This strategy will deal not only with the critical first implementation stages, but also with the broad implementation guidelines for moving the organization forward in a coherent and well-managed manner. Other important areas relating to strategy include the manner in which selection of information opportunities will occur, the use of resources, and the use of prototyping and rational justification methods for new applications.

PUT AN EFFECTIVE INFORMATION POLICY IN PLACE

The implementing organization must have an active policy that makes very concrete its commitment to a general information strategy, and that supports a multitrack, open development environment where Information Automation capabilities are implemented under a gradual and transitional approach based on business need. Technology professionals establish the information infrastructure upon which future capabilities are implemented by users.

A *multitrack process* enforces the notion that Information Automation is placed on its own track separate from Business Automation, that both tracks are pursued equally and are designed to converge long-term. Under this policy, each side uses the appropriate technologies and practices for building needed capabilities.

New business systems will not be designed to meet EIT needs, except insofar as they are an inherent part of the production system's requirements. Instead, new systems will be designed to meet standard EIT interfaces, and will add capabilities to provide more usable information for EIT users. Wherever possible, such systems should be designed to use an EIT's Information Database instead of creating and maintaining their own databases.

Open development refers to the manner in which new EIT capabilities are made available. It encourages an entrepreneurial approach to seizing new uses of information by giving business units the incentives (and means) to implement capabilities as part of their normal business responsibilities. In an open development environment, users move forward with both planned and unexpected information objectives, constrained only by common-sense justification practices and a single information infrastructure. As users become adept at implementing their own capabilities, the company will see several development efforts underway at one time, controlled and managed by each area in much the same way as other business activities are handled currently. Possible redundancies and inefficiencies are kept in check by the inherent reusability built into the EIT Design and by the central control of information by the information infrastructure itself.

The policy also calls for the establishment of a *basic information infrastructure by technology professionals*. Working under the management of a senior line executive, these people lay the technological groundwork to meet the identified business objectives of the first opportunity area *and* to provide the basis for a common information utility. Hence, this first implementation stage is overseen by senior management because its initial stage is critical to all future uses.

Once that initial capability is in place, further Information Automation moves forward in uneven increments according to *a gradual and transitional approach based on business need*. Each new capability builds on what has gone before, adding to or revising the contents of an EIT's Information Database. With more of the company's information available, each new requirement requires increasingly less effort, as users get immediately to the issues confronting them. As other users add to that central resource, all stand to benefit.

REMAKE THE INFORMATION PLANNING PROCESS

Planning the EIT implementation environment is a far more dynamic process than what occurs in Business Automation. Three-year formal statements of direction and meticulous action plans do not work well in the world of Information Automation, where changes in the business and the marketplace affect requirements drastically and immediately. Certainly, building the initial information infrastructure must be carefully planned. But once that is done, further development cannot be planned in the conventional sense, only sketched in the broadest of terms. And with users driving the process, things *really* get exciting. A company implementing EIT capabilities must establish a healthy tension between free-wheeling innovation and formal planning.

One approach is to cut planning down to size by delegating it to middle and business unit management to perform as they see fit. Another is to create flexible and changing review bodies that seek to share and coordinate the best of the proposed capabilities. Still another is to impose a minimum amount of formal central planning, perhaps limited to summary business cases regarding the proposed new capabilities and how they impact the company's larger goals and operations. Yet another approach is to remake the information technology planning process for the company (see Figure 13-1, An Open and Iterative EIT Planning Process).

In such an environment, top-down strategic and enterprisewide requirements are held in check by matching pressures from tactical, day-to-day requirements (as articulated by employees and line managers), opportunity-driven, tactical market and customer requirements (as articulated by outside agents and people on the front lines), and by constant assessments of new strategic possibilities in emerging technologies (as articulated by technology professionals and users).

The ideal EIT planning environment is based on a top-down guided, bottom-up activated approach that encourages maximum participation and loosely coordinated implementation. It relies heavily on user-managed efforts to set targets and priorities. The top-down guidance should deal primarily with getting the EIT implementation process off the ground and with providing the necessary policies and controls to see that the spirit of the process is maintained. Top-down direction should also include the ongoing identification of information areas of greatest competitive opportunity, and articulation of the company's general information strategy. Within that general framework, an EIT moves forward,

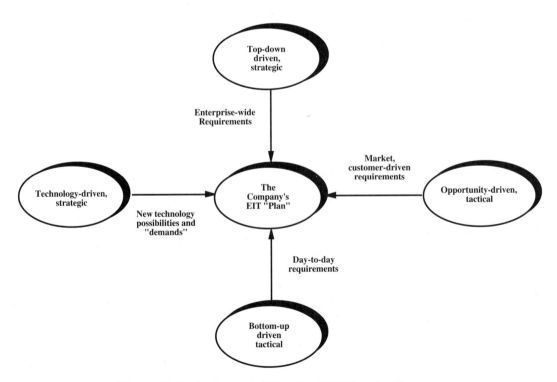

Figure 13-1. An Open and Iterative EIT Planning Process

dynamically influenced and altered by all the relevant forces—from the top, the bottom, and the sides.

PROVIDE THE NECESSARY INCENTIVES

Creating meaningful incentives is probably the single largest force for success. Each business enterprise must establish its own most appropriate incentives, keeping in mind that information should be viewed both as a means for seizing new opportunities and as a vehicle for better control of operations.

The most basic incentive is in enabling the use of information to drive business strategies, tactics, decisions, and organizational effectiveness. Another incentive is providing true information autonomy, wherein top management gives business units the authority and maneuvering room to deal with their own information requirements. Yet another incentive is providing serious funding assistance when one unit's efforts are expected to generate improvement beyond its immediate area, benefiting the company as a whole.

SET TOUGH BUT REALISTIC EXPECTATIONS

An important element in creating the right implementation environment is setting tough but realistic expectations. These are used to help judge the success of each information application, and for measuring progress against major objectives. A central expectation is that an EIT application be instrumental in achieving competitive advantage, and that a major business success is then directly attributed to that capability. Another expectation has to do with the level of success in accumulating and reusing Information Automation applications and related information, helping users by building on what exists. Still another expectation deals with empowering the user. Finally, there is the expectation that the use of information can help guide the application of all technologies in the company, providing greater accessibility and higher quality information.

USE APPROPRIATE CONTROLS

An attractive implementation approach permits users and organizations much latitude in determining the areas of information opportunity to exploit. Believing that the greater the overall participation, the greater the payback, a company exercises minimal control over information implementation and use. The areas where controls are appropriate are discussed below.

Applications and Technology Selection

Except for the initial application, applications selection is completely left to the judgment of each business unit. If Sales and Marketing wants to improve customer satisfaction through the use of Information Automation capabilities, that should be part of their business plan. If World-Wide Warehousing Operations wants on-line, real-time 24-hour-a-day distribution and inventory capabilities, that's a judgment for the head of that organization.

Technology selection, however, should be coordinated by flexible but effective guidelines. Some of these were mentioned in Part IV, especially the desirability of employing technologies that are open, industry-standard, and cost-effective. Information infrastructure and transformation technologies should be scrutinized by a peer-review process from the major organizations.

EIT information analysis and delivery technologies, however, should be left to the complete discretion of each using organization, subject only to a handful of general guidelines and standards. An advanced technology review capability should be established to keep the company up-to-date on new capabilities and developments, either performed by an internal group or by an outside organization.

Justification and Funding

Justification and funding of EIT capabilities must also be left to each using organization, since it will be asked to justify and pay for the cost of new capabilities. However, in the case of the EIT infrastructure and initial application areas, a rational business case must be completed, as its scope exceeds the boundaries of any one organization, and funding will probably be provided by corporate sources.

Design and Installation

The design and installation of the EIT infrastructure and the initial application is managed by key users and technologists under the control of the primary business unit head. The manager should be as high up the chain of command as possible, and the project should be independent of existing Business Automation standards and practices. Once that base is implemented, management of the design and installation of new capabilities will be provided by flexible controls appropriate and natural to the enterprise, with basic responsibility for development in the hands of the user.

Ongoing Support

Controls for supporting the EIT capability should be limited to major functional components and to information itself. *Support for technology components* should be exercised to ensure full availability of changes and upgrades as they occur. This can be performed by technology specialists. As organizations implement applications, *the control of the information resource* is provided mostly by the infrastructure itself and by "information ombudsmen" and "information architects." Information, already captured and available for exploitation, is used freely, subjected only to simple, common-sense controls.

Unnecessary or grossly inefficient approaches, however, should be prevented. Information conflict management, automatic aging, archiving, validating information meanings and usages—these and other capabilities provide an ever-vigilant control of information. A growing dependence on the information resource also tends to create a self-regulating process. Information quality will improve as users subject information to constant use, increasing the demand for ever greater integrity, meaning, and availability.

Controlling access to information involves adequate safeguards that do not hamper legitimate access. These safeguards should be established through the use of information-user authorization controls, although an EIT's information contents should be open to any interested employee. Except for obviously sensitive areas, access to information should be virtually unlimited. There should be no monitoring or tracking of use, except by those individuals who manage the performance of the overall infrastructure. There must be as much concern for *opening* access to information as there is for *limiting* it.

ASSIGN IMPLEMENTATION RESPONSIBILITIES

EIT implementation requires the melding of skills of several types of business, information, and technology professionals. The people in charge of selecting, justifying, and implementing applications are the line business executives, the ones best equipped to provide the authority and accountability to be successful. This is especially pertinent in managing the delivery of the first application area. The responsibility for the definition, content, and quality of the information resides with the users in each business area. Professional technologists are responsible for designing and integrating the core EIT capabilities in concert with users.

HEAD OFF THE EXPECTED BLOCKERS

No matter how much consensus appears to exist, for an initiative as far reaching and as fundamental as this one, every company will find itself with a small army waiting to detour or derail the effort at the first opportunity. It is critical to understand who these people are, what motivates them, and how a company may anticipate and head them off.

On the Business Side

On the business side, resistance from managers and executives—to doing business differently, to relying more heavily on hard facts to run the business—will be a major problem in implementation. Managers with an excessive reliance on personal style or intuition will refuse to accept the larger role of information in making decisions and in managing performance. Part of this is due to failure to perceive the true value of information; part to the leveling effect of information, as anyone with intelligence can use information to second-guess decisions made in the heat of battle. A good part of the resistance is due to a certain safety factor that exists in making decisions without all needed information. While executives beg for better information, they are also protected by the lack of it, an excuse for those (inevitable) poor decisions.

There is also resistance to changing at all. People will ask, "Why fix things if they're not broken?" "What if changing makes things worse?" "What's so bad about the way things are now?" There is validity in these concerns, especially if a company is not hurting a lot, if it is coasting along and meeting its numbers with little pressure from customers, competitors, or shareholders. But if there is pain, if it appears that things are not all that right, then this resistance can be deadly. It can be a major force for paralysis and blindness—until the pain gets so bad that action has to be finally taken, despite all the fears and excuses. Of course, by then the cure may be too late to do any good.

There is also likely to be resistance by management to the idea of aggressive use of information technology, perhaps because executives are uncomfortable with it or because they have been misled before. Finally, there are executives who will resist this kind of program because they really don't want to know the facts, because they really don't want to know what's going on. If they did, perhaps, they would be forced to take action. These managers live at the pinnacle of the status quo, albeit a false and dangerous one.

On the Technical Side

While the apparent threat to the status quo from an EIT capability appears greatest from those whose responsibilities are most affected by information, the large and powerful information systems groups—the MIS departments—will also resist implementation. Basically, MIS is an organization chartered to uphold the current technology order.

Chapter 2 looked at the inadequate and even misleading practices found in almost every MIS department. These attitudes not only prevent skilled people from helping users meet their needs for information; they also serve to resist any approach that threatens their own status quo. The EIT approach threatens MIS with new information technology paradigms. For example:

- Current systems keep MIS in charge of information; EIT hands it to the user.
- There is an MIS penchant for expensive and long-term programs; EIT proceeds in controlled and incremental steps.
- MIS manages things according to rigorous methodologies; EIT uses just enough to keep information at the highest level of usability.
- MIS wants to ration information; EIT wants to maximize its availability.
- MIS wants to plan the future; EIT believes in dynamic planning and in responding to challenges as they happen.
- MIS wants to centralize processing (or decentralize processing); EIT wants to centralize information and decentralize processing.
- MIS doesn't trust users to understand their information needs; EIT lives and dies by the user.

These contrasts, while certainly not true for every company, help explain why MIS is likely to resist an EIT implementation. Even more than the PC revolution, an EIT capability promises a revolution in the use of automation. A few technology vendors have grasped this sea-change: they no longer sell to MIS managers, but direct their marketing at users, line managers, and CEOs.

Among the Dreaded Formalists

Finally, there is a class of blocker that isn't so much threatened by an EIT as it is simply opposed to what it stands for on principle. These are the *formalists,* people who vigorously insist on stale formulas and set-in-stone ways. Many of the EIT approaches appear heretical and dangerous to these people, taught, as they have been, to believe only in the known, the logical, and the precise.

Formalists may be accountants, planners, staff analysts, technologists, statisticians, and occasionally executives. They are well-meaning but overly structured minds who impose inappropriate and process-threatening approaches before allowing a program to move forward. These are people caught up in the rigid thinking associated with the controller mentality—to protect rather than to provide. This is the kind of thinking that limits the availability of information and the means for using it in the interest of protecting its integrity and privacy.

Also in this category are people who resist any attempt that stretches the "feasibility envelope." These are the laggards, people who are content to wait forever for definitive proof before taking that all-important first step. When dragged kicking and screaming into a new technology, they take just as long to accept it. They are also the ones found praising the benefits of a technology long after it is ten years out-of-date (laggards, lost sheep, and the thundering herd will be discussed in a larger context in the last chapter).

GUARD AGAINST LOSS OF MOMENTUM AND COMPLACENCY

Once a certain degree of success has been obtained, it is not unlikely that there will be a momentary loss of forward movement. The organization still has to: absorb the impacts of recently completed implementation; make sense of what has occurred; and permit a changing of the guard as players shift responsibilities. In addition, a more serious problem prevents a company from moving forward—confusion about how to best capitalize on the initial information success. This lapse can widen into a general failure to move forward at all, and perhaps a falling back into isolated and conventional approaches that limit an EIT program to a one-application or single-purpose existence. At a minimum, a second area of opportunity should be anticipated from the beginning.

Another danger is that early success leads to a paucity of desire to move forward altogether, perhaps because the prime movers, their immediate information agenda satisfied, believe that the major advantages have been obtained and additional efforts will not be worthwhile. This complacency prevents further exploitation of the information resource, serves to hoard the newfound benefits and advantages, and invalidates the underlying premise of the EIT vision.

Failure to keep an alert stance and to insist on forward movement, no matter how incremental, may result in top management losing its interest and allowing an unsympathetic organization to assert control over the system. Until an EIT capability is an integral part of an enterprise, management cannot afford to take its collective eye off the Information Automation ball.

14

Prototype and Justify the Implementation

With the general EIT environment prepared for implementation, the next stages involve selecting and prototyping the information opportunity that appears most likely to create important benefits. This targeted area will be the basis for establishing core infrastructure and transformation functions. With success of the prototype, the implementing organization is in a position to justify the overall investment in the EIT implementation.

SELECT THE MOST ATTRACTIVE INFORMATION OPPORTUNITY

Selecting the correct initial information opportunity area (information opportunities were reviewed in Part II) is critical to the success of implementation, because that area will be the primary factor in whether the firm will be successful in creating important competitive benefits. Smart targeting of the first area is also important because it is essential in establishing the cornerstone capabilities needed for leveraging the information resource for use in other areas as well.

It is therefore important that the targeted application be one that requires a wide swath of rich and detailed information. This is information captured at the most detailed level (or one notch up from that), and it is almost always the basic transaction of the business—in banking, the ATM and teller transaction; in a utility, the basic service used and billed; in insurance, the policy premium and claims activity; in transportation, the basic travel ticket; in retail, the POS transaction.

High-volume consumer-related businesses, almost certainly equipped with automatic scanning and collection devices, have an inherent advantage in getting started, for they must collect these massive amounts of detailed information to run their businesses. They have an excellent basis for creating a solid core of a central information resource with their first application, whether it be targeted to marketing, customer purchase tracking, inventory and logistics control, or some other business function. Knowledge of their business can come from this rich stock of information.

For those who lack the business need and justification for collecting detailed information, they must incur the cost of gathering it. That must be either an act of faith, or, preferably, part of a carefully-justified strategic effort.

BUILD A PROTOTYPE

Prototyping helps to assure a company that the first area selected for implementation and the general approach will work. It tests important notions about the value of transforming existing data, the feasibility of the design and selected technologies, and the problems and costs to be encountered once underway. It delivers concrete results quickly, creating a spotlight under which important premises and assumptions can be viewed more clearly.

While company management is obviously concerned with creating capabilities for a major business area—new account marketing for a bank credit card company, for example, or consumer behavior analysis for a retailer, telephone company, or utility—this approach calls for first building a prototype that focuses on a critical subset of the application. This approach quickly tests the core functionalities and technology performance issues before it implements the larger and final version. An adequate prototype, probably a throwaway, should not take more than a few months to build, yet it must be capable of providing insights into the problems and payoffs of EIT implementation.

Once the implementation team is assembled, it proceeds to lay out the specific objectives and deliverables that constitute successful completion of the prototype. It makes initial judgments about the information needed, the processing required, the technologies of greatest value, and the time frames involved.

Only the information needed to satisfy a subset of the initial application will be placed in the prototype database, although the Business Information Model will have all the hooks for future relationships and structures. Functional capabilities will be limited to those identified as critical to the application. With success of the prototype, these capabilities will be either rebuilt, built anew, or retrofitted by fine-tuning and expansion. The steps for implementing the application prototype are described below.

Kickoff

Made up of the implementation team, the sponsoring line executive, and the responsible technology executive, the kickoff assures there is unanimity and shared purpose among the participants. Expectations, formal and otherwise, are expressed and documented, preliminary business objectives and tradeoffs are reviewed and updated, a basic timetable developed, and approval and policy authorizations laid down. This group will meet at the completion of the prototype, expected to be no more than six to eight months in length, to evaluate results.

Define Applications Requirements

Using team-building workshops, this activity defines the information required to satisfy the objectives of the application. It creates a view of information that corresponds to the way business professionals look at that part of the company. It is articulated with little regard for implementation, and provides the starting point for the application. The problem is put clearly in focus. This step builds consensus as initial awareness is raised, feasibility determinations are made, and mechanisms for review and guidance put in place.

The workshops identify the most pressing questions about the applications area and the critical decisions that need support. The members identify what information is needed to answer those questions and to promote effective decisions. Laying this information out in the form of columns, rows, and tables, the team adds information about volumes and dynamics, creating a complete information statement. Decisions are made about the scope and level of information needed to meet the objectives of the application. If the application is to be the basis for a buyer decision support system, for example, this statement will contain the rationale and approach needed to support the buyer organization in a different manner than the current one. It will indicate that the application will provide information to help buyers focus on better markdown management, better next-season planning, quicker discovery of out-of-stock conditions, better understanding of new product introductions, greater leverage in vendor negotiations, and more comprehensive, automatic, and precise tracking of regional, district, store, and item performance.

The basis for the application's design is established at this point—the requirements that will be used to construct the Business Information Model. This step also builds the base for the EIT Justification Model, pinpointing specific payoffs, and having the responsible line executive place defendable dollar estimates on the value of the application. It documents these benefits along with the identified business and information requirements.

Order Prototyping Technologies

Working with the EIT Design and Integration Model, the technologies needed for the first application are decided upon and prototype components are ordered. This includes technology needed for core EIT hardware and software components and the means for connecting them.

For example, the technologies employed in the prototype will most likely be limited to a small version of the central database server, connections to one or two LANs, and perhaps a half-dozen client workstations. EIT infrastructure capabilities will probably be restricted to core functions, such as relational database, industry-standard GUIs, and user information views, and perhaps limited object technologies. EIT transformation functions will have capabilities considered essential for prototyping, such as rudimentary extraction and conditioning programs, and standard analysis tools such as 4GLs and SQL front-ends. None of these functions need to be full-functioned or general-purpose at this stage.

Accurately sizing the central database server is an important requirement, for the implementation team must ensure there will be sufficient capacity to handle the volume of information expected in the application. A technology implementation plan, including diagrams, identified devices and functions, network addresses, and other descriptions, is produced, along with delivery dates that coincide with the prototype schedule. Operational benchmarks using live production information may be performed off-site at this time.

Design Information Structures and Model

The Business Information Model is reworked with an eye towards implementation. Users and designers work through their understanding of the information and decide how to construct an organized and detailed model. This analysis includes the transformation needed to extract and condition information from source systems.

At the same time, an effort is made to establish the major points of connection between the segments of information needed by this application and other information areas and segments. These connections become the hooks mentioned earlier, the basis for integration of information in the first application with other information sectors as implementation continues. For example, if the first application starts with current quarter activity, later extensions may incorporate additional months and information elements. Or a subsequent application may need to link sales activity to warehouse inventory information to manage product distribution.

However, no attempt is made to model all business and functional areas of the company. As discussed earlier, that objective will be accomplished over time by the incremental addition of information segments as part of each new application. The idea of an exclusive top-down information modeling process (like top-down planning) is anathema to the EIT approach.

Install Prototyping Technologies

The ordered prototype technology is installed. Network, workstation, and server setups are performed based on the technology implementation plan established earlier. Software is installed on the hardware. Tests are made to validate connectivity and functionality. Personnel are assigned to support the technology. Initial versions of the prototype are run to validate the configuration.

Build and Test the Prototype

At this point, users test the prototype. The Business Information Model is subjected to query, navigation, and manipulation. This is followed by tests of extraction and conditioning. Changes in specifications and rules are constantly made as the full extent of the source data and its quality is unveiled. Unexpected problems with the information are almost certain to occur, with new functionality added as needed. Finally, a workable version of the information is established and testing of the information analysis functions commence.

While this is going on, technologists are testing basic infrastructure capabilities, such as database management and control, objects management by the Information Directory, performance and quality measures, operating issues, links to the source systems, and so on. When both groups are ready, a series of complete tests are run, successively adjusting and refining the application and underlying components. Preliminary business, operational, and technical results are compiled and reviewed. Flags, red and green, are posted as results start coming in.

Fine-tune the Prototype

Reviews are held to study the initial results. Additional tuning and adjusting may be necessary before final conclusions can safely be drawn and presented to management. Surprises, positive or otherwise, are discussed and hopefully resolved. Interim results that may have use in the business are released with the necessary caveats. Tuning goes on until results and performance are satisfactory, or if not, until future corrections are defined. All this is documented and validated with vendors and experts in their respective areas.

EVALUATE PROTOTYPE

The group from the kickoff meets to review the prototype results. Original expectations are compared to reality, application results are checked against the business case and updated, the actual timetable is compared against the planned one, and issues of implementation policy are assessed. Cost and operational issues are also reviewed, with new projections made for applications implementation. Recommendations are discussed and the following answered: Were the prototype objectives met? Did the technology work? Did the prototype validate the concept of the application? Were there surprises, and are any of them potentially fatal to the overall effort? And is it reasonable to believe that the general benefits from an EIT implementation will be forthcoming if the program continues?

JUSTIFY THE EIT INVESTMENT

With the prototype results arguing for success in achieving implementation objectives, the next step is to build a convincing business case. Justifying the investment requires a rational business case that takes qualitative and organizational enabling benefits into account without ignoring traditional ROI and cost/benefit analysis. This expanded business case blends strategic, economic, and alternatives analysis, while accounting for expected benefits, costs, and risks.

Using technology to exploit information for greater business advantage requires new paradigms of business justification, in which enlightened risk balancing dominates the decision. There is a need to recognize the importance of taking greater risks for important "soft" business opportunities. Investing in an EIT capability, partly because of its potential for delivering unexpected effects and benefits, must be anchored in a more open-ended, flexible, and tolerant justification model.

EIT Strategic Analysis

While the strategic application of technology generally delivers large impacts only with commensurate risk, strategic bets are often the smart bets. Strategic justification of an EIT capability requires that executives develop, validate, acknowledge, and commit to achieving the benefits they believe will follow its implementation.

These benefits may be mostly quantitative, as when a line executive states "there will be a three percent increase in overall market share within nine months of rollout." Or they may be chiefly qualitative, as when that same executive adds that "no matter the cost, without this capability the company is putting itself at a serious competitive disadvantage. This system is a strategic necessity."

There are great difficulties in evaluating proposals that promise strategic impact. If a venture is attractive to one firm, it is probably attractive to competitors. Since technology is readily acquired or copied, unless it can be used in conjunction with other unique assets (as when it produces a significant barrier to competition), it is unlikely to be sustainable. Given that, the benefits will not endure; they may even backfire. Yet, the temporary benefits may still be worth the investment.

EIT capabilities hold the promise of large beneficial impact with relatively little risk. Further, because of their general-purpose nature, they have the potential for sustaining those important benefits, primarily by accumulating power, sophistication, and knowledge. If this is used by a company to leverage key assets not readily available to competitors (market dominance, scale of operations, diversity of capabilities and so on), there is an excellent likelihood that the benefits will be large and sustainable.

A company needs a reliable way to assess the true strategic payoffs of EIT implementation. Management needs to understand how the application of that information technology can provide strategic advantages that help it to meet its critical objectives. This will include clarifying the technical and managerial factors, and accurately assessing the hard and soft costs and benefits.

If an EIT implementation can be linked to a critical business strategy, such as was true for Smarter Stores, its strategic value is more obvious and substantiable, taking justification from the program's business attractiveness. If this is not possible, then an EIT implementation must have its own rational basis for strategic justification. This would include the benefits and costs of the initial application, any identifiable follow-on applications, as well any important generic benefits.

EIT Economic Analysis

In addition to justifying an EIT on strategic factors, it is important to make an economic business case. Standard cost/benefit analysis is the most fundamental method. It estimates savings brought by the investment and incorporates the value of money, invested and saved over time, to provide a measure of rate of return. It is especially effective when used to decide issues involving saving money or avoiding costs.

Economic analysis can be used to assess more qualitative factors, such as weighing the cost of an investment against the benefits of better decisions, higher quality products and services, and improved customer satisfaction. An EIT has some very definite quantifiable cost and benefit aspects, especially those that deal with the different financial, operational, and technical areas.

Quantifiable *financial benefits* could include increases in revenue, profit, book value, and shareholder value. *Operational benefits* might be shorter product delivery times, higher rates of customer acquisition and retention, increases in market share, or reduction in complaints and support services. *Technical benefits* might include reducing the costs of technological operations and equipment, increased functionality, and higher levels of performance.

EIT Alternatives Analysis

All programs have alternatives. EIT implementation must include an assessment of its viability compared to other alternatives. A rigorous analysis of alternatives helps a company better understand the value of a proposed capability and whether to support it. There may, for example, be an interest in expanding current Business Automation capabilities or in creating an Information Center. Others within the company might lobby for distributing information to local departments as part of an effort to downsize business applications. Still others might argue for better tools to manipulate information in production systems.

Management must review each of these proposals individually and against the others, judging the merits of each against their basic business case, issues of technical and functional quality, the enterprise's priorities and goals, and assessments of different technology strategies. Each alternative is weighed and given measures that represent its potential value to the company. The alternatives are then ranked. The decision to proceed with a particular alternative does not need to be positive in absolute terms; it just must be superior to the others.

THE EIT JUSTIFICATION MODEL

Since traditional justification does not give full credit to an EIT vision's radical enabling capabilities, an organization must use creative justification to assess its likely impact and value. An EIT Justification Model includes a statement of the company's business strategies, its critical success factors, and key performance measures. It explains how an EIT capability supports them and includes a statement of its key enabling capabilities. EIT Justification is accomplished by making quantitative and qualitative assessments of the benefits, costs, and risks associated with implementation.

EIT Benefit Analysis

Benefit assessment includes both hard and soft measures, so that savings in mainframe processing can be pegged at a fairly hard value, whereas the worth of improving the quality of decision-making is likely to be far less precise. Management must put their best estimates on the value of these benefits, especially on the all-important business benefits. For example, what's it worth (in revenue and in margins) to seize opportunities that improve customer satisfaction and retain customers? What should the company estimate is its worth (on the bottom line) to facilitate management decision-making capabilities that over the long-term help to increase revenues, raise profit levels, and push up shareholder values?

Since each company's EIT implementation will vary, several benefit checklists are offered: business financial, business operational, informational, technology financial, and technology operational. These checklists are listed in five tables, with the items intended to be more suggestive than comprehensive or final. The reader will want to refer to earlier sections of the book for a fuller treatment of benefits.

Business financial and *operational benefits* are listed in Tables 14-1 and 14-2. *Informational benefits* are equivalent to the idea of receiving a return on the information asset and are shown in Table 14-3. *Technology financial benefits* derive their effect from enabling technologies such as those discussed in Chapters 10 and 11, and are described in Table 14-4. The same is true for *technology operational benefits,* this last category an example of a company's return on its technology asset (described in Table 14-5).

EIT Cost Analysis

Most EIT implementation costs are incurred up-front, absorbed in prototyping, building the first application, and implementing core technologies for the information infrastructure. It is during this initial phase that the basic hardware and software are installed and tested, and the transformation software designed and put to use.

If a company already has most of the basic components (relational database, interconnected LANs, client workstations, information analysis technologies, and

TABLE 14-1   EIT BUSINESS FINANCIAL BENEFITS

Increasing revenue from current sources

Generating new sources of revenue

Improving gross and profit margins

Improving book value and shareholder value

TABLE 14-2   EIT BUSINESS OPERATIONAL BENEFITS

Improving general responsiveness to change

Accelerating communications flows and reporting relationships

Surpassing competitive offerings

Raising customer satisfaction levels

Raising rates of customer acquisition and retention

Reducing customer complaints

Improving distribution and inventory management

Increasing employee productiveness

Providing drill-down executive information

Providing information access for running the business

Improving management decision making and control

Increasing market share

Improving merchandising capabilities

Downsizing or resizing the organization structures

Increasing personnel motivation and expertise

Increasing product and service quality levels

Shortening new product delivery times

Improving tactical responsiveness

so on), the initial costs will be considerably less. Subsequent costs will then be incurred for incremental expansion of capabilities beyond that first application, some of which represent new costs, and others possibly considered part of ongoing operating costs. For example, adding new information to the Information Database and proceeding to transform that new information is executed by the information user and can be considered part of normal working responsibilities. The cost of extracting and conditioning information is relatively minor compared to the costs of acquiring it in the first place. Additional storage capacity will be required, as will information processing cycles. But these are relatively minor costs and will generally not require new hardware.

If, however, a major business area is added, it would certainly involve major new costs for workstations, LANs, expansion and connectivity attachments, and possibly new software. Also, costs beyond the first phase must include any expenses incurred for upgrades or additions of new EIT functions, applications, and technologies.

TABLE 14-3   EIT INFORMATIONAL BENEFITS

Accessibility

Greater accuracy

More adaptability

Greater availability

Fewer copies

Greater consistency

More flexibility

More integratable

Improved integrity

Greater meaning

Richer organization

Higher relatability

Greater sharability

More timely

Greater usability

TABLE 14-4   EIT TECHNOLOGY FINANCIAL BENEFITS

Simplifying the business automation development process

Reducing administrative support

Reducing data administration costs

Reducing disk space (say, from 25 to 2 copies)

Cost avoidance or deferral due to modularity

No displacement costs by using existing information sources and systems

Mainframe processing offload

Requiring less people to support

Preserving existing information and skills investments

More efficient performance on special-purpose platforms

Excellent price-performance from low-cost microprocessor-based technology

Greater user productivity from faster response times, etc.

TABLE 14-5   EIT TECHNOLOGY OPERATIONAL BENEFITS

Reducing application backlog for information automation

Providing automatic and unsupervised operations

Greater connectivity by integrating existing heterogeneous hardware platforms

Effective capitalizing on existing computers and expertise

Simplified distribution of information processing

Simplifying coordination and administration of information

Improving modularity by smaller, lower-cost upgrades with less disruption

Improving performance by the use of dedicated platforms and divided work loads

Improving productivity by ease of use, simpler operations, and greater power

Providing processing expansion linearity

Increasing reliability by automatic recoverability and fault tolerance

Improving response time

Enhancing standardization by effective using of open technologies

Enhancing system availability

Improving throughput times

Providing uninterrupted operations

Enabling comprehensive user capabilities

An EIT implementation's total cost includes: (1) the costs for the initial application and core infrastructure, (2) the costs for major new application areas, (3) the costs for major functional or technological expansion, and (4) the costs (generally minor or none) for each user application. (For a larger list of cost areas, see Table 14-6, EIT Cost Factors.)

The total cost of an EIT capability should be spread over its life cycle, a period possibly as long as 15 years. Since that is not acceptable financial practice, it is necessary to have the first application justify the entire cost. Once justified, subsequent use of that infrastructure requires no additional major expense and is essentially free, except, as noted above, for major increases in function, capacity, or technology.

The EIT Justification Model must also compare the operating costs of EIT capabilities against the costs of current Information Automation applications. In such a comparison, the costs of doing business in the inefficient, ad hoc, one-at-a-time world of conventional automation will stand out starkly. These include the costs of building and operating each and every extract system, and the efforts to make changes for new requirements as they occur. The cost of duplication of effort

TABLE 14-6   EIT COST FACTORS

General cost factors
Costs to achieve EIT implementation Costs if prevented from doing so: Lost business opportunity costs and current Information Automation costs
Implementation cost factors
Costs for infrastructure: equipment, software, installation and testing Costs for initial application: definition, design, prototyping and implementation Costs for major subsequent applications Costs for major functional or technological expansion Costs (minor or none) for each "user application" User training or retraining costs Disruption costs due to transition to an "information-based environment"
Operating cost factors (replaces costs of current methods)
User information transformation costs Productivity costs (professional staff eliminated or reduced)

and reconciliation between competing versions of information must be factored in as well.

When the costs to produce EIT capabilities with current approaches are calculated, the contrast is even more dramatic. It is conceivable that current methods would break down entirely after several hundred extracts, or else make it increasingly expensive for each new requirement. In any case, there is no improvement in cost reduction from extract to extract—each must start from scratch, whereas an EIT capability becomes more cost-effective with greater use.

In completing the cost picture, the analysis must take into account the costs of undertaking the program versus the costs of being frozen out of future opportunities. A company must size the costs to the business of not being able to respond effectively to business opportunities and challenges as they occur. This is, of course, a much less quantifiable type of cost assessment, and perhaps anecdotal evidence may help to drive home the true costs of not having an EIT capability. Losing one critically important business opportunity (such as an emerging new market segment), or winning over a customer from a competitor (through superior responsiveness), can more than justify the entire cost of an EIT capability.

EIT Risk Analysis

EIT implementation, like any large, innovative undertaking, entails risks, some subject to analysis and planning, others outside the limits of predictive abilities (see Table 14-7, EIT Risk Factors). The risk of proceeding must be first tested against the risk of not making the investment. As with a yes decision, there are many dimensions to a no decision. Continuing to rely on inadequate information and ineffective automation means handicapping the company in its ability to wage economic war with competitors, and in its effectiveness to deliver greater growth, profit, and earnings.

TABLE 14-7   EIT RISK FACTORS

Extended risk factors

The risk of not proceeding
Systemic risk by introducing unexpected changes
Environmental risk due to uncertainties

Traditional risk factors

Financial risk
Technical risk
Implementational risk
Functional risk

Given that proceeding is preferable, a closer look at the risks of implementing an EIT capability is necessary. In general, the level of risk corresponds to the level of return. The reason why EIT implementation has a potential for high risk is not so much due to traditional risk factors (financial, technical, etc.), but for the very reason it has such potential in the first place—its potential for impact is so deep and far-ranging that no one can accurately estimate its true outcomes. Thus, EIT implementation has its greatest risk in the unknown effects it brings in its wake, where its own success may lead to new assumptions about needs, costs, benefits, and strategies. It is often in such success that the rules are so changed and the conditions so altered that the very accomplishment leads to effects that may negate or diminish the gained improvements.

Allied with the risk of unexpected effects is the risk of environmental uncertainty, of radical shifts in the business and market. Although one of an EIT's objectives is to seize value from information to help it deal with rapid and profound change, nonetheless, shifts in technology and business practices can surprise even those targeting the phenomenon of change itself.

Traditional dangers are not as major for EIT implementation. *Financial risks* exist where the costs for new capabilities are greater than the value of the benefits realized or provided. The costs for EIT implementation should be quite attractive, at least when compared to the expected benefits or to building comparably sized Business Automation systems. Financial risk is also minimized because implementation is pursued in small, self-justifying steps.

Technical risks arise where the proposed capabilities cannot be feasibly supported by current technologies. It was seen in Part IV that feasible technologies exist to support EIT capabilities, and in fact, they offer significant power and effectiveness over what is being employed today to perform similar abilities. An EIT capability is based on technologies that are both available and proven. There is no element or component that has not been used in comparably sized situations or under similar levels of demand.

Implementation risks are present where the system simply cannot be completed, either because it is too complex, expensive, or large, or it is beyond the skills of the developers. The risks of EIT implementation should be quite small because most of the capabilities are acquired rather than developed. Its implementation is based on incremental design and development, to be built and used when people are ready and technologies available. It also benefits by enlisting the capabilities of an army of users who know their needs and will devote the energy to making it happen.

Functional risks come into play when implemented capabilities do not meet the needs of the business, being either wrong, out-of-date, or inappropriate. An EIT capability is especially resistant to functional risks. In fact, its guiding motivation is to provide the ability to meet unanticipated needs for information. Even if requirements demand information beyond the range of an EIT's information capabilities, it is poised to accept new information when available.

As in any large implementation program, all areas of risk, traditional and extended, must be actively managed. These include issues such as deciding when specific capabilities are to be available, how they should be achieved, where the effort should begin, and who should be responsible for developing them.

15

Implement the General Information Solution

This chapter presents strategies for implementing EIT capabilities. These strategies include charting the company's *implementation vectors* and constructing a staged and incremental approach for moving forward on several implementation fronts. Such implementation must not only respond to business needs and priorities, it must also satisfy EIT objectives as well. The chapter makes a strong case for starting immediately down the yellow brick road to a companywide information capability, and for building the competitive capabilities needed to survive and prosper in today's marketplace.

CHART THE EIT IMPLEMENTATION VECTORS

There are five vectors or dimensions involved in EIT implementation. (Figure 15-1, EIT Implementation Vectors, shows the vectors for a consumer goods manufacturing company.) These are: the information opportunity areas (the applications vector), the information subject areas needed to support those applications (the information vector), the users or functions supported (the organization vector), the capabilities needed to support those users and applications (the functions vector), and the computing and communications resources needed to support these other vectors (the technology vector).

Each of these vectors needs to be understood and factored into the implementation program at different stages and levels of fulfillment, for each contains its own set of priorities, sequences, and considerations that must be part of the overall program. As implementation moves the EIT program along these vectors,

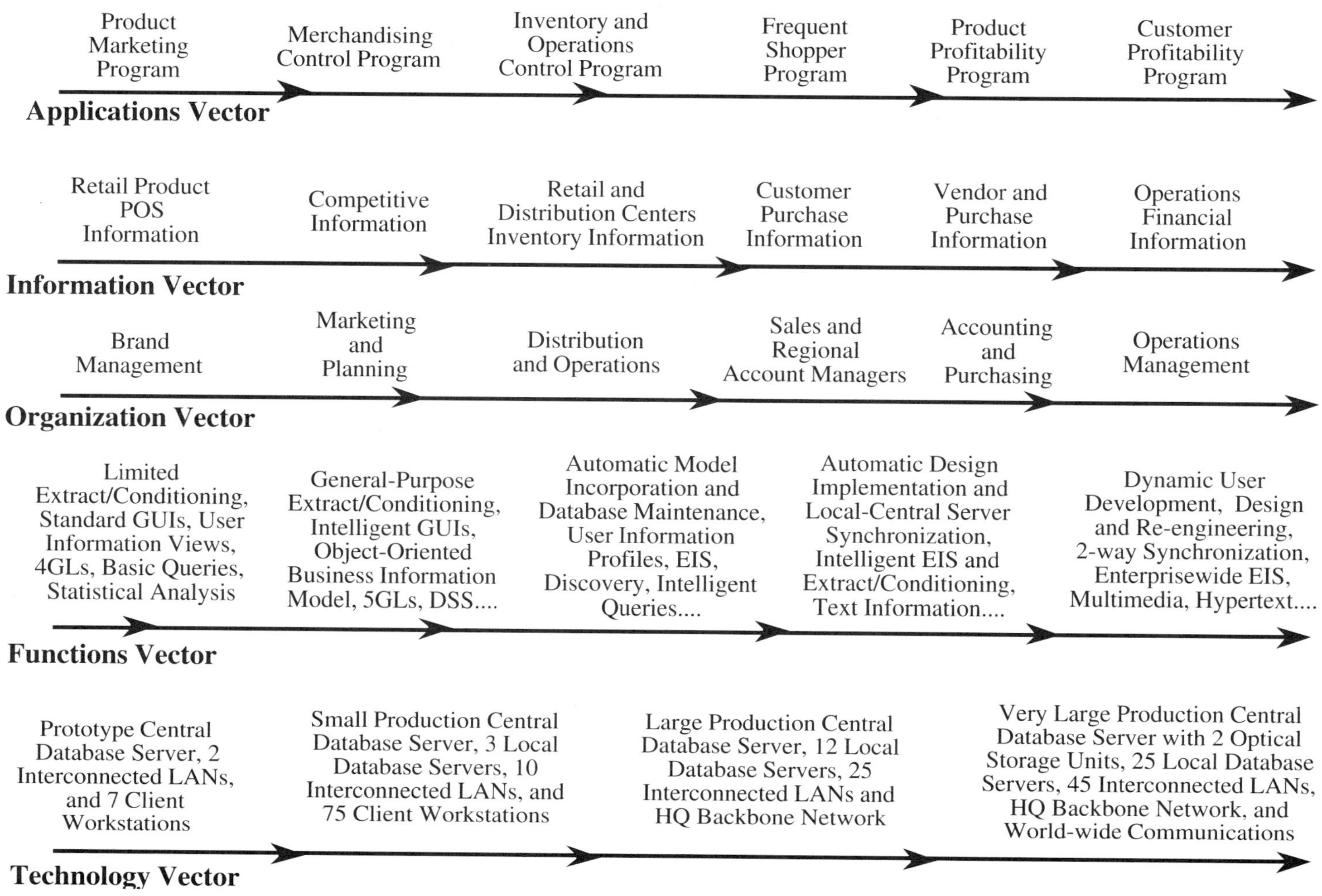

Applications Vector
Product Marketing Program · Merchandising Control Program · Inventory and Operations Control Program · Frequent Shopper Program · Product Profitability Program · Customer Profitability Program

Information Vector
Retail Product POS Information · Competitive Information · Retail and Distribution Centers Inventory Information · Customer Purchase Information · Vendor and Purchase Information · Operations Financial Information

Organization Vector
Brand Management · Marketing and Planning · Distribution and Operations · Sales and Regional Account Managers · Accounting and Purchasing · Operations Management

Functions Vector
Limited Extract/Conditioning, Standard GUIs, User Information Views, 4GLs, Basic Queries, Statistical Analysis · General-Purpose Extract/Conditioning, Intelligent GUIs, Object-Oriented Business Information Model, 5GLs, DSS.... · Automatic Model Incorporation and Database Maintenance, User Information Profiles, EIS, Discovery, Intelligent Queries.... · Automatic Design Implementation and Local-Central Server Synchronization, Intelligent EIS and Extract/Conditioning, Text Information.... · Dynamic User Development, Design and Re-engineering, 2-way Synchronization, Enterprisewide EIS, Multimedia, Hypertext....

Technology Vector
Prototype Central Database Server, 2 Interconnected LANs, and 7 Client Workstations · Small Production Central Database Server, 3 Local Database Servers, 10 Interconnected LANs, and 75 Client Workstations · Large Production Central Database Server, 12 Local Database Servers, 25 Interconnected LANs and HQ Backbone Network · Very Large Production Central Database Server with 2 Optical Storage Units, 25 Local Database Servers, 45 Interconnected LANs, HQ Backbone Network, and World-wide Communications

Figure 15-1. EIT Implementation Vectors

progress occurs at different rates; at times, progress in one vector may come to a temporary standstill. Long-term, however, EIT implementation will traverse the length of all five vectors to fully satisfy its long-term information objectives.

The Applications Vector

This is the primary vector. It describes the major stages of Information Automation and its progress in bringing important and sustaining benefits to the organization. The *applications vector* will be different for each industry and enterprise. One retailer may believe, for example, that customer purchase behavior is the most critical area; another may focus on faster, more flexible distribution of standard, high-volume products; still another may target customized goods and services for higher but fewer profit sales.

Despite the area of emphasis, any company has to eventually confront all aspects of its business, whatever the sequence and priority of the individual areas they start with, develop, and evolve over time. The total set of information opportunities discussed in Part II makes up a company's applications vector. In tracing the outlines of the implementation program later in this chapter, it is the applications vector that is central, the driving force behind the other vectors.

The Information Vector

As applications are implemented, an EIT's information resource "fills out" and expands as additional information elements, structures, and meanings are added to support new applications. The *information vector* is made up of information that is part of the company's major assets or entities: its customers, products, locations, people, equipment, vendors, and money.

Around these major information entities cluster the functions and operations of the business, and these, the orders and shipments that make up the product category, for example, collectively make up the contents of the company's information vector. While the general outline of the Business Information Model is established in the beginning stages of implementation, the actual information (its contents, definitions, structures, etc.), is incorporated gradually and incrementally as a result of the successive automation of all of a company's information applications.

The Organization Vector

The *organization vector* identifies the type, range, and order of information user clusters that are brought on-line as information applications are implemented. Assuming that in the full EIT implementation a company wishes to put all of its white-collar and management personnel directly in touch with an EIT's information resource, then the organization vector defines how that will occur, both in reference to the other vectors and to other organizations. This vector is driven by the applications vector and in turn drives the functions and technology vector.

The Functions Vector

Despite the need for core infrastructure and transformation functions (the Information Database, Desktop GUIs, information design, acquisition, and analysis capabilities, etc.), the *functions vector* recognizes that each enterprise has its own set of priorities in this area as well. This causes some functions to be available sooner and at different levels of sophistication. For example, a company may eschew intelligent GUI workstations and full-text capabilities in order to concentrate on enabling a powerful Information Directory or information discovery capabilities.

As is true for the information vector, the functions vector is primarily governed by the requirements of information applications, although there are important relationships between functions that must be taken into account. After the core capabilities are put in place, an EIT's functions, like other vectors, are implemented incrementally over time. How and when functions are activated depends on the needs and resources of the implementing organization.

The Technology Vector

The *technology vector* identifies the computing and communications hardware needed to support the other vectors, especially the applications and organization aspects of implementation. Beginning with an inventory of the company's existing hardware environment, the technology vector describes the additions and changes that must be put in place to support implementation. All needed technologies are defined, grouped, and ordered for implementation as part of this vector.

DOWN THE YELLOW BRICK ROAD

With the implementation vectors delineated, it is possible to begin the activities that will lead to full production implementation. Unlike the detailed and inflexible plans drawn up for Business Automation, the EIT implementation roadmap provides general guidance, describing what is needed to accomplish planned business objectives without sacrificing the ability to seize unplanned opportunities or to respond to surprises that will undoubtedly occur.

The goal of implementation is to create a general information solution and to achieve four major objectives: to transform data into competitive advantage, to sustain competitive advantage by building on what exists, to empower the information user, and to use information for guiding information technologies.

But these objectives are attainable only for a time, as there will always be an ongoing need for using information to gain new and different advantage, for sustaining those new advantages, for further empowering users, and for using information as the continuing focus for applying better information technologies. While greater or lesser levels of success can be attained in satisfying these objectives, they really represent a moving target for an organization determined to squeeze the greatest value out of its information asset.

Hence, the journey itself is as important as reaching its end-state goals, for along the way, an organization achieves benefits and value that are the essence of the EIT vision. Recognizing that, a company will follow an implementation course that is basically incremental, and that favors quick business results with low-investment, low-risk intervals. This path provides an environment conducive to improving people's understanding of information and the associated implementation issues before they're carved in stone. It incorporates their ideas and knowledge, and delivers increasing leverage with each step of the way.

The company taking the yellow brick road to implementation is not only going to benefit along the way; it is far more likely to arrive at its final destination. The best implementation plan takes these factors into account and lays out the major stages and choices leading to the successful establishment of a general information capability. Immediately following are suggested stages and routes leading to full EIT implementation.

IMPLEMENTATION STAGE ONE: SINGLE-PURPOSE APPLICATION

This is the first stage towards production implementation, where, despite the scope and range of the first application, there is primarily a single-purpose orientation to the program. While the application, organization, and information boundaries are never firm and likely to shift with new results, the implementation effort initially confines itself to the requirements defined during the prototype stage (see discussion in the previous chapter on prototyping).

With detailed and concrete results from the EIT prototype and the Business Case in hand, the implementation team makes the necessary corrections, adjustments, and expansions to the prototype capability and readies it for production implementation. Most important is identifying the full set of information needed to satisfy the application requirement.

Building on the subset used in the prototype, the implementation team determines what additional information is needed, and how and whether to change the information structures already defined. The Business Information Model is further reworked, and the full set of extraction and conditioning mappings established through information re-engineering. Major relationships and connections between the segments of information and future segments are defined.

Processing considerations are taken into account, fine-tuning both the design and physical placement of information in order to get the best flexibility and performance out of the resulting capabilities. With installation of the underlying hardware technologies, these capabilities are tested under production conditions. Any additional information that is needed is also collected and made part of this testing.

Initial production infrastructure and transformation functions are established at this time, based on the needs of the application and the results of the prototype. Core EIT functions are implemented based on production needs, with an eye towards fulfilling the general intent of the functions vector charted above. Even where such capabilities are only partially implemented, they should be capable of meeting requirements while serving as a platform for future expansion.

Finally, the production hardware is configured, installed, tested, and shaken down for use. Any additional hardware, extensions to prototype hardware, and other needed connections are put in place. Full-volume stress and crash-and-burn testing is performed, with hands-on participation by all major users. Tuning continues until adequate performance is obtained, with any changes to functions and information based on these results.

Stage One Example

For the consumer goods manufacturing company used as an example in Figure 15-1, EIT Implementation Vectors, the first application is a product marketing program that collects POS information on product purchases by its retailer outlets. This information provides daily sales activity for each individual product, with sales quantity, unit, and total price by retail store or outlet. The information is used primarily by company brand managers.

Initial transformation functions are limited to rudimentary (mostly custom-written) extraction and conditioning programs, standard information analysis tools (4GLs, statistical and spreadsheet applications, etc.), and an interactive SQL facility. EIT infrastructure capabilities consist of a standard Desktop GUI, a relational database system (with standard user information view capabilities), and limited use of object technologies for the Business Information Model.

The Information Directory is decidedly *static,* requiring professional technologists to intervene to incorporate new segments of the information design as well as to physically implement them for the user. The technologies employed in this stage are limited to an initial central database server configuration, connections to two local area networks, and a half-dozen client workstations.

Expand the First Application Area

After a reasonable period of time in production, an audit is performed to determine how much of the projected benefits from the application have actually materialized. Also identified is whether there have been unplanned benefits or other unfavorable effects. An objective assessment is made to determine if the basic approach is still valid, and if continuing with implementation appears to be the right thing to do. Both soft and hard benefits are accounted for at this time, and they must span the full range of possibility—from valuing higher-quality information, to faster response to business requirements, to meeting the objectives set out for the program. Opinions should come from the business area and implementation team.

With success of the initial application, a company is in an excellent position to capitalize on its investment. Moving beyond the limits of the first application is as important to the overall success of the program as the completion of the initial application itself. But as mentioned above, there is often a tendency at this point to lay back and absorb the benefits before investing again for additional benefits. Such loss of momentum can be deadly, and there must be a program in place that immediately drives the company forward.

The next implementation area should not be a totally new application or business function. This stage should be looked upon as a consolidation and extension of the first implementation area rather than as a fundamental shift or expansion in orientation. Movement into areas clearly beyond the scope of the original implementation vectors should be deferred until a critical mass of users, functions, technology, and information is established. Too small a base makes major expansion difficult, for not enough has been learned about the information infrastructure and transformation cycle. And problems are best solved when the environment is still small enough to be corrected with ease. If a major feature suddenly deletes the Information Database, it is far better that it happen in a controlled environment.

Rather than wait a year or more to test everything (and lose potential business advantage), it is better to expand an EIT's capabilities in small increments based on the mapped implementation vectors. This allows the time and opportunity for shaking out bugs while building a solid base for future expansion. This next implementation step could be a reasonable extension of functionality by providing, for example, additional capabilities for information analysis and discovery, or more powerful information conditioning. These would be made available to the same set of users based on the original information contents and supporting technologies.

Carefully leveraging the initial application could also be done by extending the same functions and information capabilities to other organizations who might benefit. This would, for example, extend the application to new clusters of users who are part of the same technology infrastructure, requiring only minor changes to client workstations, LANs, and existing database servers.

Another possibility for moving gently beyond the first application is to extend information from its original contents into closely related areas. This could be done, for example, by extending the Information Database contents from 3 to 15 months, by including descriptive information, or by adding adjunct sales activity not originally collected. This would be implemented while freezing in place the current set of users, functions, and technology.

Finally, a company may nimbly expand the first implementation by extending technology capabilities, perhaps by adding more powerful client workstation capabilities, better networking facilities, more robust directory and navigating capabilities, or using expert systems technologies to aid information query. This would be done holding steady the starting cluster of users, information, and functionality.

IMPLEMENTATION STAGE TWO: MULTIPURPOSE APPLICATIONS

The next implementation stage moves a company into a true multipurpose environment. With a second major application, preferably one related to the first application, the EIT capability begins to take on the shape of a common information utility, with a central information resource (replicated from production databases) and a wide set of general-purpose information capabilities. That next implementation step opens the door for serving expected needs from several areas and meeting a host of unexpected requirements as well.

This next stage is best executed by implementing a closely related second application. This allows for a natural progression based on existing information as well as on continued expansion of one or more of the other implementation vectors. This second application should ideally complete the automation for a major business area, and in doing so, create a jumping-off place for expansion into other business areas.

As this work proceeds, the team should be addressing other implementation vectors, attempting to bring them up to the same level of completion. The goal is to emerge from this application with a capability powerful enough to support all future implementation directly by business users. This will require having a satisfactory level of functional and technological capabilities in place. For the information vector, it means creating critical mass.

Stage Two Example

The consumer goods manufacturing company's second application is a merchandising control program, in which competitive information is added to the POS information already available in the Information Database. While this information was used extensively by brand managers, it was primarily intended for marketing and product planning organizations concerned with creating capabilities for better store-level ordering, improved item performance, greater out-of-stock prevention, more effective in-store promotion, and tighter expense control.

This second application completed the Information Automation of a major segment of the merchandising function of the company. It resulted in connecting as many as 100 users in 15 departments to the Information Database. Adding these users changed the mix of demands, moving from mostly simple requests to more complex ones, and from narrow interests to broader, multi-organizational ones as users' knowledge and sophistication increased. It also required the addition of more information, more details and history, and more complex relationships between the information elements.

As the Information Database grows to include additional information segments, it begins to reach the hard-to-define but very real state of *information critical mass*. Having this critical mass provides an almost irresistible base for information use by other organizations and applications. The second application moved the company much closer to this state.

The minimum amount of information needed to provide critical mass is a complete information subject area. This might be all customer or product information, or depending on the approach to implementation, it may be all the information needed to satisfy the needs of a major business function such as marketing or inventory control. Completing the customer subject area for this company was expected to require information from over a dozen production systems.

To match these capabilities, the company expanded its functions to provide general-purpose extract and conditioning capabilities, additional intelligence on top of the standard GUIs (they also added two more Desktop GUI systems), a full object-oriented Business Information Model, the extensive use of 5GLs and natural language systems, and a comprehensive decision support capability. These went a long way towards empowering information users and liberating them from technical intervention procedures.

The larger number of users increased operating demands, necessitating an increase in the underlying hardware technologies. This resulted in the introduction of three local database servers (primarily to ease processing bottlenecks on the central database server), a more powerful central database server (upgrades to 250 gigabytes), and increases that came to a total of 10 interconnected LANs and more than 75 client workstations.

IMPLEMENTATION STAGE THREE: BEYOND CRITICAL MASS

Information critical mass ushers in the third implementation stage, in which users are the primary source of knowledge for transforming information and for developing applications. This is the mature stage, where, with information at critical mass and the other implementation vectors at a comparable level of completion, the company's general information capability is ready to explode in all directions, allowing users in all business functions to satisfy their information needs.

In this stage, multiple Information Automation applications are aggressively pursued, either consecutively or in parallel. Additional applications or user groups do not have to tie directly into the areas of information already in the Information Database, for as long as the informational hooks are in place in the Business Information Model, any business group can take advantage of the information infrastructure and its transformation capabilities. And management, that special class of information user, now has an especially excellent opportunity for employing truly powerful executive information and decision support capabilities—for better planning and management, for more insightful decision-making, for more responsive organization redesign, and for much more tightly focused operations tracking and control.

Further development of an EIT's implementation vectors consist of adding and refining features and functions, and expanding into information areas missed or ignored the first time around. New technologies will make replacements of hardware and software components likely. This may include the addition of truly massive storage capabilities that allow a company to keep years of detailed information on-line for immediate access.

Over time, the information resource is expanded to the point where it embraces all major functions and business areas and is used to meet all information needs as business demands dictate. At that point, for all practical purposes, all information about the company is in the Information Database. With the phase out of independently extracted databases, the number of copies of information in the company goes from dozens to two: the copy in the source systems and the copy in the Information Database. This brings implementation to the point at which the Information Database is now considered *the official system of record of the company,* the only official representation of information accepted throughout the organization (this corresponds to Level 2 described in Chapter 3).

Stage Three, Example #1

Several examples of possible implementation applications for this third stage are given. The consumer goods manufacturing company launched an inventory and operations control program, building on the excellent marketing information available. They added inventory information from their retail and distribution centers to create a powerful on-line support system for managers in their distribution and operations organizations.

Those responsible for inventory management use the information to link with new areas to provide insight into managing shrinkage, upgrading spot level physical inventory control, and creating advanced perpetual inventory capabilities. Warehouse managers add their information to the growing database and get a leg up on delivering better vendor management and sell-thru order replenishment. Corporate planning managers grab hold of the detailed historical sales and channel information and merge it with their planning information to gain a better handle on next year's store expansion program, since they now know exactly what's selling where and for how long in all the major product, brand, store, and geographic categories.

This stage also makes available some extremely powerful functional capabilities: automatic information incorporation capabilities allow users to create new information designs (or change existing ones) and have them automatically made part of the Business Information Model; onboard trigger capabilities provide automatic maintenance functions, especially for aging and archiving and providing integrity control management; user information profiles greatly expand the intelligence of the Information Desktop and its associated user functions; executive information systems regularly tap into the information and provide precise tracking and control of business operations. In addition, extensive information discovery capabilities further improve the company's ability to learn more about their business operations. Finally, intelligent query capabilities help users get better response to requests that were poorly defined or lacking in specificity.

The hardware support for this stage called for a massive increase in information storage capacity, creating a large production central database server of close to 500 gigabytes. There were other increases that brought the equipment infrastructure to 12 local database servers, 25 connected LANs, and a complete HQ backbone network.

Stage Three, Example #2

Following the inventory program, the company decided its next highest need was to provide the operational basis for a frequent shopper program. This necessitated a huge increase in information, as each POS transaction had to carry household information, and additional outside information described that same customer's activities with competitors products. The users primarily satisfied by this program were sales and regional account managers.

Additional functional capabilities were added: automatic information design implementation (eliminating the need for database administrators), the availability of automatic local-central server synchronization (that reflects changes to the Information Database), intelligent EIS (where powerful expert systems sift and analyze the detailed information results prior to use by managers), similarly intelligent extract and conditioning functions (where sophisticated rules help scrub and upgrade the quality of incoming information), and the inclusion of text information for technical product information access.

By this time, the technology infrastructure had expanded to include a very large production central database server of over a terabyte, 2 optical storage units to handle archival information over 3 years in age, 25 local database servers, 45 interconnected LANs, an HQ backbone network, and world-wide communications capabilities. Effectively, every organization in the company was on-line to the Information Database at this point.

Stage Three, Example #3

The company approached the stage in which its Information Database was considered the official system of record by launching two closely related programs for increasing product and customer profitability. These required the addition of vendor and purchase information as well as detailed financial information on product costs and operating margins. The new users were people in accounting, purchasing, and operations.

These new applications were matched by advanced functions that provided dynamic user development capabilities and fully supported information design and re-engineering functions (i.e., the user as applications designer), two-way information synchronization (for posting changes from the Information Database to source systems), an enterprisewide EIS capability (that tracked every critical success factor in the company), multimedia on the Desktop (for specialized user needs), and the first use of a hypertext capability (for power users).

From this point on, the consumer goods manufacturing company will continue to evolve its EIT capabilities along the lines sketched in Chapter 3. Further Business Automation development and re-engineering would seek every opportunity to directly use the EIT Information Database, gradually phasing out separate collections of production databases, and moving the company ever closer to the end-state goal of a single image of information.

GET STARTED . . . NOW

This completes the discussion of the EIT implementation roadmap, and with it, the major components of the EIT Enabling Framework. Progress towards achieving the company's most critical information objectives is best ensured when working within this framework, by seizing the most attractive sectors of the company's information opportunities based on the EIT Design, Integration Model, and implementation roadmap.

Much ground has been covered since first postulating the notion that within a company's production data lies the potential for significant competitive advantage. And while the EIT vision is not offered as a panacea, it nonetheless represents an important way to boldly use technology to advance a company's important goals and strategies. Even assuming that executives agree fully with that provocative notion and find the enabling approaches appropriate for their business, none of that is going to do any good until somebody in the company actually does something, until some manager decides to bite the bullet and get started. *Taking those all-important first steps is what ultimately separates the doers from the talkers, and the winning from the losing enterprises.*

Seizing the Information Opportunity

This book has looked at the power of information and the approaches and enablers needed to harness it. It has demonstrated how companies can transform their abundant computer data into a heavily exploited asset for continuing competitive advantage. The book has explained the reasons why enterprises that want to compete successfully in the marketplace must take advantage of all their assets, and especially their information asset. The book has described designs, technologies, and vendor programs that offer the means to rechannel the flood tide of data into usable business information. Case histories of information-astute companies have demonstrated how that might be done. The enormous quantities of information and the technologies needed for transforming it are available to every large business enterprise.

The key to unlocking information's potential lies with the information users in the company. These information experts must be given the very best tools and information to satisfy business needs on their own using a single source of high-quality information. As users increasingly take control of their information destiny, the quality of information improves, its usage increases, the number of applications multiplies, and the impact of the many business benefits widens dramatically. With increased success, there is greater willingness to accept more responsibility for delivering a business result with information. That willingness leads to increased participation in technology uses and investment decisions.

Blocking the way to realizing information's full potential are problems with information itself and the lack of an adequate vision. The vision of a company-wide information capability requires going well beyond the ineffective practices in place today and articulating a workable framework for enabling the solution. *Enterprise Information Technologies* is the vision and framework that gives a company the power of information.

Out In Front of the Thundering Herd

The early adopters of EIT capabilities will be positioned as the future winners in the marketplace. Today, organizations are establishing these capabilities. At this very moment, companies are betting the farm on this strategy, using it to raise ever higher their capabilities for business success.

While efforts to implement this capability are neither common nor widespread, they are happening. Realizing the EIT benefits is possible for a company that understands the value of information and the importance of being an early adopter. The general availability of enabling technologies should convince even the most timid or skeptical that harnessing the power of information is not only possible but necessary.

Which companies will be the first to gain compelling competitive advantages from their information asset? They will be those with the insight to understand the deepest potential of the opportunity, and the skills and determination to apply the needed technologies, just as Citicorp's early adoption of ATM technology led to the tripling of its marketplace in the first three years of use. The companies that run the risks and master the challenges will get to pocket the initial information edge. Given the accumulating nature of an EIT capability, there is an excellent chance they will get to keep that edge.

It is expected that adoption of the EIT vision will follow normal technology adoption patterns. There will be the early adopters, the popularizers, the followers (the thundering herd), the conservatives (the lost sheep), and the resistors (the laggards). Early adopters will see the opportunity and move ahead despite the temptation to wait for prices to come down, for technology to be improved, or the "next generation" to appear.

Those that decide to wait may wait too long. Like the companies in the airline, retail, and banking industry that didn't keep up with earlier technological innovation, they will be forced to run with the thundering herd. They will miss the window of opportunity and have to work just as hard to hold on and to keep from sustaining competitive harm. For the lost sheep and laggards, the future holds only a series of desperate responses—of selling below cost, of living permanently with skeleton crews, of hoping for the best.

Implementing the EIT vision will be one of the key differentiators of future business prowess, resilience, and resourcefulness. As information becomes as important to a company as its flagship products, the management and exploitation of that asset will help enterprises triumph at the expense of those "less fortunate." Competitive power will accrue to those who first recognize information's fundamental role in the success of the enterprise.

Appendix

Recommended and General Readings

The Peter Drucker quote on page one is from "The Economy's Power Shift," *Wall Street Journal*, Sept. 24, 1992.

CHAPTER 1   **THE HIDDEN POWER OF INFORMATION**

Ginzberg, Eli and Vojta, George. *Beyond Human Scale, The Large Corporation At Risk*. New York: Basic Books, 1985.

Hoover, Gary, et al. *Hoover's Handbook of American Business*. Austin, Texas: The Reference Press, Inc., 1992.

Flanigan, James. "Retailer Forgot What It's About: Wal-Mart Didn't." *The Los Angeles Times*, Feb. 29, 1992.

Keen, Peter. *Shaping the Future: Business Design Through Information Technology*. Boston: Harvard Business School Press, 1991.

McFarlan, Warren. "Information Technology Changes the Way You Compete." *Harvard Business Review*, May–June, 1984.

Medina, Diane. "Sears Cuts to the Paper Chase." *Information Week*, April 1, 1991.

Moskowitz, Milton, et al. *Everybody's Business: A Field Guide to the 400 Leading Companies in America*. New York: Doubleday, 1990.

Networking Management. "Satellite Network Benefits Retailer on Many Fronts." Nov., 1990.

O'Reilly, Richard. "Software Can Map Out the Future." *The Los Angeles Times,* Jan. 16, 1992.

Peters, Tom. *Thriving on Chaos.* New York: Harper & Row, 1987.

Porter, Michael and Millar, Victor. "How Information Gives You Competitive Advantage". *Harvard Business Review,* Jul.–Aug., 1985.

Schwadel, Francine. "K mart Testing 'Radar' to Track Shopper Traffic." *Wall Street Journal,* Aug. 9, 1991.

Tinsley, Tom and Power, Andrew. "Why Information Systems Should Matter to CEOs." *Datamation,* Sept. 12, 1990.

Tucker, Robert. *Managing the Future.* New York: G.P. Putnam, 1991.

Tumulty, Karen. "Global Competition: Can U.S. Still Play by Its Rules?" *The Los Angeles Times,* June 8, 1992.

Ulrich, Walter and Rabkin, Barry. "Technology Offers More Than Speed." *The Los Angeles Times,* July 24, 1991.

Weiss, Michael. *The Clustering of America.* New York: Harper & Row, 1988.

Wiseman, C. *Strategy and Computers.* Homewood, IL: Dow Jones-Irwin, 1985.

Zuboff, Shoshana. *In the Age of the Smart Machine.* New York: Basic Books, 1988.

CHAPTER 2   OBSTACLES TO EXPLOITING THE INFORMATION ASSET

Donovan, John. "Beyond Chief Information Officer to Network Manager." *Harvard Business Review,* Sept.–Oct., 1988.

Editors. "Executives Lead Development Process at United Technologies." *PC Week,* May 28, 1990.

Eskow, Dennis. "Andersen Poll Says 'Leadership Gap' Is Emerging (Survey of MIS Managers)." *PC Week,* Nov. 5, 1990.

Fiore, Amy, et al. "Critical Issues of Information Systems Management for 1991." *Fourth Annual Survey by the Index Group,* Dec., 1990.

Lucky, Robert. *Silicon Dreams: Information, Man, and Machine.* New York: St. Martin's Press, 1989.

Rothfeder, Jeffrey and Driscoll, Lisa. "CIO Is Starting to Stand for Career Is Over." *Business Week,* Feb. 3, 1990.

Ryan, Bob. "The Data Swamp: Bill Gates Talks About Information At Your Fingerprints." *Byte,* May, 1991.

Andrew Seybold's Outlook on Professional Computing. "A Technological Metaphor: Taking Advantage of New Technologies." Dec., 1988.

CHAPTER 3 **A NEW VISION: ENTERPRISE INFORMATION TECHNOLOGIES**

Gibson, Cyrus and Bund Jackson, Barbara. *The Information Imperative.* Lexington, Mass: Lexington Books, 1987.

Head, Robert. "IS Execs See Information Technology as Tool of Change." *Government Computer News,* March, 1991.

Hopper, Max. "Rattling SABRE—New Ways to Compete on Information." *Harvard Business Review,* May–June, 1990.

Newman, William and Brock, Floyd. "A Framework for Designing Competitive Information Systems." *Information Executive,* Spring 1990.

Reeves, Ross. "Architecture Can Free Banks From High-Tech Bondage." *Computing Canada,* Oct. 11, 1990.

Reid, Richard and Bullers, William. "Strategic Information Systems Help Create Competitive Advantage." *Information Executive,* Spring 1990.

Schrage, Michael. "IBM Should Use Japan's Formula." *The Los Angeles Times,* Nov. 28, 1991.

Sloan, Kenneth. *The Information Factory.* New York: Teradata White Paper, 1989.

Straub, Detmar and Wetherbe, James. "Information Technologies for the 1990s." *Communications of the ACM,* Nov., 1989.

Toole, Jay. "Architectural Strategy: System Models for Hospitals." *Computers in Healthcare,* Nov., 1990.

Wallace, Scott. "Databases: Crossing Networks and User Needs." *Communications Week,* Feb. 25, 1991.

CHAPTER 4 **INFORMATION FOR CRITICAL BUSINESS STRATEGIES**

Alexander, Suzanne. "New Frequent-Flier Program Promises." *Wall Street Journal,* Sept. 8, 1991.

Bekey, Michelle. Series of customer profiles for Teradata Corporation, including "Requiem for an Era," "Growing an Information Pyramid," "Collecting Dividends on Data," "Navigating a Global Transportation System." 1988–1991.

Betts, Mitch. "Romancing the Segment of One: Database Marketing." *Computerworld,* Mar. 5, 1990.

Couger, Daniel. "E Pluribus Computum." *Harvard Business Review,* Sept.–Oct., 1986.

Curtice, Robert. "How Future Information-based Firms will Cut the Fat." *The Los Angeles Times,* Feb. 14, 1990.

Drucker, Peter. "Where the New Markets Are." *Wall Street Journal,* April 9, 1992.

Ehrensberger, Mike, et al. *Solutions Marketing: Teradata Database Computing in the Consumer Packaged Goods and Retail Market Segments.* Los Angeles: Teradata Position Paper, Jan., 1989.

Hammer, Michael. "Reengineering Work: Don't Automate, Obliterate." *Harvard Business Review,* Jul.–Aug., 1990.

Howard, R. *Brave New Workplace.* New York: Penguin, 1985.

The Index Group. "Business Re-engineering: The End of Business as Usual." *Indications,* Jan.–Feb., 1990, Vol. 7, No. 1.

Johansen, R. R. *Groupware: Computer Systems for Business Teams.* New York: Free Press, 1988.

Johnston, Russell and Lawrence, Paul. "Beyond Vertical Integration—The Rise of the Value-Adding Partnership." *Harvard Business Review,* Jul.–Aug., 1988.

Kanter, Rosabeth. *When Elephants Learn to Dance.* New York: Simon & Schuster, 1989.

Krass, Peter. "The Delta Difference." *Information WeeK,* Jan. 21, 1991.

Layne, Richard. "John Watson Revs British Airways' Engines." *Information WeeK,* Mar. 27, 1989.

Miles, R., and Snow, C. C. "Designing Strategic Human Resource Systems." *Organizational Dynamics,* AMA, 1980.

Pepper, Jon. "Get Off My Cloud: The MIS Chiefs at American and United are fighting for IT Supremacy." *Information WeeK,* Feb. 11, 1991.

Pomice, Eva. "Stores for the 1990s." *US News and World Report,* May 13, 1991.

Schrage, Michael. *Shared Minds.* New York: Random House, 1990.

Walton, R. *Up and Running.* Boston: Harvard Business School Press, 1989.

Winslow, Ron. "Insurers Move to Cut Piles of Paper Work." *Wall Street Journal,* March 13, 1992.

CHAPTER 5   INFORMATION FOR TACTICAL RESPONSE

Armstrong, Larry. "Teradata Gets Magic from a Gang of Microchips." *Business Week,* Nov. 21, 1990.

Cash, James and Konsynski, Benn. "IS Redraws Competitive Boundaries." *Harvard Business Review,* Mar.–Apr., 1985.

Cohen, Gary. "Can Sears Recover?" *US News and World Report,* May, 1991.

Dahl, Jonathan. "Agents Rankle Airlines With Fare-Checking Programs." *Wall Street Journal,* May 20, 1991.

Fulwood III, Sam. "Data Crunchers: Marketing Boom or Threat to Privacy?" *The Los Angeles Times,* May, 19, 1991.

Keen, Peter. *Competing in Time.* Cambridge, Mass.: Ballinger, 1988.

Lodish, Leonard and Reibstein, David. "New Gold Mines and Minefields in Market Research." *Harvard Business Review,* Jan.–Feb., 1989.

Moriarty, Rowland and Swartz, Gordon. "Automation to Boost Sales and Marketing." *Harvard Business Review,* Sep.–Oct., 1987.

Nonaka, I. "Toward Middle-Up-Down Management: Accelerating Information Creation." *Sloan Management Review,* Spring 1988.

Ries, Al and Trout, Jack. *Bottom-Up Marketing.* New York: Penguin, 1990.

Rothfeder, Jeffrey, et al. "How Software is Making Food Sales a Piece of Cake." *Business Week,* July 2, 1990.

Taylor, Thayor. "Xerox: Who Says You Can't Be Big and Fast?" *Sales and Marketing Management,* Nov., 1987.

CHAPTER 6   INFORMATION FOR EFFECTIVE MANAGEMENT

Applegate, Lynda, et al. "Information Technology and Tomorrow's Manager." *Harvard Business Review,* Nov.–Dec., 1988.

Blattberg, Robert. "Assessing and Capturing the Soft Benefits of Scanning." A study conducted for the Coca-Cola retailing research council, May, 1988.

Bruns, William and McFarlan, Warren. "Information Technology Puts Power in Control Systems." *Harvard Business Review,* Sep.–Oct., 1987.

Bullen, Christine and Rockart, John. "A Primer on Critical Success Factors." Working Paper No. 69, Center for Information Systems Research, Sloan School of Management. Cambridge, Mass.: MIT, June, 1987.

Cole, Robert. "Target Information for Competitive Performance," reprinted in *The Information Infrastructure.* Cambridge, Mass.: Harvard Business Review paperback No. 90078, 1991.

Conners, Dennis. "Decision Support Systems at Mervyn's." National Retail Merchants Association Information Systems Conference, Oct., 1988.

Davenport, Thomas, et al. "How Executives Can Shape Their Company's Information Systems." *Harvard Business Review,* Mar.–Apr., 1989.

Friend, David. "EIS: Successes, Failures, Insights, and Misconceptions." *DSS-86 Transactions.* Providence, R.I.: The Institute of Management Science, 1986.

Howard, Bill. "Commentary to the Dominion–Swann Case Study." *The Information Infrastructure.* Cambridge, Mass: Harvard Business Review Paperback No. 90078, 1991.

Judis, John. "Innovation, a Casualty at IBM." *Wall Street Journal,* Oct. 17, 1991.

Keen, Peter and Hackathorn, Richard. "Decision Support Systems and Personal Computing." Working Paper No. 47, Center for Information Systems Research, Sloan School of Management. Cambridge, Mass: MIT, Oct., 1979.

Konopolsky, Irwin. "Specifications for a Decision Support Presentation." New York and Los Angeles: Teradata White Paper and Presentation, Feb., 1990.

Lazzareschi, Carla. "Woolworth to Unload 450 Stores." *The Los Angeles Times,* Jan. 9, 1992.

Marx, Gary. "The Case of the Omnisicient Organization." *Harvard Business Review,* Jul.–Aug., 1990.

McCann, John. *The Marketing Workbench.* Homewood, IL.: Dow Jones Irwin, 1986.

Meyer, Dean and Boone, Mary. *The Information Edge.* Toronto: Holt, Reinhart and Winston of Canada, Limited, 1987.

Rockart, John and DeLong, David. *Executive Support Systems,* Homewood, IL.: Dow Jones-Irwin, 1988.

Rogers, T.J. "No Excuses Management." *Harvard Business Review,* Jul.–Aug., 1990.

CHAPTER 7   PROTOTYPES FOR AN EIT DESIGN

Betts, Mitch. "Feds to Break Reservation Lock on Computerized Flight-Reservation Systems." *Computerworld,* Apr. 1, 1991.

Clements, David. "The Strategic Advantages of Data Base Computing." Los Angeles: Teradata White Paper, Oct., 1989.

Devlin, B. and Murphy, P. "An Architecture for a Business and Information System." *IBM Systems Journal,* Vol. 27, No. 1, 1988.

Donovan, John. *Crisis in Technology: Strategic Weapons and Tactics for Executives.* Cambridge, Mass: The Cambridge Technology Group, 1989.

Heterick, Robert. "A Single System Image: An Information Systems Strategy." *Professional Paper Series, #1,* CAUSE Publications, May, 1988.

Inmon, William. "Building the Perfect Beast." *Decision Support Systems,* Spring 1991.

Johnson, Demarco. "Life Cycle Management: It's Already Broken." *Journal of Systems Management,* Feb., 1991.

Madron, Thomas. "Enterprise Computing in Higher Education." *T.H.E. Journal,* June, 1991.

Marshak, David. "Filters: Separating the Wheat from the Chaff." *Patricia Seybold's Office Computing Report,* Vol. 13, No. 11, Nov., 1990.

Martin, James. *Information Engineering.* Englewood Cliffs, N.J.: Prentice Hall, 1989.

Martin, James. "Software's Future Lies in Cooperative-Processing Systems." *PC Week,* May 21, 1990.

Mead, Tim. "The Information Systems Innovator at DuPont." *Datamation,* April 15, 1990.

Radding, Alan. "The Best Laid Plans Blend Old and New." *Computerworld,* Jan. 7, 1991.

Treacy, Michael. "Death of the Data Center: The Coming Revolution in Technology Architecture." Dallas, TX: Paper and Presentation, April, 1990.

CHAPTER 8   THE EIT INFORMATION INFRASTRUCTURE

Barsalou, T. and Wiederhold, G. "Complex Objects for Relational Databases." *Computer-Aided Design,* Oct., 1990.

Bernknopf, Jeff. "Repository Race Getting Crowded." *Software Magazine,* July, 1990.

Caldwell, Tom. "Using Corporate Data Models Saves Time and Effort." *Computing Canada,* Dec., 1990.

Carlson, David and Ram, Sudha. "HyperIntelligence: The Next Frontier." *Communications of the ACM,* March, 1990.

Chen, Peter. "The Entity–Relationship Model." *ACM Transactions,* 1976.

Coad, Peter and Yourdon, Edward. *Object-Oriented Analysis.* Englewood Cliffs, New Jersey: Yourdon Press, 1990.

Codd, E. "A Relational Model." *ACM Communications,* 1970.

Hales, Keith and Guilfoyle, Christine. *The Future of the Database.* London: Ovum Ltd., 1989.

Harding, Elizabeth. "Applications Enabling CASE Support." *Software Magazine,* Oct., 90.

Hein, K. "DevelopMate, A New Paradigm for Information Systems Enabling." *IBM Systems Journal,* June, 1990.

Martin, Robert. "Comparing Relational and Object Database Management Systems." *Hotline on Object-Oriented Technology,* May, 1990.

Neches, Phil. "The Anatomy of a Data Base Computer System." *13th IEEE Computer Conference Proceedings,* Spring 1985.

Prabandham, Mohan, et al. "A View of the IRDS Reference Model." *Database Programming and Design,* March, 1990.

Robinson, Mike. "Through a Lens Smartly." *Byte,* May, 1991.

Targowski, Andrew and Rienzo, Thomas. "Managing Information Through Systems Architecture." *Information Executive,* Summer 1990.

Zachman, John. "A Framework for Information Systems Architecture." Paper presented at Database World, Los Angeles, July, 1991.

CHAPTER 9   EIT INFORMATION TRANSFORMATION

Aranow, Eric. "Modeling Exercises Shape Up Enterprises." *Software Magazine,* Jan., 1991.

Ashby, Len. "Artificial Intelligence Helps Retailers Measure Bang for Their Advertising Buck." *Computing Canada,* Jan. 3, 1991.

Briggs, George. "Quaker Oats Builds Decision Support System to Gain Marketing Edge." *MIS Week,* June 10, 1990.

Brown, James. "A Machine Learning Approach to Studies of Recovery Efficiency." Dallas, Texas: Society of Petroleum Engineers Paper and Presentation, June, 1991.

Brown, Robert. "Logical Database Design Techniques." Manhattan Beach, CA: Paper from the Database Design Group, 1982.

Carroll, Paul. "Software Helps Managers Find the Data They Need." *Wall Street Journal,* Oct., 1990.

Eckles, Wesley. "AI Software Analyzes Databases." *PEI Softtalk and Hardware,* Dec., 1990.

Gleason, Bernard. "Open Access: A User Information System." *Professional Paper Series, #6,* CAUSE Publications, 1991.

Harding, Elizabeth. "Building MIS Into the Business Plan." *Software Magazine,* Oct., 90.

Immel, Richard. "McKesson's Monster 1-2-3 Profitability Models." *Lotus,* Sept., 1990.

Jacobs, Sheila and Keim, Robert. "Knowledge-based Decision Aids for Information Retrieval." *Journal of Systems Management,* May, 1990.

Katz, Robert. "Business Enterprise Modeling." *IBM Systems Journal,* Dec., 1990.

Korzeniowski, Paul. "Gleaning Executive's Data Glut Remains an EIS Potential." *Software Magazine,* July, 1990.

Leonard-Barton, Dorothy and Sviokla, John. "Putting Expert Systems to Work." *Harvard Business Review,* Mar.–Apr., 1988.

Loomis, Mary. "Data Modeling." IEEE Proceedings, 1986.

Lorenz, Mark. "Object-Oriented Development: Not Business as Usual." *Hotline on Object-Oriented Technology,* May, 1990.

Mahnke, John. "IXL Tool Discovers Database Patterns." *MIS Week,* Dec., 1988.

Maletz, Mark. "KBS Circles: A Technology Transfer Initiative." *MIS Quarterly,* Sept., 1990.

Mallach, Efrem. "Without a Data Model, Everything Falls Down." *Computerworld,* Aug. 8, 1990.

Merlyn, Vaughan and Boone, Greg. "The CASE Experience." *Publications of the CASE Research Corporation,* 1988–1989.

Parsaye, Kamran, et al. *Intelligent Databases.* New York: John Wiley & Sons, 1989.

Schmitz, John, et al. " 'CoverStory': Automated Newsfinding in Marketing." *MIT Management,* Winter 1990.

Stein, Richard. "Browsing Through Terabytes." *Byte,* May, 1991.

Strapko, William, "Knowledge Management: A Fit with Expert Tools." *Software Magazine,* Nov., 1990.

Watkins, Ronald. "Decision Support Delivers Bottom Line Results." *Information Executive,* Spring 1991.

Williams, Joseph and Nelson, James. "Striking Oil in Decision Support." *Datamation,* March 11, 1990.

Wood, Lamont. "CASE—Divided It Stands." *Andrew Seybold's Outlook on Professional Computing,* Sept., 1989.

CHAPTER 10   AN EIT INTEGRATION MODEL

Ambrosio, Johanna. "Airline Builds Scheduler on Client/Server Model." *Computerworld,* Feb. 4, 1991.

Bartl, Jan. "Information-Intensive Firms Move to Enterprise Networks." *Computing Canada,* Sept., 1990.

Buzzard, James. "The Client–Server Paradigm." *Data Based Advisor,* Aug., 1990.

DeBoever, Larry. "New Animal for MIS: Very Large-Scale LANs." *Software Magazine,* Dec., 1988.

Finklestein, Rich. "When Worlds Collide: Client Server Architecture Integrates Microcomputer and Mainframe Technologies." *LAN Magazine,* Sept., 1990.

Gates, Bill and McNealy, Scott. "What Does 'Open Systems' Really Mean?" *Computerworld,* May 13, 1991.

Moriarty, Terry. "Planning an Application Architecture." *Computer Language,* Sept., 1990.

Neuhold, Erich and Stonebreaker, Michael. "Future Directions in DBMS Research." *International Computer Science Institute Proceedings,* May, 1988.

Toperczer, Tom. "From Pyramids to Peers: Data Management Takes on New Importance." *Byte,* May, 1991.

CHAPTER 11   ENTERPRISE INFORMATION TECHNOLOGIES

Anthes, Gary. "Expert Systems Plus Chaos Equals Better Control Systems." *Computerworld,* June 29, 1992.

Brewin, Bob. "Data Base Machines." *Federal Computer Week,* Feb. 19, 1990.

Brown, Bob. "Retailers Stock Stores with LANs." *Network World,* June 18, 1990.

Butler, Martin and Bloor, Robin. "Client–Server Engines." *DBMS,* June, 1991.

Halsall, Fred. *Data Communications, Computer Networks and OSI.* Wokingham, England: Addison Wesley, 1988.

Janson, Jennifer. "Chevron Chemical Plans to Grow Worldwide Network." *PC Week,* Aug., 1990.

McCusker, Tom. "Teradata Revs Up Its Database Machine." *Datamation,* July 23, 1990.

Musich, Paula. "New DEC Options Recast VAX Models as Servers." *PC Week,* July 30, 1990.

Orfali, Robert and Harkey, Dan. Client–Server Programming. New York: Van Nostrand Reinhold, 1991.

Polilli, Steve. "Greetings at Hallmark: Use Common Sense in Software." *Software Magazine,* March, 1990.

Editors. "Banquet-Hall Dining Replaces the Corporate I/S Cafeteria." *IBM Directions,* Winter 1990/91.

Watterson, Karen. "Making the Move to Database Servers." *Data Based Advisor,* April, 1991.

Wilke, John. "Parallel Computing Finds Mainstream Uses." *Wall Street Journal,* Jan. 6, 1992.

Zdonik, Stanley and Maier, David, editors. *Readings in Object-Oriented Database Systems.* San Mateo, CA.: Morgan Kaufmann Publishers, 1990.

CHAPTER 12   VENDOR INFORMATION VISIONS

Brown, Bob. "NCR Unveils Scalable Server Line." *Network Line,* Sept., 1990.

Buckler, Grant. "Follow Standards, But Don't Be Paralyzed By Them." *Computing Canada,* Nov., 1990.

Carlyle, Ralph. "Assessing Computer Associates' New Architecture." *Datamation,* Aug. 29, 1990.

Cini, Al. "A Survivor's Guide to User-Centered Systems." *DEC Professional,* Jan., 1991.

Editors. "The Big Ten Enterprise Architectures." *Systems Integration,* June, 1990.

Moffat, Susan. "AT&T Buying Teradata to Tap Into Database Computer Arena." *The Los Angeles Times,* Dec. 3, 1991.

Newman, William. "SAA: IBM's Commitment to the Future." *Information Executive,* Winter 1989.

Schulman, Marc. "Teradata Corporation: A Larger Vision." UBS Securities Equity Research Report, March, 1990.

Sperling, Ed. "DEC Advances Interoperability." *Computer Systems News,* Dec., 1990.

CHAPTER 13   ESTABLISH THE IMPLEMENTATION ENVIRONMENT

Best, Laurence. "Building Software Skyscrapers." *Datamation,* March 20, 1990.

Curtice, Bob and Stringer, Dave. "Visualizing Information Planning." *Computerworld,* Jan. 19, 1991.

CHAPTER 14   PROTOTYPE AND JUSTIFY THE IMPLEMENTATION

Clemons, Eric. "Evaluation of Strategic Investments in Information Technology." *Communications of the ACM,* Jan., 1991.

Diebold Research Program. "A Sampling of Justification Methods," as reported in *Computerworld,* Nov., 1991.

Goldberg, Adele and Rubin, Kenny. "Talking to Project Managers—Case Studies in Prototyping." *Hotline on Object-Oriented Technology,* May, 1990.

Gurbaxani, Vijay and Whang, Seungjin. "The Impact of Information Systems on Organizations and Markets." *Communications of the ACM,* Jan., 1991.

Jenkins, Chris. "Justifying Expenditure on Information Technology." *Which Computer?,* April, 1990.

GENERAL READINGS

Braudel, Ferdnand. *Capitalism and Civilization.* New York: Harper and Row, 1985.

Drucker, Peter. "The Coming of the New Organization." *Harvard Business Review,* Jan.–Feb., 1988.

Feigenbaum, Edward and McCorduck, Pamela. *The Fifth Generation.* Reading, Mass.: Addison-Wesley, 1983.

Gilder, George. *Microcosm.* New York: Simon & Schuster, 1989.

Jastrow, Robert. *The Enchanted Loom.* New York: Simon & Schuster, 1984.

Manzi, Jim. "MIPS and Metaphysics." *Release 1.0,* Annual issue, 1990.

Naisbitt, John. *Megatrends.* New York: Warner Books, 1982.

Noble, David. *Forces of Production.* New York: Knopf, 1984.

Porter, Michael. *Competitive Advantage.* New York: Free Press, 1985.

Roszak, Theodore. *The Cult of Information.* New York: Pantheon Books, 1986.

Toffler, Alvin. *The Third Wave.* New York: William Morrow, 1980.

Index

Acquisition technologies, 165
Ad hoc solutions, repeating, 64
Alternatives, to EIT, 145
American Airlines, 4–6
Analysis technologies, 165–68
Applications:
  multi-purpose, 230–32
  single-purpose, 228–30
  selection of, 205–6
  vector, 226
Archetypes, of EIT, 145
Architectures. *See specific types*
ATM (automated teller machines), 3, 5
Automatic teller machines (ATMs), 3, 5
Automation:
  of business operations. *See* Business automation
  conventional. *See* Conventional automation
  of information. *See* Information automation
Availability, of information, 137

Banks:
  buying, 56–57
  customers and, 51–53
  design prototypes for, 83–85
Benefit analysis, for justification model, 217
Business automation:
  case studies of, 3–4
  conventional, 19–22

implementation of, 199–200
  information automation separated from, 28–30
Business Information Model, 99
  design information structures and, 213
  case study of, 116
  implementation of, 228–30
  information design and, 112
  technologies, 157–58
Business organizations. *See also* Management
  challenges facing, 47–48
  critical strategies for, 47–60
    competitive strategies, 39, 48–54
    organizational strategies, 54–60
  external challenges to, 48
  internal conflicts of, 48
  reshaping the basics of, 10
  resistance to implementation of EIT by, 207–9
  revitalizing by using information strategies, 59–60

Call churning, 70
CA90s (Computer Associates), 188–92
  compliance with EIT integration model, 191
  general observations, 191
  generic and infrastructure technologies, 189–90
  overview, 188–89
  transformation technologies, 190
CASE (Computer-aided systems engineering), 80, 163–64

Case studies:
  critical mass stage of implementation, 233–34
  information analysis, 125–26
  information conditioning, 119–20
  information delivery, 129–30
  information discovery, 127–28
  information enhancement, 118
  information extraction, 119
  information incorporation, 117
  information maintenance, 121–22
  information navigation, 123
  information organization, 115, 117
  information population, 120–21
  Information Transformation, 114–15
  multi-purpose applications, 231–32
  single-purpose application, 229
Central database server, 152–55
Central information resource, 32–33
  replicating, 37–39
Citibank, 3, 5
Client/server architecture, 139–40
  large-scale, 140–44
Client workstation technologies, 159–60
COBOL, 78–79
Common information utility, 35–37
Competitive advantage:
  information automation as, 12–15
  possibilities for exploiting information for, 7–12
  sustaining, 14–15, 30–31, 235–36
  transforming data into, 30
Competitive strategies. *See also* Organizational
      strategies
  critical, 39, 48–54
  customer relationships as, 48–49, 51–54
  information automation as, 12–15
  marketing strategies and, 49–51
  organizational strategies and, 54–60
Complex information representation, 99–100
Complex information technologies, 158–59
Computer-aided systems engineering (CASE), 80,
      163–64
Computer Associates' CA90s, 188–92
  compliance with EIT integration model, 191
  general observations, 191
  generic and infrastructure technologies, 189–90
  overview, 188–89
  transformation technologies, 190
Connectivity, 137
  technologies for, 161–63
Conventional automation, 20–22
  Enterprise Information Technologies versus,
      106–11
Cost/benefit analysis, 216, 217–21
Critical mass, 232–34
Culled information, 101

Customers:
  banking on, 51–53
  nurturing frequent, 53–54
  relationships with, 48–49
  shifting the emphasis from products to, 60
Cypress Semiconductor Corporation, 68–69

Data:
  harnessing power of, 6–7
  transforming into business information, 5–6
  transforming into competitive advantage, 30
  transforming into strategic resource, 11–12
Data analysis and inquiry systems. *See* Information
      automation
Data Base Computer/1012 (DBC/1012), 181–84
Database-directory interface, 104
Database interface, 104
Database management systems, 103
Databases:
  distributed, 25
  drawbacks to conventional, 17–19
  storage capacity of, 135–36
  uncovering vital relationships in massive, 8–9
Database servers, 140
Database technologies, 152–56
Data extraction and conditioning systems. *See*
      Information automation
DBC/1012 (Data Base Computer/1012), 181–84
Decision support systems. *See* Information automation
DEC's Information Network, 184–88
  compliance with EIT integration model, 187
  general observations, 187
  generic and infrastructure technologies, 185–86
  overview, 184–85
  transformation technologies, 186–87
Deductive analysis, 125
Delivery technologies, 168–69
Design prototypes, 77–94, 89–90. *See also* Case studies
  applicability to other companies, 90–91
  for banks, 83–85
  building, 211–14
    defining applications requirements, 212
    designing information structures and models, 213
    fine-tuning, 214
    installing prototype technologies, 213
    kickoff, 211–12
    ordering prototyping technologies, 212–13
    testing the prototype, 213–14
  evaluating, 214
  for retail companies, 85–89
Design technologies, 163–65
Desktop-directory interface, 103
Desktop interface, 103
Desktop technologies, 159–61
Directory technologies, 156–59

Discovery technologies, 167–68
Distributed databases, 25
Domino's Pizza, 62

Economic analysis, 216
EIT. *See* Enterprise Information Technologies
Employees:
    empowering, 10–11, 31, 72–73
    information for effectiveness of, 73–74
Enabling Framework, 42–44
    general information solution and, 77–130
    getting started, 234–36
    implementing the general information solution and,
        199–236
    information opportunity terrain and, 47–60
    integration strategies and, 133–44
Enterprise Information Technologies, 27–44. *See also*
        specific topics
    categories of, 145–69
      acquisition technologies, 165
      analysis technologies, 165–68
      database technologies, 152–56
      delivery technologies, 168–69
      design technologies, 163–65
      desktop technologies, 159–61
      directory technologies, 156–59
      generic technologies, 148–52
      interface technologies, 161–63
    components of, 31–37
      central information resource, 32–33
      common information utility, 35–37
      general information strategy, 32
      general-purpose information capability, 33–35
    constructing the design for, 91–92
    conventional automation versus, 106–11
    crucial premise of, 28–29
    design summary, 92–94
    developmental levels of, 37–42
      official system of record, 39–41
      replicated central information resource, 37–39
      single information image, 41
    expanding the information payoff with, 81–82
    framework of, 42–44
      designing the general information solution, 42–43
      identifying the information opportunities, 42
      implementing the general information solution, 44
      integrating the information technologies, 43–44
    ideal first applications of, 39
    objectives of, 30–31
    separating information automation and business
        automation with, 29–30
    underlying philosophy, 27–30
Executive information systems. *See* Information
      automation
Expert knowledge, information directory and, 100

Expert systems technologies, 150–52
External challenges to business enterprises, 48
Extract files, 17

Financial risks, 222
Formalists, resistance to implementation by, 209
Functionality, 137
Functional risks, 223
Functions vector, 227
Funding, 206

General Information Solution:
    designing the, 77–130
      information infrastructure, 95–104
      information transformation, 105–30
      prototypes for an EIT design, 77–94
    implementation of, 224–36
      charting EIT implementation vectors, 224–27
      getting started, 234–36
      stage one: single-purpose application, 228–30
      stage three: beyond critical mass, 232–34
      stage two: multipurpose applications, 230–32
General Information Strategy:
    establishing the, 202
    implementing the, 44
    policy for, 202–3
General-purpose information capabilities, 33–35, 83
Generic technologies, 148–52
Graphical user interfaces (GUIs), 10–11, 97, 160–61
Graphic information, 100
GUIs (graphical user interfaces), 10–11, 97, 160–61

Hypertext, 100

IBM:
    Information Center, 79
    Information Warehouse, 171–76
      compliance with EIT integration model, 174–75
      general observations, 175–76
      generic and infrastructure technologies, 172–74
      overview, 172
      transformation technologies, 174
Image information, 100
Implementation process:
    cost analysis for, 217–21
    establishing the environment, 196–209
      assigning responsibilities, 207
      creating information vision, 202
      enlisting information users, 201–2
      general information survey, 202
      general preparation, 200
      guarding against loss of momentum and
        complacency, 209
      heading off expected blockers, 207–9
      management's role in, 200–201

providing necessary incentives, 205
putting an effective information policy in place, 202–3
remaking the information planning process, 203–5
setting realistic expectations, 205
using appropriate controls, 205–7
of general information solution, 224–36
charting EIT implementation vectors, 224–27
getting started, 234–36
stage one: single-purpose application, 228–30
stage three: beyond critical mass, 232–34
stage two: multipurpose applications, 230–32
prototype and justifying the, 210–23
building a prototype, 211–14
evaluating the prototype, 214
justification model, 216–23
justifying the EIT investment, 214–16
selecting information opportunity, 210–11
risks of, 222–23
vectors for, 224–27
applications, 226
functions, 227
information, 226
organization, 226
technology, 227
Industrial Strength Database Computing (Teradata), 181–84
compliance with EIT integration model, 183
general observations, 183–84
generic and infrastructure technologies, 181–82
overview, 181
transformation technologies, 182–83
Information:
applications for, 50
controlling access to, 207
for critical business strategies, 47–60
competitive strategies, 39, 48–54
organizational strategies, 54–60
for employee effectiveness, 73–74
identifying opportunities of, 42
for management effectiveness, 65–74
management styles and, 66–68
for monitoring the business, 69
obstacles to exploiting, 16–26
for redesigning the company's structures and processes, 58
to revitalize the heart of the business, 59–60
for tactical response, 61–64
Information acquisition, 118–22
Information analysis, 122–28
case study, 125–26
Information analysis technologies, 165–68
Information applications, for Information Desktop, 97–98
Information applications repository, 101–2
Information architectures, existing, 44

Information automation:
business automation separated from, 28–30
as a business strategy, 12–15
dead-end capabilities of, 79–80
defined, 6–7
early capabilities of, 77–81
expanding information requirements through, 81–82
harnessing power of, 6–7
implementation of, 200
major developments in, 78
overview of possibilities, 4–5, 8–12
liberating information users and empowering employees, 10–11
opening new windows for management, 9–10
reshaping the basics of the business organization, 10
transforming operational data into a strategic resource, 11–12
uncovering vital relationships in massive databases, 8–9
precursors to, 78–79
single-domain capabilities of, 80–81
transforming data using, 5–6
Information Center (IBM), 79
Information central, 23
Information chaos, 23
Information conditioning, 119–20, 165
case study, 119–20
Information Database, 102–3, 231–32
Business Information Model technologies and, 157–58
database technologies and, 152–56
engines for, 103
Information definition, 114
Information delivery, 128–30
case study, 129–30
technologies for, 168–69
Information design, 112–18, 163–65
Business Information Model and, 112
Information Desktop, 96–98
information applications for, 97–98
user interface for, 97
Information Directory, 98–102, 229
Business Information Model and, 99
Complex Information Representation, 99–100
information applications repository, 101–2
user information profiles, 101
user information views, 100–101
Information discovery, 126–28
case study, 127–28
technologies for, 167–68
Information enhancement, 117–18
case study, 118
Information extraction, 118–19
case study, 119
technologies for, 165

Information feedback, 129
Information incorporation, 117
  case study, 117
Information Infrastructure, 95–105
  components of, 96
    information database, 102–3
    Information Desktop, 96–98
    Information Directory, 98–102
    information interfaces, 103–4
  design and installation of, 206
Information interfaces, 103–4
  technologies for, 162–63
Information interpretation, 128
Information maintenance, 121–22
  case study, 121–22
Information navigation, 122–23
  case study, 123
  technologies for, 165
Information Network (DEC), 184–88
  compliance with EIT integration model, 187
  general observations, 187
  generic and infrastructure technologies, 185–86
  overview, 184–85
  transformation technologies, 186–87
Information objects, 99–100
  object technologies and, 149–50
Information opportunity, 210–11
  seizing the, 235
Information organization, 115, 117
  case study, 115, 117
Information population, 120–21
  case study, 120–21
Information presentation, 128–29
Information re-engineering, 114
  technologies for, 164–65
Information scatterplot, 23, 25
Information technologies:
  breakthroughs in, 3–4
  harnessing the power of information, 6–12
  integrating, 43–44, 133–96
    classes of Enterprise Information Technologies, 145–69
    evaluating and configuring, 133–44
    vendor information visions, 170–96
  limits of, 19–22
    conventional automation's diminishing returns, 19–20
    crippling myth of information linkage, 21–22
    inaccessibility of conventional systems, 21
    revenge of the frustrated user, 22
    same tired old approaches, 22
    unresponsiveness and rigidity of conventional designs, 20–21
  possibilities for exploiting information for competitive advantage, 7–12
  prevailing visions of, 22–26

    distributed databases, 25
    information central, 23
    information chaos, 23
    information scatterplots, 23, 25
    single information image, 25–26
  transforming data into business information, 5–6
  using information for guiding, 31
Information topics, 100
Information Transformation, 105–30
  altering opinions for effective business action, 128–30
  automatic monitoring and, 110
  capabilities drill down and, 109–10
  case study, 114–15
  combining several forms of information, 109
  comprehensiveness of, 107–9
  creating quality information from production data, 118–22
  creative work paradigms and, 111
  cycle for, 111–12
  important questions to be answered, 106–8
  modeling the form and nature of, 112–18
  testing and creating opinions, 122–28
  user's style and, 110–11
Information users:
  authorization controls for, 207
  desktop technologies and, 159–61
  empowering, 31
  enlisting, in implementation, 201–2
  Information Transformation and, 110–11
  liberating, 10–11
  profiles of, 101
  views, 100–101
Information vector, 226
Information Warehouse (IBM), 171–76
  compliance with EIT integration model, 174–75
  general observations, 175–76
  generic and infrastructure technologies, 172–74
  overview, 172
  transformation technologies, 174
Infrastructure. *See* Information Infrastructure
Integration model, 133–44
  CA90s (Computer Associates) compliance with, 191
  enabling criteria for, 135–39
    availability, 137
    connectivity, 137
    functionality, 137
    modularity, 138
    price-performance factors, 136–37
    processing performance, 136
    productivity, 138
    reliability, 138
    security, 138
    sharability, 137
    standardization, 139
    storage capacity, 135–36

fully integrated environment, 143
Industrial Strength Database Computing (Teradata)
    compliance with, 183
Information Network (DEC) compliance with, 187
Information Warehouse (IBM) compliance with,
    174–75
integrating architecture into existing systems
    environment, 144
objectives and limits of, 134–35
Open Cooperative Computing (NCR) compliance
    with, 179–80
Oracle Parallel Server compliance with, 194–95
processing architecture and, 139–43
Intel chips, 148
Intelligent user interface technologies, 160–61
Interconnected local area network technologies, 161–62
Interface technologies, 103–4, 161–63. *See also specific
    interfaces*
Internal conflicts of business enterprise, 48

Justification, of EIT product, 214–16
    alternative analysis, 216
    economic analysis, 216
    model for, 216–23
        benefit analysis, 217
        cost analysis, 217–21
        risk analysis, 221–23
    strategic analysis, 215

K Mart, 3, 5, 61–62

LANs (local area networks), 140–41, 161–62
Large-scale client/server architecture, 140–44
Local database servers, 155

McKesson Corporation, 4, 6
Mainframes, central database server and, 153–55
Management. *See also* Business organizations
    information opportunities for, 42, 65–74
    opening new windows for, 9–10
    resistance to implementation, 207–8
    role of, 15
        in implementation, 200–201
    styles of, 65–68
Marketing strategies, 49–51
Microprocessor technologies, 148–49
    central database server and, 153–55
Modularity, 138
Monitoring, of business, 69
Multi-purpose applications, 231–32
Multitrack process, 202–3

NAS (Network Application Support), 184–85
NCR's Open Cooperative Computing, 176–81
    compliance with EIT integration model, 179–80

general observations, 180
generic and infrastructure technologies, 177–78
overview, 176–77
transformation technologies, 178–79
Network Application Support (NAS), 184–85

Object technologies, 149–50
Open Cooperative Computing (NCR), 176–81
    compliance with EIT integration model, 179–80
    general observations, 180
    generic and infrastructure technologies, 177–78
    overview, 176–77
    transformation technologies, 178–79
Oracle Parallel Server, 192–95
    compliance with EIT integration model, 194–95
    general observations, 195
    generic and infrastructure technologies, 192–94
    overview, 192
    transformation technologies, 194
Organizational strategies, 54–60. *See also* Competitive
        strategies
    bridging organizational islands, 57–58
    buying banks, 56–57
    carrying excess organizational baggage, 55
    driving the need for organizational redesign, 56
    information for redesigning the company's
        structures and processes, 58
    information to revitalize the heart of the business,
        59–60
    performing operational open-heart surgery, 55–56
    redesigning the organization, 54–55
    shifting the emphasis from products to customers,
        60
    turning applications into revenue, 58–59
Organization vector, 226

Parallel systems, central database server and, 153–55
POS (point-of-sale) technologies, 3, 5, 14, 86
Price-performance factors, 136–37
Processing architecture, 139–43
Processing performance, 136
Productivity, 138
Products, shifting the emphasis to customers from, 60
Prototypes, design, 77–94, 89–90. *See also* Case
        studies
    applicability to other companies, 90–91
    for banks, 83–85
    building, 211–14
        defining applications requirements, 212
        designing information structures and models,
            213
        fine-tuning, 214
        installing prototype technologies, 213
        kickoff, 211–12
        ordering prototyping technologies, 212–13

testing the prototype, 213–14
evaluating, 214
for retail companies, 85–89

Records, official system of, 39–41
RDBMSs (relational database systems), 155–56, 163
Redundancy, of information, 17
Relational database technologies, 155–56, 163
Relationship banking, 5
Reliability, 138
Replicated central information resource, 37–39
Retail companies, design prototypes for, 85–89
Risk analysis, for justification model, 221–23

Sabre system (American Airlines), 4–6
Security, 138
Sharability, 137
Simulation models. *See* Information automation
Single-domain Information Automation capabilities, 80–81
Single information image, 25–26, 41
Single-purpose application, 228–30
Standardization, 139
Statistical analysis. *See* Information automation
Storage capacity, 135–36
Store traffic, 3, 5
Strategic analysis, 215
Strategic information opportunities, 42
Support capabilities, 206–7

Tactical information opportunities, 42
Tactical response, information for, 61–64
Technical risks, 222
Technologies. *See also specific types*
installing prototyping, 213
ordering prototyping, 212–13
selection of, 206
Technology Integration Model, of EIT, 43–44
Technology vector, 227

Teradata's Industrial Strength Database Computing, 181–84
compliance with EIT integration model, 183
general observations, 183–84
generic and infrastructure technologies, 181–82
overview, 181
transformation technologies, 182–83
Text information, 100

User information views, 100–101
constructing, 124
User interfaces:
for Information Desktop, 97
technologies for, 160–61
Users of information:
authorization controls for, 207
desktop technologies and, 159–61
empowering, 31
enlisting, in implementation, 201–2
Information Transformation and, 110–11
liberating, 10–11
profiles of, 101

Vectors, for implementation process, 224–27
applications, 226
functions, 227
information, 226
organization, 226
technology, 227
Vendor information, 170–96
CA90s (Computer Associates), 188–92
distributed database computing and, 196
Industrial Strength Database Computing (Teradata), 181–84
Information Network (DEC), 184–88
Information Warehouse (IBM), 171–76
Open Cooperative Computing (NCR), 176–81
Oracle Parallel Server, 192–95
Virtual view, 101